THE WAY OF THE
RONIN

THE WAY OF THE
RONIN

A Guide to
Career Strategy

Beverly A. Potter, Ph.D.

Illustrations by Matt Gouig

American Management Associations

This book is available at a special discount when ordered in bulk quantities. For information, contact Special Sales Department, AMACOM, a division of American Management Associations, 135 West 50th Street, New York, NY 10020.

Library of Congress Cataloging in Publication Data

Potter, Beverly A.
   The way of the ronin.

   Bibliography: p.
   Includes index.
   1. Vocational guidance.   2. Career changes.   I. Title.
HF5381.P675 1984   650.1'4   84-45203
ISBN 0-8144-5798-3

Printing number

10 9 8 7 6 5 4 3 2 1

To the Ronin
in each of us

Acknowledgments

A special thanks to Sebastian Orfali, who as midwife nurtured and fussed over *The Way of the Ronin*; to Matt Gouig, whose imaginative illustrations gave Ronin physical form; to Gary Dexter, whose suggestions added dimension; to Doug Pies and Suzanne, who enthusiastically cheered it on; to Rob Kaplan, who championed on its behalf; and to all those who showed me the Way of the Ronin.

We are living in the *time of the par-enthesis,* the time between eras.

Those who are willing to handle the ambiguity of this in-between period and to anticipate the new era will be a quantum leap ahead of those who hold on to the past. The time of the parenthesis is a time of change and questioning.

Although the time between eras is uncertain, it is a great and yeasty time, filled with opportunity. If we can learn to make uncertainty our friend, we can achieve much more than in stable eras.

In stable eras, everything has a name, and everything knows its place, and we can leverage very little.

But in the time of the parenthesis we have extraordinary leverage and influence—individually, professionally, and institutionally—if we can only get a clear sense, a clear conception, a clear vision, of the road ahead.

My God, what a fantastic time to be alive!

—John Naisbitt
Megatrends: Ten New Directions Transforming Our Lives

Introduction

Serious problems have developed in the workplace since the peak of industrial growth in the early 1970s. Productivity declined, unemployment increased, and people were increasingly discontent. Much of the underlying problem can be traced to the way working in organizations is arranged. The vertical chain of command and the vassal-like relationship between worker and company limited mobility and effectiveness in accomplishing assignments. Organizations became rigid, stifling innovation, unable to respond creatively to the ever quickening rate of technological and economic change. Capable workers at all levels began colliding with a feudal work system. The problem was exacerbated by the baby-boomers, an enormous number of highly educated, ambitious, and talented people, trying to squeeze into the upper levels of a shrinking corporate pyramid.

Out of this chaos is emerging a new breed of worker, the Ronin, who has broken with the tradition of career feudalism. Guided by a personally defined code of adaptability, autonomy, and excellence, Ronin are employing career strategies grounded in a premise of rapid change. By making lateral moves that follow their interests, they become generalists with specialities.

Organizations are searching for a way to revitalize, to become more flexible and innovative. Obviously, the solution lies in the synergistic efforts of those who populate the workplace. With the Ronin lies hope for a corporate renaissance. Properly managed, Ronin can be catalysts. Their breadth of experience combined with their self-generated motivation to accomplish project goals promises to increase productivity and corporate profits.

Ronin is used here as a metaphor based on a Japanese word for lordless samurai to describe the optimal career strategy for the 1980s. As early as the eighth century, the word *ronin*, translated literally as "wave-people," was used in Japan to describe people who had left their allotted stations in life. Most commonly, it refers to samurai who left the service of their feudal lords to become masterless. When a samurai was severed from his lord, he had two choices: to commit *seppuku* (ritual disembowelment) or to *do ronin*. If he chose to *do ronin*, he lost his stipend and forfeited all formal affiliations and duties, because no provisions were made in feudal Japanese society for those who were dislodged. Just earning enough to survive was exceedingly difficult, and being disavowed in a society built upon rigidly defined relationships was a challenge to develop self-directedness. Dislodged from their niches, *ronin* were considered thrown on the waves of a difficult and uncertain destiny. Doing *ronin* was accepted as a spiritual trial thrust upon one by misfortune. Those who passed the tests did so by following *bushido*, the way of the warrior, and mastering *bujutsu*, practice of martial arts.

Under the rule of the Tokugawa dictatorship (1600–1867), citizens of feudal Japan were subjected to a stringent system of control. Farmers were registered in their villages and forbidden to leave. Merchants and artisans had to be registered with appropriate guilds, and any activity considered irregular was reported to shogunate officials. Affiliated warriors were closely monitored through a chain of supervisors linked vertically by the institution of vassalage, which was built upon a tight master–subordinate unit. Vassals were expected to exhibit unquestioning loyalty to the superior. Control over movement in the cities was maintained through special gates installed across the intersections of every two streets, with passes required of even the highest officials. Penalties for unauthorized movement and other crimes were harsh and inflicted upon the entire family of the guilty party. The intolerance of anything that might have forced a person to confront individual values different from those of society made it extremely unlikely that anything unexpected could happen.

In a land made up of hundreds of competing fiefs, warriors were essential for more than four centuries. Eventually the Tokugawa dictatorship closed the borders, stamped out Christianity, and suppressed the incessant conflict. Without wars, the warriors' role changed as they were slowly domesticated by their many nonmilitary duties. By 1700, the samurai, the affiliated warriors, had been surreptitiously turned into civil bureaucrats hidden beneath swords, military titles, court rituals, and a host of routine guard duties. This is when the *ronin*, who continued to live by *bushido*, stood out most starkly and were regarded with awe and suspicion. It is from this period that the Ronin metaphor as it is used here is drawn.

Severe restrictions were placed on *ronin*, forcing them into outlaw status. To survive, some became scholars, many hired themselves out as bodyguards to rich farmers, some banded together and terrorized the countryside, and a few started schools to illegally teach martial arts to people outside of the warrior class. One such *ronin* was Miyamoto Musashi, an illustrious undefeated fighter who in 1645 wrote *Go Rin No Sho*, which was selling briskly in the West in three editions in the early 1980s under the title of *The Book of Five Rings*.

Reasons for doing *ronin* were numerous and varied. Children of masterless samurai who maintained their warrior status were born *ronin*. Changes in a samurai's master's or clan's circumstances could force him to do *ronin*. He might be dismissed from service or request dismissal to be free to embark upon a spiritual trial of self-development or an adventure that otherwise might have discredited or involved his former master. Revered in legend are the tales of samurai who joined the ranks of *ronin* willingly in order to avenge themselves or their masters. Most frequently, a samurai became masterless through a stroke of misfortune as when his master lost in war and was executed or exiled or when his master's clan was disbanded by order of the shogun. The progressive elimination of clans that were considered dangerous by the Tokugawa dictatorship eventually increased the *ronin* in this group to over 400,000. After the opening of Japan to the West, many samurai chose to become unaffiliated in order to serve in the Western compounds and learn from the barbarians, later returning to their clans to share their newly acquired knowledge. In time, a number of these errant warriors came to prefer this more difficult but generally more exciting mode of existence, which taxed their wits and imagination and forced them to develop their potential more fully. They became addicted to a life of comparative freedom. *Ronin* traveled all over Japan, meeting and accepting challenges, often going out of their way to seek them.

Forced by necessity to be individuals, *ronin* had to rely almost entirely upon themselves and their martial skill. As such, they were prime targets for anyone seeking a duel, because slaying an unaffiliated samurai carried no threat of retribution from state or clan. Consequently, those *ronin* who did not continually hone extraordinary skills and discipline met a speedy demise.

Ronin played a key role in Japan's abrupt transition from a feudal society to industrialism. Under feudal rule, warriors were not allowed to think freely or act according to their own will. On the other hand, having been forced by circumstances to develop independence, they took more readily to new ideas and technology and became increasingly influential during the transition because they made up a substantial percentage of the faculty in the independent schools. These private schools, which taught science, mathematics, and commerce, were more liberal than were the official government schools, which taught only the traditional curriculum. Consequently, *ronin* were more acquainted with Western developments and the avant-garde.

Many were instrumental in chauffeuring in industrialism by founding some of the great Japanese corporations. Traditionally, it was considered demeaning for samurai to be involved in mercantile activity, so only those who had broken out of the old beliefs attempted to develop astute business skills. A good example is Yataro Iwaski, who in 1870, three years after the overthrow of the Tokugawa rule that formally marked the end of feudalism, founded Mitsubishi. Mitsubishi, over a hundred years later, is one of the world's greatest corporate empires, with revenues exceeding $65 billion in the early 1980s.

In contemporary Japanese usage, the word *ronin* refers to would-be students who have not yet passed the entrance exams for the university. Mistakenly, many assume that these *ronin* are equivalent to the Western high school dropout. Actually, in this context, doing *ronin* refers to a time of independent study. Although most students prepare for the stiff entrance exams by attending institutionalized cram schools, similar to our prep schools, *ronin* have a more self-directed strategy in which they hire tutors to help them prepare for the exams.

Occasionally, these *ronin* choose to leave college to form corporations. Kazahiko Nishi, or "Kay" as he is commonly called, is an example of such a contemporary *ronin*. Instead of completing his degree at Tokyo's Waseda University, he founded the successful Japan ASCII Corporation and later joined with Bill Gates, a *ronin* from Harvard who started Microsoft Corp., which rapidly became the world's largest microcomputer software company. In 1983, for example, 40 percent of all the personal computers sold contained Microsoft's software.

The West has many historical parallels to the *ronin* archetype. The term *free lance* has its origin in the period after the crusades, when a large number of knights were separated from their lords. Like their Japanese counterparts, they had to use their skills and live by their wits. Many lived by the code of chivalry and became "lances for hire." Renaissance man refers to a multiskilled person, concerned with self-development and educated in both science and art. Similarly, *ronin* often composed haiku poems, arranged flowers, practiced calligraphy, and developed inner discipline in addition to wielding a sword.

The American frontier was fertile ground for the *ronin* archetype. *Maverick*, derived from the Texan word for unbranded steer, is used to describe a free and self-directed individual. The Western character that most closely embodies the archetype you'll meet in *The Way of the Ronin* appeared in the famed 1960s television series "Have Gun Will Travel," in which Palladin, a sophisticated strategist as well as a hired gun, made a career out of adventure.

Leland Stanford is an example of an American frontier Ronin. From humble origins and with only limited formal education, he emerged to make millions in the industrialization of the West. When his only son died unexpectedly, he decided to start a university in his name. Leland Stanford Junior University has become one of the world's great universities, and a hundred years after its founding, it spawned the booming Silicon Valley.

The Ronin model is especially relevant in the 1980s because it is a time of transition from one era, industrialism, to another, the information society. With change comes chaos, uncertainty, and confusion. And in times of change, the Ronin archetype emerges. The Ronin can handle the ambiguity unavoidable during such in-between periods, and those who employ new strategies and new definitions of success will be the winners. The traditional approach to conceptualizing and planning careers, which involved specializing and following a linear career strategy to move up the promotional ladder, is no longer optimal because it does not factor in the unexpected. The optimal career plan in a time of transition must take the fact of change into account.

Although many of the Ronin's roots, such as the *bushi*, are in male culture, most career women are well acquainted with the Way of the Ronin. Career women have left their traditional stations and battled their way into the recesses of the male-dominated workplace. Most women's careers are characterized by a multiplicity of experiences and back-and-forth moves between home, work, and school, causing them to confront the crisis of self-direction. Like the *ronin* who had no clan, professional women often feel excluded from the corporate cliques' inside tracks, without ally or mentor.

We must be prepared to *"do ronin"* because our futures are unpredictable. Telecommuting and the electronic cottage are changing the face of the workplace. Relationships between bosses and employees and the way people are managed at work are undergoing scrutiny and alteration. Technology is ushering in new specialities and rendering old ones obsolete. To prepare, we must become more flexible and develop a new work ethic, one that meets the needs of both the company and the individual. And with this in hand, we can leap into the adventure of the Way of the Ronin.

Contents

1   The Waves of Change   1

2   Career Feudalism   31

3   The Way of the Ronin   60

4   Have Skills Will Travel   90

5   Career Strategies   122

6   Doing Ronin: Riding the
        Waves of Change   153

7   Corporate Ronin   186

    Suggested Readings   217

            Index   223

THE WAY OF THE
RONIN

The Waves of Change

The baby boom transforms each institution through which it passes. The pig is now devouring the python.

—John Naisbitt
Megatrends[1]

The big question when we were children was "What do you want to be when you grow up?" No one ever thought to ask, "What sort of life do you want to be living when you grow up?" The question assumed that the life created by following a linear path up the corporate or professional ladder toward affluence would satisfy all of us. Our task was to choose from a smorgasbord of possibilities one vocational speciality for our entire work lives. Without realizing it, we have been set up to experience frustration and disappointment, and have been forced to make dramatic

changes without warning or preparation. By following the linear
career strategy, we've whittled ourselves down to fit a slot in an
intricate pattern—a pattern that is changing in unprecedented
and unpredictable ways.

To a far greater degree than we realize, our work molds our
entire lives: where we live, who our friends are, how we enter-
tain, what we do for leisure, the values we live by, and the way
we think. Consequently, choice of a career becomes a necessary
and fateful process, because in choosing an occupation, we also
select an identity and a way of life.

So we went to college to become teachers, lawyers, or business managers. Or we entered technical school to learn a trade.
And once made, this educational training commitment became
our vocation for life. We were expected to follow a strictly linear
career path within the corporations where we worked. After an
appropriate number of years of shopping around, we were to
settle down into a corporate structure and build a career. We
were expected to be established on our career path by our late
twenties, certainly no later than our early thirties. Then we
started advancing up the corporate ladder.

It was in moving from management trainee up the various
rungs toward top management that we were expected to achieve
success and satisfy our needs for esteem and personal growth.
During the postwar growth era, following this linear strategy
made it relatively easy for a young professional to ride the growth
curve all the way to the top. From 1950 to 1970, the total number
of jobs in the United States grew by 20 million, a 33 percent
increase. Jobs were plentiful, especially at the top of the occupational career ladder. The need for highly prestigious and well-
paid professionals grew faster than the need for any other category of worker.[2]

But now the linear pattern is no longer an optimal career strategy. Large corporations and government agencies are finding it
difficult to create enough opportunity to keep young and eager
managers and professionals on an upward career track. Companies are no longer creating jobs and sufficient growth opportunities for all those who want fulfilling work. Says economist
John Oliver Wilson:

> When there are four college graduates competing for every new
> professional job opening; when three million college graduates
> have had to settle for low-skilled, clerical or blue-collar jobs; when
> thousands of mid-level managers will be competing for a limited

number of higher management and professional positions, it is rather naive to continue to talk of upward mobility in the traditional sense of linear careers.[3]

WE WANT SOMETHING MORE

In our youth, we enjoyed affluence and possessions. We found them nice but not satisfying. We watched our fathers in their gray flannel suits and our mothers confined to PTA meetings and coffee klatches in the suburbs. We sensed that we had been indoctrinated with a rigid understanding of success and personal growth. So in the 1960s, we tuned in, turned on, and dropped out. We went to sensitivity groups, learned massage, experienced weekends at Esalen, expanded our awareness with Zen, meditated, and became assertive. Most of us dropped back in during the 1970s, but many did not. Some have tried to be both in and out of the World Game of making an impact on the mainstream of our businesses, professions, and society.

In the space of only two decades, from 1060 to 1980, many Americans rejected the notion that affluence and possessions alone yield a "successful" life[4] and adopted new values pivoting around self-fulfillment. While our parents placed their emphasis on getting ahead and adjusting to the mores of the corporate structure, today we question the traditional postwar work ethic, insisting there must be something more to life than making money, accumulating possessions, and struggling to get ahead. We want greater flexibility in our lives, with more opportunity to express ourselves and develop our potential. Increasingly, we define our own internal measures of success and failure and are far less accepting of the external gauges society and organizations imposed on our parents. We manifest our desire to develop our full potential in our life-styles, in our attitudes toward work, and in a great mistrust of our large institutions and their leaders.

The change can be characterized in one word: diversity! And we are carrying our new attitudes toward work and our increasing unwillingness to conform over into our jobs. Although work is still a major part of our lives, we are less willing to sacrifice everything for the sake of the job just to make it to the next rung on the ladder. Increasingly, we insist that work be an integral part of the whole of who we are in addition to providing an economic base for rich, full, and balanced lives. We have moved

ourselves onto center stage. We are rewriting the script so that
self-realization rather than social conformity becomes the theme
of the play.

> Americans tend to equate living expensively with liv-
> ing well. This is not really true. People who labor at work
> they don't like are not living well no matter how much
> money they make. These people are wasting the most
> precious commodity they own—one they can't buy: time.
> Each person has only so much of it. Any use of it which
> isn't fulfilling and enjoyable is a waste.
>   —Ed Rosenthal and Ron Lichty
>   *132 Ways to Earn a Living Without*
>   *Working (For Someone Else)*[5]

The once unquestioned trust in the major institutions of our
society is being challenged. We want more freedom from the
economic power of corporate plants and office bureaucracies. We
are not willing to leave our new sense of self and our new social
values in the suburbs. Instead, we bring with us to the office the
yearnings for flexibility, for greater freedom in thought and dress;
the desire for nonfinancial rewards, recognition, and respect; and
the sense of belonging and contributing. We want to find fulfillment and personal satisfaction in conventional careers, while
at the same time enjoying the financial rewards that will enable
us to live full and rich lives.

More than a 100 studies over the last 20 years have shown
that what we want most from our work is to feel that it, and thus
we as individuals, are important.[6] We do not want just a job; we
want employment that offers challenge, growth, and fulfillment.
We want to feel that what we do is important, that we make a
contribution to some meaningful objective. We want balance and
are less willing to continue the split between work life and personal life, less willing to sacrifice the family to the corporation,
and less accepting of a fractionalized existence.

All over America, we are weighing the rewards of conventional success and the traditional notions of work, and finding
them lacking. And to our horror, we are discovering that we are
locked in. We are trapped. Our future is dictated by choices we
made in high school and college. Our specialized vocations have
become comfortable cells that we cannot get out of without sac-

rifice to either/or choices. After years of specialization and climbing the rungs of the ladder, we find that in order to make a change we must step down and start at the bottom of yet a new ladder. We must accept a tremendous drop in pay, status, and sphere of influence or return to school for lengthy training or even drop out of the World Game altogether.

We are told this is the price we must pay if we want something more. It is *either* a conventional career of climbing the ladder and becoming ever more specialized with ever fewer options *or* accepting a less lucrative but more satisfying endeavor outside of the World Game. Some, who are locked into mortgage payments, credit cards, and the kids' college bills, would like to reach for self-realization but believe they cannot. Others, not willing to give up affluence, attempt to realize themselves with hobbies or volunteer work, part-time around the edges of their jobs. They are finding that they cannot actualize their self-realization goals at work after all. They are not free. The linear career is a master who permits little deviation from a straight line. These people become trapped in career feudalism!

Consider Bill:
    My parents worked hard. They struggled so that I could have what they never had. And they expected me to become a professional. I didn't question it. It seemed like the thing to do, and law seemed like the best option. I figured I'd get a lot of respect and a lot of money. So I pushed through the grind of law school. And now I've been a lawyer for nearly a decade. It's O.K. I've done well. But I'm tired of it. It's not that I don't like it. It's just that it doesn't meet all of my needs. A lot of people think I'm a hired gun. And I don't like that. There are certain inequities in the court system, and I don't like that. And I have a hard time with the values of some of my colleagues. And then there's the paperwork, the endless, endless paperwork. But when I think about my options, I get depressed. Ever since I got my home computer, I've gotten more and more interested in electronics and programming. But when I look in the paper at the job openings, I'm not qualified. Oh, maybe with a couple courses at the local college I could talk myself into an entry-level position. And I've considered it. I really have! But, you know, I'd never get far, and I'd get only about a quarter of what I make now. The money's not that important,

really. And I've got some savings. But what's the point? I may as well be pumping gas for all the impact that I'd make. Of course, I could go back to school and get a degree in engineering. But it seems like I spent a lifetime in school already. I don't want to do that again. And I'm not sure I'd be any better off after I got the degree anyway. I'd probably want to do something else after a while. No, I can't start over. It's too late for that. I guess I just have to accept law and make the best of it. And find some satisfaction playing around with my home computer. It's depressing really. And I feel trapped.

(This and the other monologues in this book are based on interviews and discussions with real people, but they have been substantially altered and rewritten to obscure the speakers' identity and to highlight their concerns.)

Some people, however, are not willing to accept this either/or choice. They are striking out of the conventional arena into the unknown. These pioneers, experimenting with their own lives, search for ways to live rich and fulfilled lives—lives in which work is not an impediment but a means to self-realization.

SLUGGISH ECONOMY

To the difficulties of making the right choices is now added the haunting fear that these choices may be futile and that our self-fulfillment goals may be unattainable because of economic reasons. For almost three decades, the U.S. economy was marked with dynamism, rapid growth, and expanding opportunity, but now things are changing. The explosive growth of professional jobs has stopped. By 1985 only 18 percent of all middle-class workers will be employed in professional occupations—far below the 25 percent level of 1970.[7]

In 1982 the first class of the baby-boom generation turned 36 years old—the heart of the prime working years, when limitless opportunity for promotion and career development promised by parents and teachers should be manifesting itself. Here is the generation endowed with the greatest affluence, the best educations, and the highest expectations of any generation in American history—indeed, in the history of the world! But the baby-boomers are discovering that the cohorts with whom they crowded the maternity wards, elementary schools, colleges, and entry-level jobs are now clogging the fast track to the top in the job market as well.

The doors of unlimited opportunity have slammed shut. The size of the 35–44-year-old age group into which the baby-boomers are now moving en masse will increase by 45 percent between 1981 and 1990, while the total number of jobs will rise by only 17.1 percent during that period.[8] It is like a group of people moving from a big room into a smaller one.

> In a matter of a few years we have moved from an uptight culture set in a dynamic economy to a dynamic culture set in an uptight economy.
> —Daniel Yankelovich
> *New Rules*[9]

The upward mobility that so characterized the occupational ladder of success during the postwar era is reversing itself. No longer are jobs plentiful at the top rung in the highly paid and

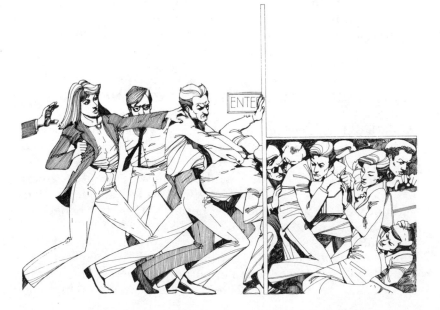

prestigious occupations. No longer is there a seemingly unlimited need for teachers, doctors, lawyers, and engineers. Many who have earned the necessary educational credentials to move into these occupations are finding the rungs full and the doors to opportunity closed.

But the problem is more than simply finding slots for a tidal wave of talented and ambitious workers. The American economy has become sluggish and taken a downturn. For over a decade, our growth has averaged just 3 percent a year.[10] The potential for the American economy to grow is far lower now than it was during the postwar era of material abundance. Since the mid-1970s, which marked the peak of our affluent society, America has been plagued by scarcity of energy and other vital resources, inflation, high interest rates, and cutbacks in government funding. Rather than unlimited opportunity, we face hiring freezes and massive layoffs. In the fall of 1982, the ranks of unemployment reached an all-time high. Even the fast-moving and highly lucrative electronics industry was hit. And the economic recovery in the spring of 1984 was clouded by the prospect of an even more severe recession looming ahead.

It has been a profoundly disorienting reversal, and even more so because there were no warning signals. There has been a change in attitude from an optimistic faith in an open-ended future to a fear that economic instability will prevent self-fulfillment and threaten security. We are hopeful and fearful at the same time. And maintaining these two states of mind simultaneously creates tension and confusion.

LIMITED OPPORTUNITY, SHRINKING CONFIDENCE

When faced with economic uncertainty, we become concerned with security. We entrench. Digging in and waiting out, we take fewer risks and become more conservative in our choices and decisions. The danger is that, while we are waiting out the slump in opportunity, we may change the way we feel about ourselves and our work as well as how we perform. This is a change that could be difficult to reverse.

Rosabeth Moss Kanter,[11] professor of organization and management at Yale, identified in her research a strong and predictable relationship between opportunity structure and how we act at work. Her results indicate that, when we are on high-mobility tracks, we are likely to develop such attitudes and values as work commitment, high aspirations, and upward orientation that propel us further along the track, whereas on low-mobility tracks we tend to disengage, becoming indifferent and willing to do only what is asked and no more. When we have little opportunity, work becomes just a job. We develop low-risk, conservative attitudes, becoming rule followers and chronic complainers. We criticize the company, the boss, the job, the commute, the pay, the politics—but never too loudly. In the process, we prove that our placement in low-opportunity jobs is justified. Limited opportunity affects self-image as well. We begin to feel and believe, "I'm nothing but a cog in the machine. But that's all I'm capable of anyway." Expectations shrink and aspirations drop as we adjust to limited opportunity.

Consider Pamela:

I started with the bank in June of '64. So in '69, when I got my first officer assignment, I felt I was doing really good. Not only was I a woman, but I was young and hadn't gone to college. In two and a half years, I was promoted to my next level and stayed there for a good five years, though I did get a promotion on site when the branch grew. So they put me in the accelerated development program, and eventually I moved from the general operations area to manager of a small branch. I did that for a while but didn't like it. When a place opened up in region operations—middle management—I took that. Then I took a break for ten months and went to school. But it didn't work out financially, so about a year and a half ago, I came back to the bank. It turned out to be a big mistake because I had to prove myself all over again. After several months, I got a position here as assistant to the vice president of operations.

But, you know, things have changed. Banks are really struggling in this economy. Now we're centralizing; all the banks are. What this means is that operations from all of the 37 branches in the northern region will consolidate in one central location. And a lot of positions will be eliminated.

What really got me was the regional VP when he came out to talk about the centralization. We all knew he was coming, and we all knew why. We can live with that. It's reality. But he gave us this bit about God helps those who help themselves and you should have seen this coming and you should have prepared and taken classes at night. Just laying the whole burden of responsibility of what happened to our careers on us. We were supposed to be able to forecast the economy! You know what I could take easier? "This is the way it is. We all think it stinks. We all feel bad about it, and we don't know what to do about it." Just be honest!

They say they're not going to terminate anybody, that they're going to find other jobs for everyone. I think, "Yeah, take half of your pay, too." And you've got to remember that every head office department is cutting back, too. There's going to be mass cuts. There'll have to be. Maybe they will have 40–60 jobs in the center. But a lot of people already commute a long distance to our branch, and the center is even further. A lot of people just can't make that kind of commute. So I don't see how they can say that they will find places for everyone. In the main branch here, there are seven of us in operations, and they'll only need three after centralization. And maybe not at the grade level we're at now. What are they going to do with all those operations people? All the banks are centralizing, too, so there's little chance of jumping to another bank at the same level. There's very limited opportunity no matter how you look at it.

I came away from that meeting feeling really discouraged. And, you know, I believed him. I felt like it was my fault somehow. I should have prepared. I started telling myself that I'm lazy. But I'm not lazy! I worked very hard to get where I'm at. I did. I worked a lot of weekends for a lot of years. My field's dried up. There's nowhere to go. I'll be lucky if I hold on to a job. I've got to start all over. Only I can't. I just don't have the energy I had when I was 23! I don't know what I'm going to do. I'll apply for the center manager position, but there are 36 others who probably will, too.

ORGANIZATIONS RESPOND

How organizations respond to downturns in the economy will have a direct impact on most of us. The economic problems America is experiencing are not the threats to modern organizations they may initially seem to be. Instead, they provide an opportunity for organizations to consolidate even more power over our lives.

Faced with uncertainty, organizations tighten up. They centralize decisions, authority, services, and planning. In short, organizations respond to uncertainty by asserting more control. It is during times of uncertainty that the feudalism of organizations becomes most apparent. But the pressures that produce conformity are often misunderstood. The precisely interlocking processes of a complex modern society require a high degree of predictability of individual behavior. As with all feudal systems, conformity and loyalty to "the Company Way" are the primary methods of ensuring predictability. And we go along with this because organizations convince us that what is good for the organization is good for us. We conform because it seems like a sensible way to keep the organization running smoothly and keeping our jobs and comforts. During hard times in particular, we buy this. In the words of William Whyte, author of the 1950s classic *The Organization Man:* "Few things are more calculated to rob the individual of his defenses than the idea that our interest and those of the organization can be wholly compatible."[12] The conflict between the individual and society has always involved dilemma and always will. The potential consequences of this direction are ominous. Many organization experts, such as Whyte, have warned that because we are bound to organizations through work there is the potential for organizations to exert totalitarian control.

Modern organizations influence us profoundly, but so quietly that we scarcely realize that they are major agencies of social control. Our commitment to organizational roles leads us to define ourselves in terms of these roles, creating even greater potential for control. The values and attitudes of the roles we play at work spill over into all other areas of our lives. While working within the organization, we *become* what we do in the sense that our personal values increasingly match those of the organization.

That organizations require strict obedience through the chain of command is obvious to all who work within one. Less obvious are the other mores of the organizational imperative. For example, modern organizations cannot tolerate an indispensable individual. If they did, organizations would become too dependent on such people, which is anathema to organizational thought and practice. So as our tenure in organizations continues, we come to accept and create, often without contemplation, our own dispensability. By embracing the linear career strategy, we become overly specialized, losing our flexibility and freedom of choice. We become standardized, interchangeable parts in a huge machine.

> The terrible paradox is that as [we] flee even more deeply into the organization, searching for security, [we] find only that [we] are the most dispensable commodity of all.
> —William Scott and David Hart
> *Organizational America*[13]

Organizations also require loyalty—loyalty that must come before our peers, friends, community, and even families. We are evaluated by the degree of our adherence to the organizational values of working to move up the occupational ladder, not by the quality of work.

> Dear Betty Harragan:
> I work for a retail jewelry chain and have done well during the past four years, getting promoted steadily. It is understood in this field that promotion depends heavily on a manager's willingness to relocate, an event that, in my company, occurs an average of three or four times a year. . . . In the past year alone I've been transferred twice to different states and now my boss has ordered another move. I just got settled in my present community, have joined some good business and sports clubs, and I hate to uproot myself so soon. . . . What effect does relocation have on one's future advancement?
> Cooperative

> Dear Cooperative:
> You are right in recognizing that physical mobility and job mobility are closely connected at the middle management level. It used to be a truism that an ambitious man who turned down a promotion because it involved relocation had effectively dead ended himself.
> In recent years, more women have been offered trans-

fer-promotions . . . but a majority of women still turn
down these offers for personal reasons. . . . Admittedly,
when the woman has a husband who cannot move with
her, plus young children, she has to weigh the pros and
cons of her relocations very carefully. Sometimes the
problem is insurmountable—she must give her primary
allegiance to her family's welfare and gamble that another job opportunity will come her way in later years.
But a surprising number of women resist geographic
transfers for specious reasons: They just "like" the city
they're in; all their friends or relatives live there; their
boyfriends live nearby. These personal and emotional ties
to a specific locale are not easily understood by bosses
or human resource planners; some managements today
can sympathize with realistic family obligations on the
part of men as well as women, but not many appreciate
undocumented excuses of "my wife doesn't want to
move," or "my husband doesn't want me to move." Such
explanations are taken as polite turndowns and get translated to the personnel file as "not interested in promotion," or "too inflexible for major responsibility."
                                                        —Betty Harragan
                                                        Knowing the Score[14]

Whyte and others claim that the ultimate outcome of the organizational imperative is to impose uniformity on all who enter
as a requisite condition of existence in an organizational culture.
The organization man and the man in the gray flannel suit may
have changed into a more contemporary garb, but they're still
with us. In the face of dwindling opportunity and intensifying
competition, we risk becoming serfs, indentured to our corporate,
professional, or academic slots as a tradeoff for golden handcuffs
of comfort and security.

Consider Jeff:
    I got into electronics years ago when it was an infant
field. I was in on the ground floor. I liked it because it
had a future and because it was exciting. I felt like I was
really doing something. Along the line, I was promoted a
number of times and finally made it into middle man-

agement, where I've been for eight years. And I hate to admit it, but I don't like my work and haven't for a long time. It's pushing papers. Every day papers, papers, papers. While I love electronics, I actually have little to do with it. The last couple of years, I've been spending a lot of time thinking that there are other things I'd rather do. I'd like to work with people, maybe in training or something like that. But I can't. If I try to transfer into that area, even within the company, I'll have to give up a big chunk of my pay and, of course, responsibility and just general clout. So I'm stuck here. I can't go out and find another job because, quite frankly, the truth of the matter is that I'm overpaid. I just don't see how I can get the same salary anywhere else. So I'm a prisoner in a plush cell. I'm wearing golden handcuffs.

Note: At the time of this statement, the mortgage on the four-bedroom modern suburban home Jeff shared with his wife was under $600 a month. And their liquid assets were more than four times Jeff's annual salary. Jeff was blind to the fact that his nest egg provided him with options few of us have. For example, he could have taken a position in a new field at half his current salary while maintaining his current life-style for eight years. But instead, Jeff was indentured to his specialized linear career track.

Earl Shorris describes the totalitarian techniques of organizations in *The Oppressed Middle: Politics of Middle Management*.[15] The most important element in any totalitarian organization is the power of the organization to assign or withdraw the means of earning a living. But organizations don't set out to be totalitarian. If they did, they would attract no more than a few lunatics to their membership. Totalitarianism evolves. We choose totalitarianism out of fear, because it holds an end to suffering and insecurity and in return it asks that we give nothing but our autonomy. University of Washington organization specialists William Scott and David Hart point out, "The benefits of the organizational imperative do not come for free; everyone must pay. And paying the debt has required us all to surrender our allegiance to the traditional American values [of individualism]."[16] But such behavioral and value alternations are not painful because we have created a society in which those who are loyal to the organizational imperative are amply rewarded.

There is no one to picket against, boycott, or turn to in appeal.
For even the leader of the organization is a dispensable human
part:

> Organizational bureaucracy or the rule of an intricate system of
> bureaus in which [no one] can be held responsible can properly
> be called Rule By Nobody. But Rule By Nobody is not no rule.
> Rule By Nobody is the most tyrannical of all, since there is no one
> who can even be asked to answer for what is being done.[17]

From the chief executive office to the clerks and assemblers,
we're all equally powerless. "We have tyranny without a tyrant.
Bureaucracy has taken on a life of its own making society answer
to a despot in the person of nobody, leaving us utterly helpless
or hopeless without the possibility of appeal."[18] We trade autonomy for material benefits and the illusion of security. Whyte
concurs, "It is not so much that The Organization is going to push
the individual around more than it used to. It is that it is becoming
increasingly hard to figure out when we are being pushed
around."[19] It is easy to fight obvious tyranny but it is not easy to
fight benevolence.

But large organizations are not to be condemned out of hand.
That is what makes the problem difficult as well as interesting.
"Organizations serve us and rule us; increase our scope and hem
us in," emphasizes social philosopher John Gardner.[20] But the
fault is not in the machine or in the pressures of industrial society;
it lies in the stance we assume before these pressures and in the
arrangement of functions that ignores our needs as individuals.
The organization is coercive to the extent that the individual has
no alternative to a given course of action. Humans are being made
to adapt to the machine, rather than the reverse. We must learn
to make technology serve people not only in the end product but
in the doing.

Nothing can be further from the values of self-fulfillment
seekers than career feudalism: the hierarchical, authoritarian, adversary attitudes that characterize the organizational outlook in
many American industries.

PREDICTIONS FOR THE FUTURE

Compounding our apprehensiveness is the energy crisis. Operating machinery, factories, and large organizations requires an

enormous amount of energy every day. Millions of people commute, many for long distances, another massive daily energy expenditure. From the 1950s through the early 1970s, we had cheap
energy in abundance, a catalyst for the unprecedented prosperity
we enjoyed. But that suddenly changed in the mid-1970s with
the oil embargo and the resulting dramatic escalation of the price
of oil. Now we pay more for energy. And all indications are that
the price will escalate again. That our nonrenewable energy resources are finite and can and will eventually run out is beginning to take on a personal meaning. We are seeing it in the prices
we pay, in the value of our money, and in our jobs. Everywhere
we turn, we hear of cutbacks and are admonished to be frugal
and to prepare for an era of scarcity.

Futurists Warren Johnson[21] and Jeremy Rifkin[22] both claim
that our industrial society as it is now will not be able to continue
as energy becomes more scarce. Ultimately, we must switch to
solar power, our one source of renewable energy. The change to
solar power will impact directly upon our industries: the way in
which we structure our workplace. Johnson and Rifkin claim that
the transition will lead to the decentralization of our economy,
because it will no longer be profitable to concentrate our industries in one location; to smaller scale technologies; and to re-
population of rural areas, thereby reducing the overload of many
of our cities.

What does decentralization of the workplace mean? Well, it's
hard to say since we don't know yet. Futurists predict that our
workplace will be more spread out geographically, that we will
work in smaller work units, and that we will live closer to work,
perhaps within walking distance, thereby reducing the energy
expenditure of commuting. It all sounds reminiscent of the "good
old days" of small-town rural America.

Johnson foresees labor-intensive industries becoming more
profitable than capital-intensive ones. The human being will become indispensable once again! Rifkin claims the solar age will
require a great conformity to the ancient rhythms of life. But we
will not go backward, says Alvin Toffler: "The diversification of
society, its shift from industrial homogeneity to superindustrial
heterogeneity, is one of the fundamental processes of our
epoch."[23]

What does this all mean? It means that there will be more
flexibility, diversity, and differences, not only in the workplace

itself, but also among those who work there. This all sounds quite good. In fact, the energy crisis may be a reprieve from the totalitarian threat of organizations. The market, after all, may become our ally, forcing us to do all the right things even if for all the wrong reasons. So while the words *frugality* and *scarcity* and thoughts of no energy are frightening, there may be a silver lining to that dark cloud. The energy crisis may result in more freedom and flexibility and in living closer to the real things in life—just exactly what we have been seeking in our quest for self-fulfillment.

But making such a transition will not be easy. The industrial era, captained by organizations, believes in centralizing and demands conformity and specialized work from specialized human parts—that's us. We complied and became specialists. But overspecialization, say biologists, is one of the most important contributing factors in a species becoming extinct. When a species becomes overspecialized in a particular type of ecosystem, it is usually unable to adapt to a change in the environment because it does not contain the flexibility and diversity to enable it to make the transition. This may be where many of us are today. Because we followed the linear career track, our ability to adapt is impaired. Having become specialized human parts for the vast organizational machine, we are now facing a crisis of adapting to an unknown future. Indeed, we find ourselves stuck on a track headed toward oblivion.

Johnson warns that the most dangerous thing we can do is to rigidly resist this change. The change is inevitable. The only option is to be open and flexible. But how can we be when we've become specialized human parts in the organizational machine, without flexibility, without a breadth of movement, without options for alternative ways of providing for our lives' needs? There are alternative ways of organizing people and producing products and services, but we can't think of them because we are so locked into our existing world paradigm that all other ways of organizing are seen as totally unacceptable. The ways in which we look at the world and the ways in which work and workers are organized conform to what can be called the Newtonian world view: Everything is cause and effect; everything is mechanistic. So it should come as no surprise that the organization itself resembles a giant machine with dispensable, replaceable human parts.

Networks

> We are participating not merely in
> the birth of a new organizational form but
> in the birth of a new civilization.
> —Alvin Toffler
> *The Third Wave*[24]

In a number of his writings, Alvin Toffler argues persuasively that the hierarchical structure of organizations is a form that is breaking down and in the future will not be the dominant way of organizing people at work. It is difficult to conceive of a new way of organizing people that is different from the feudal chain of command. The feudal system is part of our belief system and the way we naturally structure people working together.

> What we are seeing today is not simply an *economic*
> upheaval, but something far deeper, something that can-
> not be understood within the framework of conventional
> economies. . . . "The old rules don't work any longer."
> What we are seeing is the general crisis of industrial-
> ism. . . . What is happening, no more, no less, is the break-
> down of industrial civilization on the planet and the first
> fragmentary appearance of a wholly new and dramati-
> cally different social order: a super-industrial civilization
> that will be technological, but no longer industrial.
> —Alvin Toffler
> *The Eco-Spasm Report*[25]

With the advent of the small computer, however, it becomes possible to connect people in different ways. In contrast to the hierarchy, a network structure of organizing becomes possible. As the accompanying diagram shows, hierarchies connect subordinates linearly to one superior. Networks, on the other hand, use the on-line capabilities of computers to interconnect individuals of equal or varying power directly. Unlike hierarchies, networks are dynamic and yield infinite shapes.

Computer technology has also increased the accessibility of telecommunications, which allows people who are not physically

ORGANIZATIONAL STRUCTURE

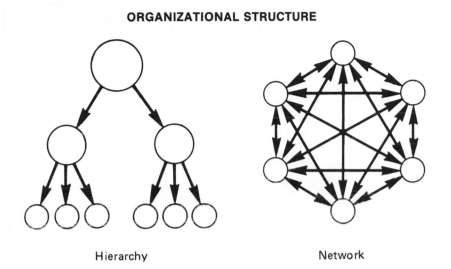

Hierarchy   Network

in the same location to connect directly. This has many ramifications for where people work and how they interface. At this writing, these new organizational forms are in a developmental state. The implications of this new and rapidly developing structure are left to our speculations. We literally do not know what the shape of new organizations will look like!

> "The central, crucial and important business of organizations . . . is increasingly shifting from up and down to 'sideways.'" What is involved in such a shift is a virtual revolution in organizational structure—and in human relations. People communicating "sideways"—i.e., to others of approximately the same level of organization—behave differently, operate under very different pressures, than those who must communicate up and down a hierarchy.
>
> —Alvin Toffler
> *Future Shock*[26]

In *Future Shock* Toffler predicts that organizations of the superindustrial society will become more and more turbulent, filled with change. He envisions a move from bureaucracy to "ad-hocracy"—changing organizational forms dictated by project goals. This will translate into a dramatic alteration in the definition of job functions. People will be differentiated, not vertically according to rank and role, but flexibly and functionally according to skill and professional training. Such changes will increase the adaptability of organizations, but will strain our adaptability. Will *you* be prepared?

> Super-industrial Man, rather than occupying a permanent, cleanly-defined slot and performing mindless routine tasks in response to orders from above, finds increasingly that he must assume decision-making responsibility—and must do so within a kaleidoscopically changing organization structure built upon highly transient human relationships.
>
> —Alvin Toffler
> *Future Shock*[27]

Computer technology is the most powerful force changing human society today. Over the next generation, every man, woman, and child will have the ability to use computers for access to facts, to organizations, and—most importantly—to other human beings. There is a new type of structure that makes this access possible. It is called a *network*.

Computer networks can be used by a repressive government to look for undesirables or to flag suspects, but they can also be used by individuals to share thoughts and facts, novel ideas, visions of humanity's future destiny. They constitute communications media unparalleled in human history. And they lead us to a momentous decision.

Computer networks are going to force us in the next few years to make a choice between two types of society: I have designated them as the "Digital Society" and the "Grapevine Alternative."

In the Digital Society, massive amounts of computer technology are used to control people by reducing them to statistics. In the Digital Society, computers are repressive tools and their use for private communication is discouraged.

In the Grapevine Alternative, on the contrary, computers are used by people to build networks. And beyond the simple use of these networks for information we find people actually communicating through them . . . it will go far beyond such applications when people in large numbers discover in these networks gateways to other minds, windows to unsuspected vistas, bridges across their loneliness, and precious understanding.

. . . for the first time, a door [has] been forced open in the bureaucracy and a new type of community [is starting] to grow.

—Jacques Vallee
The Network Revolution[28]

The Electronic Cottage

The technology of the computer allows us to have a distinct and individually tailored arrangement with each of thousands of employees.

—John Naisbitt
Megatrends[29]

With computers comes hope for a new way of working: the electronic cottage. What Alvin Toffler and other futurists envision is millions of people working in their homes at their computer terminals rather than in centralized office complexes. Such an arrangement would not require commuting or providing offices and other facilities with energy-gobbling lights and air conditioning. Yet, because of telecommunications, the worker could plug directly into the central office of the company. Indeed, it becomes possible for one to live in San Francisco and "work in" New York City.

That worksteads [home workplaces] are feasible and timely seems clear; that they are also enormously beneficial to their participants is the payoff. . . . Perhaps most important, the worksteader usually doesn't make a distinction between "living" and "working." . . . Economic factors are certainly a primary impetus for worksteads, as well as the most tangible measure of the movement's impact on society. In addition to its money-saving features, a home-based career offers the individual comfort, freedom from commuting, a sense of independence, and

the opportunity to be closer to family. Collectively, worksteads offer society the example of entrepreneurs who
emphasize conservation of resources, question the use
of energy-intensive technology, and urge a scaling down
of most institutions. . . . In short, worksteads are the
ground where a certain kind of economics meets a certain kind of humanism. . . .

—Jeremy Joan Hewes
Worksteads[30]

Perhaps we will be saved from the totalitarian thrust of the
organization by the electronic cottage. Perhaps we will have
more flexible work styles, working at different times and in different ways, better integrating work and home, not having to
dress for work, not having to buy all those expensive success
costumes, and contending with fewer demands for conformity.
Perhaps it will happen; perhaps it won't. There is only one thing
we can count on with absolute certainty: Our futures are uncertain. Like the *ronin* of feudal Japan, we're all being cast upon
the waves of change. We don't know which way change will go.
Perhaps we will become serfs in the totalitarian organization, or
perhaps we will be set free by our electronic cottages. The only
security is our ability to adapt to the coming changes even though
we don't yet know what they will be. The problem is that many
of us are ill prepared. We are not adaptable; we are not flexible.
We are specialized human parts, having prepared ourselves for
one career for our entire lives, a career that may soon be obsolete.

THE EMERGING RONIN

And out of the collision between the quest for more flexibility,
self-fulfillment, and opportunity to develop our full potential and
the economic reversal, the increased pressures for conformity,
the reduced opportunity, the uncertainty, and the confusion is
emerging a new breed of worker: the Ronin.

Who are the Ronin? If you take a look around, you will see
them everywhere, emerging in every industry and in every walk
of life. Perhaps even you, yourself, are an emerging Ronin.

The end of the feudal period in Japan brought with it great
social change. Traditionally indentured to a feudal lord or pro-
vincial army, many samurai became *ronin* when the armies were

disbanded. Like the ancient counterpart, the modern American Ronin has broken out of the bonds of the linear career track or the one-life-one-profession imperative to which so many of us are indentured, following instead irregular, nonlinear career paths.

Ronin look like other people. The difference is in attitude and life planning strategy. Ronin project an aura of autonomy, of being guided from a center within. They take command and direct their lives. Ronin don't just react to change; they take the initiative and direct their futures. Ronin do not believe it is possible to find security in one job, in one place, doing one thing. Guided by the belief that change is the only constant, Ronin develop skills, attitudes, and habits of mind that become adaptable instruments of continuous change and growth. Ronin do not exhibit fealty to organizational goals. Instead, they strive for project goals and excellence even if it means going against the Company Way.

He who wishes to undertake the path of Heiho should always:

First: Do not harbor sinister designs.
Second: Diligently pursue the Way of the Warrior; the Way is in the pursuit.
Third: Cultivate a wide range of interests in the arts.
Fourth: Be knowledgeable in a variety of occupations.
Fifth: Be discrete regarding one's commercial dealings.
Sixth: Nurture the ability to perceive the truth in all matters.
Seventh: Perceive that which cannot be seen with the eye.
Eighth: Do not be negligent, even in trifling matters.
Ninth: Do not engage in useless activity.

If one consistently devotes one's energies to Heiho, and aggressively pursues Truth, one should be able to win by the hand and to be obviously superior, and since one's body is completely under one's control due to the training, it is possible to be physically superior, and furthermore, if one disciplines one's spirit sufficiently, it is possible to be psychologically superior. If one can achieve this, how can one lose?

—Miyamoto Musashi
Ronin, circa 1645
The Book of Five Rings[31]

Like Palladin, the frontier gunslinger whose famed calling card read "Have Gun Will Travel," Ronin use their skills, whether they be sword fighting, gunslinging, selling, doctoring, or teaching, as tickets to adventure. For Ronin, it is the adventure

of self-actualization: developing oneself to the fullest by encountering and overcoming challenges and risk.

Being able to change, Ronin do not resist. Instead, expecting
change, they prepare by developing a broad base of expertise
and skills. Ronin do not pay allegiance to any one career track.
Instead, using their interests as a guide, they follow one, then
another, becoming generalists with many specialities. Ronin can
wear many hats and often do. And they can bring their diverse
skills together in creative and profitable ways. So while the linear-track specialists lose the capacity to adapt, which is so essential in our changing world, Ronin are able to reorient themselves when the economy takes a downswing putting them out
of work or when technologies change making their specialities
obsolete. Ronin have a basic confidence, a sense of potency or
personal power. This is their security. Ronin believe they will
be able to deal adequately with whatever might arise and will
be able to earn the money they need.

Don Juan, the famed Yaqui Indian sorcerer who taught Carlos
Castaneda the Way of the Warrior, warns:

> Does this path have a heart? If it does, the path is good; if it doesn't,
> it is of no use. Both paths lead nowhere; but one has a heart, the
> other doesn't. One makes for a joyful journey; as long as you follow
> it, you are one with it. The other will make you curse your life.
> One makes you strong; the other weakens you.[32]

Ronin know that the adventure is in traveling on the path and
not in reaching the destination. Consequently, when making career decisions they are less compromising than linear careerists,
who often find themselves trapped on paths with no heart. Ronin
refuse heartless paths because they expect work to provide an
experience for growth through challenge. Ronin want a sense of
contributing and belonging, and they expect work to be ener-
gizing while serving as a vehicle of self-discovery, a way to test
one's contribution and limits, as well as providing for the basic
necessities of life and for delightful comforts. Although all these
ingredients may not exist at any given point in time in the desired
amounts and mixes, Ronin use the disappointments and setbacks
as lessons in the quest to realize their potential.

As Ronin advance along their irregular career paths, gaining
more experience and more expertise, options multiply. When
blocked in an existing job with no place for advancement, Ronin
move laterally in any number of directions. Ronin are resistant

ITHACA

When you start on your journey to Ithaca,
then pray that the road is long,
full of adventure, full of knowledge.
Do not fear the Lestrygonians
and the Cyclopes and the angry Poseidon.
You will never meet such as these on your path,
if your thoughts remain lofty, if a fine
emotion touches your body and your spirit.
You will never meet the Lestrygonians,
the Cyclopes and the fierce Poseidon,
if you do not carry them within your soul,
if your soul does not raise them up before you.

Then pray that the road is long.
That the summer mornings are many,
that you will enter ports seen for the first time
with such pleasure, with such joy!
Stop at Phoenician markets,
and purchase fine merchandise,
mother-of-pearl and corals, amber and ebony,
and pleasurable perfumes of all kinds,
buy as many pleasurable perfumes as you can;
visit hosts of Egyptian cities,
to learn and learn from those who have knowledge.

Always keep Ithaca fixed in your mind.
To arrive there is your ultimate goal.
But do not hurry the voyage at all.
It is better to let it last for long years;
and even to anchor at the isle when you are old,
rich with all that you have gained on your way,
not expecting that Ithaca will offer you riches.

Ithaca has given you the beautiful voyage.
Without her you would never have taken the road.
But she has nothing more to give you.

And if you find her poor, Ithaca has not defrauded you.
With the great wisdom you have gained, with so much
      experience,
you must surely have understood by then what Ithacas
      mean.

                                   —C. P. Cavafy
                                   Rae Dalven, Translator[33]

to job burnout and suffer less trauma or psychological setback
when they are passed over for promotion or miss out on a desired
job. Viewing life as a voyage of exploration, Ronin welcome unexpected turns. Changes, even negative ones, are accepted as
opportunities to conquer new challenges.

> All a person can do in this life is to gather about him
> his integrity, his imagination, and his individuality—and
> with these ever with him, out in front, leap into the dance
> of experience.
> "Be your own master!
> "Be your own Jesus!
> "Be your own flying saucer! Rescue yourself!
> "Be your own valentine! Free the heart!"
> —Tom Robbins
> *Even Cowgirls Get the Blues*[34]

Ronin do not measure success by the rungs on the ladder or
the digits on the paycheck. For like their ancient prototype, they
are accountable to their own standards based on growth and realization. In contrast to linear careerists, especially those on the
fast track, who often picture their accomplishments on a football-
type scoreboard, Ronin view their lives as a giant canvas upon
which they, the artist, paint with each experience.

When working in organizations, Ronin are not as vulnerable
as linear specialists to organizational control because their sense
of confidence and autonomy are vital buffers. Although Ronin
don't like layoffs, cutbacks, or being fired, they know they can
survive them. But do not assume they are nonconformists; rather
they are autonomous in the sense that they know how to act
appropriately and will do so if it does not violate their internal
guidelines. And Ronin are not rebels. Instead, they consider
work a medium for self-realization, the barbells that develop the
skills muscles. Ronin view themselves, much like a vendor or
independent contractor, as working for themselves within the
company. Stated another way they work through the company,
not for it. Ronin integrate their personal goals with company
goals. Although Ronin like comforts and the good things that
money can buy, obtaining these is not their primary motivator.
Instead, they are propelled by the quest for self-development.

Being their own masters, Ronin are self-directed, using work as an opportunity to set high goals to create a challenge and also to learn. Rarely do they allow their jobs to become static, instead they tend to rework the job constantly in response to the needs of the company or marketplace. In the following chapters, we will explore why Ronin are resistant to job burnout and the mid-life crisis and how Ronin are valuable performers in organizations. We will then explore more deeply the attributes of Ronin, their attitudes, their training, and their career strategies and how they overcome fear of change.

Consider Clayton:

A lot of people are surprised when they find out about my doctorate in psychopharmacology. They think it contradicts my publishing growth books for kids. For me, it seems like a natural progression.

When I was in school, I had a lot of problems choosing what I wanted to do. There were just too many things I enjoyed, and I resented having to pick one for the rest of my life. I was very much into science, chemistry in particular. At the same time, people and why they did things fascinated me. Education seemed like a way to have an impact on the society. And I dabbled a little in poetry and writing. As I said, I resented having to pick just one of these and give all the others up. I thought teaching psychopharmacology in the university would be a good way to combine the psychology, the education, and the chemistry and promised to provide some money, some credibility—in essence, the good life. So that's what I did. I got my degree and my first assistant professor job in an East Coast university. I taught and did research.

But I became disillusioned with the university. It was stifling in many ways. Psychopharmacology seemed to be my best ticket, and I quickly landed a job as a salesman with a pharmaceutical company. I was good at selling because I was good with people; I listened and all of that. It didn't take me long to learn just about everything there was to learn about selling drugs to doctors. So this time I used selling as my ticket, and I landed a job as marketing director of a big toy manufacturer. What did I know about toys? Nothing. But it didn't take me long to learn. It was fascinating because I saw the connection with kids and the power that toys had over them.

One thing led to another, and I started leading sales

training classes. At the same time, I'd gotten interested in the human potential movement in psychology. I belonged to a growth group and went through a number of personal changes. And I wanted to integrate them into my work. So I left the toys and began leading self-development and growth workshops. It worked out perfectly because I was getting restless and wanted to travel. So I got into the lecture circuit, which took me all around the country. But before long, I decided I'd rather not be spending my weekends on a plane or in a hotel. So I packaged some of my stuff and started selling it. I got a number of big accounts with schools and businesses and expanded into a publishing house.

Now I have a substantial list of self-development books for children and adolescents. I'm interested in the adjusting person, not the adjusted person—that's static. I'm interested in teaching kids adaptive skills that will serve them their whole lives. I'm really proud of our books.

You know, when I left the university, people told me that I'd ruined my whole life, that I'd never get anywhere and that I'd always be poor. But they were wrong. I've had a hellava good time; I'm anything but poor and I think I'm doing something important—helping kids have quality lives.

Oh, I won't stay in publishing forever. One day, maybe soon, I'll sell the company and do something else. I don't know what it might be. Oh, I have been getting a yearning to get back into science, and I've started to develop an interest in some of the problems in the medical industry. There are a lot of them, you know. So my psychopharmacology degree combined with my training experience might be a perfect ticket into the medical world. Who knows?

Notes

1. *Megatrends: Ten New Directions Transforming Our Lives* (New York: Warner Books, 1982), p. 53.
2. John Oliver Wilson, *After Affluence: Economics to Meet Human Needs* (New York: Harper & Row, 1980), p. 13.
3. Ibid., p. 201.
4. Daniel Yankelovich, *New Rules: Searching for Self-Fulfillment in a World Turned Upside Down* (New York: Bantam, 1982), p. 16.

5. New York: St. Martin's Press, 1978, p. viii.
6. Wilson, *After Affluence,* p. 196.
7. Ibid., p. 18.
8. Thomas L. Friedman, "The Baby Boomers Run Head On into Reality," *San Francisco Chronicle,* May 26, 1982.
9. New York: Bantam, 1982, p. 19.
10. Wilson, *After Affluence,* p. 66.
11. *Men and Women of the Corporation* (New York: Basic Books, 1977), p. 134.
12. New York: Touchstone, 1956, p. 397.
13. Boston: Houghton Mifflin, 1980, p. 68.
14. *Knowing the Score: Play-by-Play Directions for Women on the Job* (New York: St. Martin's Press, 1983).
15. New York: Doubleday/Anchor Press, 1981.
16. *Organizational America* (Boston: Houghton Mifflin, 1980), p. 50.
17. Hannah Arendt cited in Earl Shorris, *The Oppressed Middle: Politics of Middle Management* (New York: Doubleday/Anchor Press, 1981), p. 84.
18. Ibid.
19. *The Organization Man* (New York: Touchstone, 1956), p. 166.
20. *Self-Renewal: The Individual and the Innovative Society* (New York: Harper Colophon, 1965), p. 63.
21. *Muddling Toward Frugality* (San Francisco: Sierra Club Books, 1978).
22. *Entropy: A New World View* (New York: Bantam, 1981).
23. *The Eco-Spasm Report* (New York: Bantam, 1975), p. 95.
24. New York: Bantam, 1980, p. 264.
25. p. 3.
26. New York: Random House, 1970, p. 123. The first sentence is quoted from William Reed of McGill University.
27. p. 127.
28. *The Network Revolution: Confessions of a Computer Scientist* (Berkeley, Calif.: And/Or Press, 1982), pp. 4–5, 102.
29. p. 43.
30. *Worksteads: Living and Working in the Same Place* (Garden City, N.Y.: Dolphin Books, 1981), pp. 1–3.
31. New York, front page. As translated by Nihon Services Corp., Bradford J. Brown, Yuko Kasaiwagi, William H. Barrett, Eisuke Sasagawa, copyright © 1982 by Bantam Books, Inc. By permission.
32. *The Teachings of Don Juan: A Yaqui Way of Knowledge* (New York: Pocket Books, 1974), p. 107.
33. *The Complete Poems of Cavafy,* trans. Rae Dalven (New York: Harcourt, Brace & World, 1961), pp. 36–37.
34. New York: Pocket Books, 1977, p. 260.

2

Career Feudalism

Without work, all life goes rotten, but when work
is soulless, life stifles and dies.
—**Albert Camus**

Although we live in a modern and free society, our freedom continues to be curtailed by career feudalism. Career feudalism is a way of organizing work that diminishes the personal power of workers. It has three characteristics that limit power. First is the divison of labor or the machine approach to designing and interfacing job functions. When jobs are standardized, people can be moved in and out of job slots like interchangeable parts in the organizational machine. Expected to act machine-like, workers learn to be cool and rational. Demonstrations of emotion or reliance on intuition are frowned upon as inappropriate. An advantage of standardization to the company is that it need invest only minimally in employee development. Rather than training its staff, the company merely has to find the correctly fitting human part. If the part is scarce, headhunters are called upon to cannibalize the part from another corporate machine.

Becoming a very special part is the optimal career strategy in such a system. By specializing, people can reduce their competition while increasing their market value. The secret of success is selecting a winning career track by specializing in a high-demand profession or trade. Once selected, the track becomes a lifelong commitment.

At first, power seems to increase with movement along the linear track. With each promotion comes more responsibility, more money, and sometimes more discretion. But enhancement of personal power is an illusion. The longer a track is followed, the more restricting it becomes. Rather than open up opportunities, linear tracks limit movement. Even when workers move to another company, they rarely switch tracks. As in all feudal societies, there are rigid barriers between classes. Serfs could not become merchants nor could clergy become samurai. Similarly, under career feudalism, secretaries cannot become executives, nor can craftspeople become professionals. Career choices made early are binding.

Not having the mobility to shift career tracks creates the effect of being a vassal, the second characteristic of career feudalism. The indentured are not free to do as they please or to do the work of their choice. Instead, they are bound by obligations in which someone (or some entity) is the final arbitrator of their fate.

Promise of security is the primary motivation for accepting the constraints of career feudalism. Peasants and knights alike were willing to be indentured because the lord, provided he was a good one, protected them from roving bands and other outsiders. The lord did more than protect, however, he also provided. He established a marketplace, supported the church, and carried out judiciary functions, for example. Similarly, companies take care of health insurance, maintain credit unions, and so forth.

The hidden price for the security provided by career feudalism is diminished freedom and personal power. Choices and mobility are limited, and corporate goals take precedence over both project and personal goals. Bureaucracies, like all feudal systems, are structured in tiers or a hierarchy that funnels power to the top. Royalty oversee the lords; the lords oversee the warriors;

and the warriors preside over the serfs. This is the bureaucratic model.

Three of the outstanding characteristics of bureaucracy were permanence, hierarchy, and a division of labor. These characteristics molded the human beings who manned the organizations.

Permanence—the recognition that the link between man and organization would endure through time— brought with it a commitment to the organization. . . . Longevity bred loyalty. In work organizations, this natural tendency was powerfully reinforced by the knowledge that termination of one's links with the organization often meant a loss of the means of economic survival. . . . To keep his job [the bureaucrat] willingly subordinated his own interests and convictions to those of the organization.

Power-laden hierarchies, through which authority flowed, wielded the whip by which the individual was held in line. Knowing that his relationship with the organization would be relatively permanent (or at least hoping that it would be) the organization man looked within for approval. Rewards and punishments came down the hierarchy to the individual, so that the individual, habitually looking upward at the next rung of the hierarchical ladder, became conditioned to subservience.

Finally, the organization man needed to understand his place in the scheme of things; he occupied a well-defined niche, performed actions that were also well-defined by the rules of the organization, and he was judged by the precision with which he followed the book. Faced by relatively routine problems, he was encouraged to seek routine answers. Unorthodoxy, creativity, venturesomeness were discouraged, for they interfered with the predictability required by the organization of its component parts.

—Alvin Toffler
Future Shock[1]

The third characteristic of feudalism is the demand for absolute fealty. European feudal kings rewarded the loyal baron just as the Japanese *shogun* rewarded the loyal *daimyo* with territorial domains or fiefs. These landlords, in return, rewarded

CAREER FEUDALISM

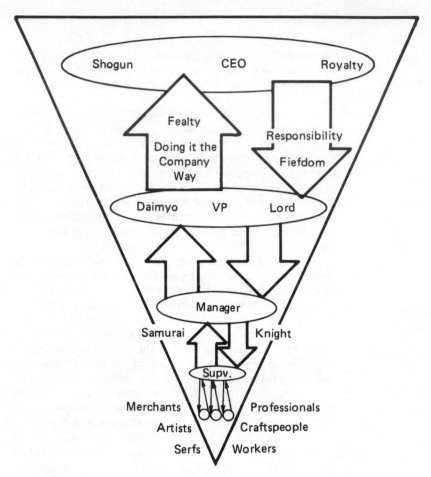

loyal subjects, usually high-ranking knights or samurai, with stipends and small land grants. Similarly, under career feudalism, loyalty to the Company Way is more important than performance as a criterion for advancement and recognition (see the accompanying diagram). Performing in line with the Company Way is paramount even when there may be pragmatically a better way. Those who are loyal to this standard are rewarded with promotions and increased responsibility domains.

Having broken out of career feudalism, Ronin do not exhibit fealty to the Company Way. Instead they focus on pragmatic project goals. When their accomplishment means doing things dif-

ferently from the Company Way, Ronin will find a route around
the company rules in search of excellence in completion of the
project.

The linear career strategy was a winner in the postwar growth
era, the heyday of industrialism. But as we specialized, we became, without realizing it, interchangeable, standardized parts
in the industrial machine, the organization. Jobs were defined,
classified, and standardized. Just as an auto mechanic can order
new plugs when the old ones misfire or replace worn wheel
bearings, the organization can replace specialized workers. At
first, the rewards were high. Once on the track, you could expect
to be carried along by the momentum. There was security in
one's niche and a fat paycheck that increased periodically, boun-
tiful luxuries and gadgets to buy, and a feeling of accomplishment
as we worked our way up through the levels in the organizational
chart toward the top. Few realized they were beholden. As long
as the economy was booming and industry was growing, everything was roses. Then things changed. The economy turned
down, industry contracted, the baby-boomers came of age and
wanted their rightful place in the pyramid, unemployment
jumped. Soon the casualties of career fedualism became epidemic.

Specialization curtails freedom. Once on the track, we can't
get off without going back to the starting place at square one. Job
functions are narrow and routine. Continuity is disrupted, and
rarely is one able to follow a project through from beginning to
end. As the range of functions gets narrower, the worker's personality becomes lopsided. Self-actualization and the development of one's full potential is impossible. We become rigid, losing the ability to learn and adapt, and we become vulnerable to
job burnout and the midlife crisis.

POWERLESSNESS

A sense of power, the feeling that we can influence the world
around us, is essential for healthy functioning. And when ability
to control our circumstances is restricted, we are vulnerable.
Consider this study: Zaleznik and two other researchers from
Harvard Graduate Business School[2] surveyed the amount of
stress experienced by 2,000 people working in three fields: staff,
management, and operations. They found that there was no dif-

ference in stress level among the three groups. Next, the stress level data were correlated with the number of stress-related disorders, such as time off the job, drug abuse, and marital problems, experienced by each group. It is commonly believed that there is a one-to-one relationship between stress level and stress-related disorders (i.e., low stress levels go with low frequencies of stress-related disorders and high levels go with high frequencies). Were this a true relationship, we'd expect the three groups to have the same number of stress-related problems. But the data did not confirm this popular assumption. Instead, one group had more stress-related disorders, and one group had fewer. Can you guess which group was high and which was low? Stop and consider this for a moment. What is the reasoning behind your guess?

Operations had the highest frequency of stress-related problems, and management had the least! The distinguishing variable was the degree of power or control over one's work. Operations workers indicated that they felt powerless. In their work, there are few markers indicating completion of a project. Instead, there is a continuous flow of work in which operations workers must live by the numbers, with stiff output standards making it easy to determine whether or not they accomplished their production quota. Yet they reported organizational conditions that sabotaged their ability to produce those numbers. For example, they complained that their supervisors were technically ignorant and that they couldn't communicate with them. Managers, on the other hand, have at least an illusion of control. The Harvard group hypothesized that feelings of personal power buffered the managers from the effects of stress.

> Bureaucratic practices set limits to the assertion of power by individuals in the organization, but the possession of power in organizations reduces the harmful consequences of bureaucracy to the individual. Therefore, survival in bureaucracies falls to those individuals who know how to negotiate a double bind situation, while advancement in bureaucracies falls to those individuals who can make an opportunity out of a paradox.
>
> —Abraham Zaleznik, Manfred Kets de Vries, and John Howard
> "Stress Reactions in Organizations,"
> *Behavioral Science*[3]

PARADOX

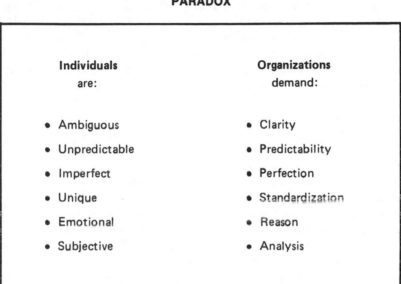

Individuals are:	Organizations demand:
• Ambiguous	• Clarity
• Unpredictable	• Predictability
• Imperfect	• Perfection
• Unique	• Standardization
• Emotional	• Reason
• Subjective	• Analysis

In discussing their results, the Harvard researchers imply that feudal organizations are toxic to the human spirit because they severely limit feelings of personal power. Feudal organizations thrust all who work within them into an unavoidable paradox, as outlined in the accompanying chart. For example, organizations are created by individuals. Yet once created, they develop an anti-individual consciousness. Individuals become a threat, and organizations will act in subtle ways to eliminate those who exhibit individuality and personal power. And this often includes the very people who birthed the organization in the first place. As the organization grows stronger, it focuses increasingly on self-preservation. Clients and customers are tolerated as necessary nuisances. Common are the stories of social agencies, for example, that neglect and in some cases even injure those they are mandated to serve. The institutions in Ken Kesey's *One Flew over the Cuckoo's Nest* is a classic example. The spirited renegade Ronin, McMurphy, was the only healthy person on Nurse Ratched's ward. He shook the patients out of their apathy and admonished them by example to assert their personal power and renew enthusiasm for living. McMurphy inspired hope in the patients and fear in the staff. The catatonic Indian spoke for the first time in over a decade—a therapeutic breakthrough! Mc-Murphy's influence actualized all that mental health authorities profess is good for mental patients. Yet, McMurphy's assertiveness upset the ward routine. No longer were the patients docile; they were unpredictable. Nurse Ratched's fiefdom was under siege. Rallying all her forces, she finally had McMurphy lobotomized and thus eliminated his spirit. Or so she thought. For so strong was his spirit that it lived on in the patients' memories. Even after McMurphy was killed, they refused to believe he was dead.

Peters and Waterman[4] chronicle the cuckoo's-nest dynamic in corporate America. Those who act too individualistic, or who challenge organizational routines, no matter how outmoded or cumbersome, are pushed out. Those Ronin who remain are continually blocked or moved into sidetracks. Never mind that the organization needs corporate Ronin to remain dynamic, innovative, and flexible. They are seen as disruptive and challenging and must be neutralized. Pledging allegiance to the Company Way is imperative.

JOB BURNOUT

Career feudalism has an adverse effect upon motivation and productivity. Territorial domains are granted for allegiance to the Company Way rather than for excellent performance. Hierarchical control limits personal control and ability to accomplish assigned goals. The demand for fealty constricts freedom of movement, action, and thought. The loss of personal power sets the stage for job burnout, a syndrome that reached epidemic proportions in the late 1970s and early 1980s.

Job burnout refers to the stressful changes that accompany the destruction of motivation. (The relationship between stress and burnout is discussed later in this chapter.) Burnout is most dramatic when it occurs among the high achievers, the front-runners, and the fast-trackers. Once infused with enthusiasm, these high performers became increasingly frustrated and disillusioned. Steadily, motivation and productivity decline. As motivation wanes, we see disruptions in five areas of functioning: intellectual, emotional, social, physical, and spiritual.

Intellectual Disruption

Cognitive problems can occur at either end of the intellectual functioning continuum. At one end is boredom, an inability to pay attention or to become intellectually involved. Instead, thinking tends to wander to daydreams. At the other end of the continuum is hypervigilance that is caused by high anxiety. Here thinking is scattered, moving erratically from one issue to another.

Emotional Disruption

Burnout is accompanied by increasingly intense negative emotions. At first, the contradictions and double binds of the feudal system engender feelings of frustration at not being able to accomplish assigned goals while being instructed to do so. Frustration ignites anger. As performance drops and interpersonal problems increase, the burnout victim begins fearing job loss. With increasing insecurity, anger turns to anxiety. Eventually, anxiety gives way to depression and apathy. The person retires on the job. Often this progression is accompanied by alcohol and drug abuse.

Social Disruption

The demotivated worker becomes touchy. Small requests are treated as unreasonable demands; minor irritants trigger emotional outbursts. Difficulty working with co-workers is the result. Increasingly, problems develop with spouse and children, often leading to separation and divorce. Withdrawal from friends and avoidance of social activities commonly happen as well. Or alternatively, the person may react by becoming hypersocial and promiscuous.

Physical Disruption

The burnout process is accompanied by a high degree of stress that impacts negatively on the body, making a person vulnerable to disease. At first, ailments are minor: gastrointestinal disorders, colds, and flu attacks, with a general feeling of being tired and run down. Later, ailments can be more serious.

Spiritual Disruption

There is a feeling of meaninglessness. "What is the point of doing this? I'm a rat on a wheel! Does this activity have any value? The hell with it all!" Such spiritual dismay is most dramatic in those making a lot of money and considered successful. Often they believe that if they make it to the next level, win the bigger fiefdom, then they'll have the promised life in the promised land. When the thrill of promotion wears off, the new territorial domain rarely yields the promised satisfaction. After repeating this disappointing cycle several times, there comes a realization that it'll always be the same old grind. The crisis of meaning sets in.

STRESS AND BURNOUT

The words *stress* and *burnout* are often used synonymously, but they are not the same. Stress is the fever of burnout. If you had pneumonia, for example, you'd have to keep the accompanying fever down or risk brain damage. But bringing the fever down does not cure the pneumonia. The same is true with the stress that accompanies burnout. We must bring the stress down to preserve health, but reducing stress does not eliminate the underlying cause of burnout, the feeling of powerlessness. You still have the pneumonia.

The accompanying diagram explains graphically why burnout is stressful. One of the most serious threats we can encounter is uncontrollability. All animals, perhaps plants, and certainly human beings are very concerned about controlling their respective worlds. We have sent rocket ships around Saturn. We have transplanted hearts. Striving to control the world around us is a survival drive. When we suspect loss of control, we feel threatened. This threat triggers what is called the "fight–flight response."

When confronted with a threat, our bodies mobilize to fight the threat or flee from it. Muscles have to be tense, blood must be circulating, and breathing has to be rapid to supply the increased demand for oxygen. But when we don't fight and don't flee, such as when we stay in a powerless work situation, fight–flight results in chronic stress. Our bodies are not made to be

STRESS AND BURNOUT

mobilized for more than a few minutes, much less all day and all night, day after day, month after month, year after year.

It is this unrelenting stress that causes many of the symptoms of burnout—the physical problems, irritability, intellectual impairment, and emotional outbursts. This is why we've got to treat the stress. Although going on a vacation or practicing deep breathing by itself does not address the core problem—the pow-erlessness caused by career feudalism—learning how to manage stress is important (see discussion in Chapter 6). It's a good idea for everyone to take a couple of courses in stress management. You'll learn how your body works and what to do to control it. And stress management workshops are fun, too!

MOTIVATION

Exploring what is necessary for motivation helps us understand how the paradoxes and double binds of career feudalism can lead to job burnout. As I described in *Beating Job Burnout*, there are two essential ingredients of motivation. The first is a "win." The second is a causal relationship between what we do and what happens to us.

Wins

The strength and nature of motivation is determined in large part by what happens after we act. If motivation is to remain high, there must be a positive outcome, or "win," for perform-ance. That's elementary. We simply do not continue to do things that make us lose or that bring nothing. But what many don't realize is there are two types of wins, one positive and one neg-ative. Both keep us moving and motivated, but one promotes growth and self-development, whereas the other can lead to mis-ery and self-entrapment.

A win is positive when something desirable is added to our experience. It can be something from the outside: a gift or re-ward, praise or other positive comments, a raise or promotion, status or fame. Or the positive can be internal: a feeling of self-respect, satisfaction, excitement, challenge, adventure, or fun. Wins are individualized; each of us has our own unique moti-vators. Work situations that provide many positive wins teach us to "work for."

The second type of win is dangerous because it has the tend-ency to ensnare us in a vicious cycle. Consider this: Suppose you have a headache. That's a negative, unpleasant sensation. So you take an aspirin, and the headache goes away. The headache going away is a win. The next time you get a headache, what are you likely to do? Probably, you will take an aspirin because it removed the headache in the past. Taking an aspirin wins because the negative is avoided or turned off. Many people work in order to avoid or escape negatives; such work includes looking busy and working to avoid criticism, to avoid losing a job, to avoid a bad relationship, or to avoid feelings of loneliness. Work situations with a preponderance of negative wins teach us to "work to avoid." This is the addictive syndrome. The alcoholic experiences a negative state of depression or anxiety, then drinks and the anxiety and unpleasant feelings go away.

Which of the two motivations, "working for" or "working to avoid," do you suppose is most likely to result in creative, quality performance? Which is more conducive to self-starting? Which requires more management monitoring? The diagram on the next page gives a clue to the answer.

Career feudalism subtly encourages working to avoid. When territorial domains are granted on the basis of loyalty, there is an implicit threat that disloyalty or acting in any way that conflicts with the Company Way will meet with reprisal, possibly loss of one's rank and fief. This engenders a subtle but pervasive fear of being demoted or fired. "If I step out of line, I'll be thrown out. I'll have no money. How will I survive?" The career feudalist learns to work to avoid this free-floating sense of insecurity.

At each step in the hierarchy, the feudal lords or organization managers are expected to keep all their charges in line and under control. Because the criterion for promotion is loyalty, not managerial ability, these lords tend to be poor managers. Rarely does the organization provide the training they need to assume managerial responsibility. Consequently, feudal managers tend to rely on punitive management techniques. Here's what happens. When productivity drops, a negative experience for managers, they tend to resort to threats and criticism. In the face of these threats, their charges work harder and productivity increases. The result is a negative win for the boss, because criticizing employees helped to avoid reprisals from above. But rarely do the productivity increases last. When productivity drops again, the boss threatens and criticizes again. Quickly a vicious cycle of police-like monitoring develops.

Because the "working to avoid" syndrome is conditioned, career feudalists often get stuck. The control and threats to security

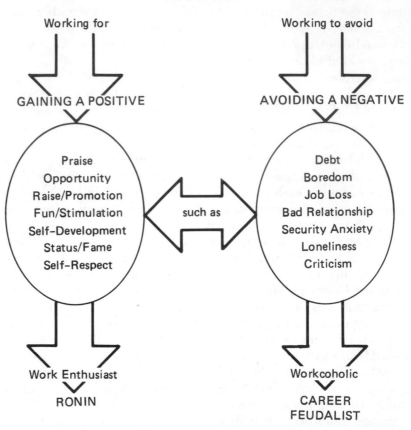

MOTIVATION

Working for

GAINING A POSITIVE

Praise
Opportunity
Raise/Promotion
Fun/Stimulation
Self-Development
Status/Fame
Self-Respect

such as

Work Enthusiast

RONIN

Working to avoid

AVOIDING A NEGATIVE

Debt
Boredom
Job Loss
Bad Relationship
Security Anxiety
Loneliness
Criticism

Workcoholic

CAREER
FEUDALIST

become necessary to keep performing. Take away the threat, and they stop performing since they don't know how to "work for."

Actually, training for the "working to avoid" motivation begins in school. Students learn to sit in study hall looking busy. They learn to stare at their books while daydreaming. They pretend to work while writing notes to friends three aisles over. If they protest this hypocrisy, they get detention and lowered grades. During this schooling process, students are prepared for career feudalism. They learn the subservient posture. Ronin, on the other hand, are more autonomous because they strive for more experience, opportunity, and skill rather than trying to hold on to their fiefs. Security for Ronin is found in self-development, learning to become their own masters.

Causality

The second factor influencing motivation is the "if–then" principle. To remain motivated, we must perceive a causal relationship between what we do and what happens to us. It is easiest to present the importance of this relationship with results from research. From hundreds of studies with animals (dogs, cats, rats, mice, and even cockroaches), research psychologist Martin Seligman[5] identified a psychological phenomenon called "learned helplessness." Here's a typical study.[6] Pairs of dogs, picked from the same litters, were matched on a number of variables. One at a time, the first dog in each pair was put in a room with a grid floor and shocked. What do you suppose the dog did? What would *you* do? The dog jumped, yelped, and tried to figure out how to turn off the shock. In the "controllable" condition, there was a way for the dog to turn off the shock, such as a lever that could be pushed, a door that could be opened, or something that could be jumped over. Quickly, the dog learned that *if* it pushed the lever, for example, *then* the shock stopped. This dog learned that there was a relationship between what it did and what happened to it. It learned that the world is controllable.

In the "uncontrollable" condition, the matched dog was put into the same room with the grid floor, only this time there was no way out and nothing the dog could do to turn off the shock. Just like the first dog, when shocked it yelped, jumped, and tried to figure out how to get away. The dog scratched the wall, chewed at the floor, and ran around. Eventually, it figured out, "There's nothing I can do. I'm getting shocked, and there's nowhere to go and no way out." What do you suppose the dog did next? The dog gave up! It lay down on the floor and just took the shock. The dog learned that it is helpless.

In the third step of the study, the dog that learned it was helpless was put into the "controllable" condition, the room with an exit. What do you suppose the dog did when it was shocked again? It apathetically lay there. It did not try to find a way to turn off the shock. Even when the door was wide open, the dog did not attempt to escape. It just lay there. Someone could stand in the door, whistle, and call, "Come on, come on, come on," but the dog wouldn't move. The dog could be pulled by the scruff of its neck out of the room to show it, "Look here's the door. All you have to do is get up and walk out the door and you're free."

Put the dog back in the room on the grid floor, shock it, and what did it do? It just lay there! The dog learned that it is helpless and continued to act as such, regardless of changes in the world around it.

To summarize, three things occurred when the dog learned it was helpless. First, motivation to try to get away was extinguished. The dog stopped trying. It lay down and took the shock. Second, the process was accompanied by a lot of negative emotion. At first, the dog yelped, then it growled and acted in other ways that we consider indications of anger. Quickly anger turned to anxiety. Then when the dog learned it was helpless, there was despair and apathy. Third, the ability to learn or to respond creatively was impaired. Something happened that interfered with the dog's ability to learn that things had changed and doing could succeed. Instead, the dog did not try. What happened when the dog learned it was helpless parallels what can happen to people who learn they are powerless at work.

Obviously, people cannot be subjected to such experimentation. However, many naturally occurring situations seem remarkably similar to this. Consider the battered wife. Many psychiatrists and others who focus on internal psychodynamics (versus those who look at behavior in relationship to environment) maintain that the wife is a masochist. She "likes" being beaten. However, a strong argument can be made that she, like the dog, has learned that she is helpless. The husband goes off to work, and she just stays there. Why doesn't she run away? Why doesn't the dog run out the open door?

We can find lots of examples of learned helplessness among people in institutions, ghettos, and concentration camps. Another situation that promotes learned helplessness is the feudal work environment.

DEMOTIVATING WORK SITUATIONS

Many are the double-bind or damned-if-you-do-damned-if-you-don't situations in the workplace that can create feelings of helplessness and thereby diminish motivation. The following story conveys the feeling. A little boy asked his father, "Daddy, what's work?" The father answered, "Billy, work is a big rock that you must push up to the top of the tallest mountain you ever saw. You sweat and struggle and strain, and *finally* you make it. Then you go home to rest. Only the next day, the rock is back on your desk!" Puzzled, the little boy asked, "I don't understand, Daddy?" To which the father replied, "You will, Billy, you will!" Perhaps you recognize the Sisyphus story. In Greek mythology, there was an evil king condemned to Hades to forever roll up the mountain a big rock that always rolled back down again. This was the Greeks' vision of hell.

Many aspects of jobs mirror the Sisyphus story. Consider the in-basket, for example. Remember those childhood fairy stories about the good little elves who came in the middle of the night to fix the shoemaker's shoes? Sometimes I wonder if bad little elves come at night and fill my in-basket. I work and work to empty the basket only to find when I come back the next day that it is full again!

The Sisyphus phenomenon can operate in any kind of work. The helping professions are a good example. The drug counselor sweats and struggles, and finally one addict shapes up and goes off into the world. The counselor thinks, "My efforts and strains have paid off. I'm a good person and a competent professional and this work is worthwhile. It doesn't matter that the other 99 percent didn't make it. At least one did!" Only, three months later there is that addict back in detox, looking exactly as before! Police and health care professionals struggle with the rock. The fact is, we can find that rock in any work, at any level. But sometimes we don't recognize it for what it is. Let's look at some examples.

The Critical Boss

The critical boss is the person who, no matter how hard you try or how well you do, always finds a nit to pick. Eventually, you begin feeling that there is no way to satisfy this boss. You become the dog on the grid floor. Nothing you do will turn off the criticism. In some jobs, it is the customers who are critical. No matter how hard you work, you cannot meet their expectations or demands. Some professions are especially prone to criticism. Consider bill collecting, repossessing, or bouncing troublemakers out of bars. People working in such jobs can get it from both sides. Supervisors tell them to collect on certain accounts, for example, but when they call to collect, they are harrassed by the debtors.

Lack of Recognition

Lack of recognition can occur in any line of work, but it is particularly prevalent in civil service. Civil servants work and work, but no one seems to notice or to care. Seniority and putting in time, not performance, seems to be the basis of recognition and reward. Workers feel like cogs in a machine. For many, inadequate pay can be a subtle form of lack of recognition because being underpaid implies a lack of appreciation of a person's contributions and lack of recognition of a person's skills.

Ambiguity

Ambiguity is so common in the electronics industry that we could call it the Silicon Valley syndrome. Electronics has been an explosive industry. Numerous are the stories of multimillion-dollar companies starting in garages. One result of such rapid growth is confusion and ambiguity. Job responsibilities are ill defined, and people move through them rapidly. Ambiguity translates into mixed messages and double binds. It is not clear who is to do what or when, which creates a great potential for working hard and failing. Corollaries to ambiguity are lack of information and unclear goals. If you don't have enough information to do the job, it is difficult to do that job well. Likewise, when goals are unclear, it is difficult to know which way to shoot to hit the target. The result can be a sense of failure and futility.

Lose–Lose Situations

Lose–lose situations are the classic damned-if-you-do-damned-if-you-don't situations, of which there are many. Consider the person caught between two different departments with different and conflicting priorities. When you meet the needs of one, the other is dissatisfied. You can't win. Those who work for more than one boss, or who interface between vendors and the company or between union and management, confront lose–lose situations.

Role Conflicts

Role conflicts could be considered a subset of the lose–lose bind. Superwoman, for example, frequently finds herself telling

the boss she can't work late because of a commitment to her
husband and kids. Reconsidering when the boss groans, "Typical
woman!" she calls home to change plans only to hear, "You always put that job first. Some wife you are!" It's easy for her to
feel like she can't win. Now in this age of enlightenment and
liberal views, men are increasingly discovering that they too are
caught in this kind of role conflict. Which is more important, work
or life? During the age of career feudalism, functioning as a machine at work took precedence.

These are only some of the ways we can feel powerless at work. There's also "topping out," "being put out to pasture," and other horror stories we hear can happen. Something is wrong in the work environment. Too many people are feeling demoralized at work to discount it as neurosis or narcissism. The workplace has become toxic and antihuman. We're talking about career feudalism.

Work, goal-oriented activity, is characteristic of the healthy person. Looking at children, we see that they are eager to learn and to do. Yet, somewhere between childhood and midlife, a large number of people lose this drive. Herbert Fruedenberger, who has been credited with coining the word *burnout*, claims an underachiever cannot burn out. I take issue with this position. I believe the underachiever has *already* burned out, probably in high school, maybe earlier. Our schools are part of the feudal system, preparing us for corporate life. A person who loses the desire to strive to reach a goal, to achieve, has a malaise of the spirit. The spirit, that which is uniquely human, has been damaged or impaired by career feudalism, being rendered powerless to accomplish work goals.

POOR MANAGEMENT

With the exception of role conflicts, the common thread running through the demotivating situations is poor management. Good work is criticized or ignored; goals are vague or conflicting. How people are managed at work exerts a tremendous impact upon their motivation and performance. This is self-evident—or is it?

The Potter Principle: There Is No Peter Principle

The Peter Principle states that people tend to rise in the organization to one level beyond their level of competence and then remain there. This principle is frequently cited as the reason for organizational inefficiencies and contradictions. The problem is that it tends to blame the victim.

How do people typically rise in the organization? Organizations take their best salespeople (as defined by the Company Way), and what do they do with them? Promote them to salesmanagers. The best engineers are promoted to project leaders;

the best teachers become administrators; the best secretaries become office managers. But is managing the same as selling? As typing? No! Rarely is the promoted person given the training necessary for success as a supervisor. Thus new managers are expected to continue performing at an outstanding level at the same time as they are trying to acquire the skills to do the job. What happens to those who master this challenge? They are promoted again, and again, and again, until they reach the point where they can no longer figure out how to do the job while doing it. Organizations then point to this casualty as an example of the Peter Principle.

Consider a question I frequently ask in my training sessions: Would you go to a dentist who had the same level of professional training as the average manager of your acquaintance? I suspect not! What does this mean? Does it mean that managing people at work is such an easily mastered, light-weight job that it requires little training? Does it mean that managers are born with the skills intact?

When people are poorly managed, motivation is damaged, productivity drops, innovation dries up, and people suffer. What a waste of human resources! Think of any employee, and try to calculate what it would cost, starting with a newborn baby, to "produce" that employee. It would be pretty costly! If an organization were installing a computer system of comparable value, operators would never be allowed to learn to use the system by trial and error. Yet this is what they do with our most valuable resource, the human resource.

Managing people involves influencing what others do. For example, substandard performance must be corrected, peak performance facilitated and maintained, conflicts mediated, participation encouraged, and so forth. In fact, there are many similarities between the behavior-change responsibilities of managers and those of counselors, social workers, and psychologists. And, a strong argument could be made that effecting behavior change at work is far more difficult than it is in a therapeutic setting. Professional helpers typically work one on one with clients for a limited time (i.e., one hour) each week. Working with couples, families, or groups or in residential facilities is considered vastly more difficult. In contrast, supervisors and managers work simultaneously with a variety of different personalities for long periods of time (i.e., 40 hours a week), often

under stressful conditions, while meeting time deadlines, output
quotas, and pressures from above.

It would seem that managing people at work requires skills
as sophisticated and complex as those of therapists and other
change agents. Yet, whereas counselors and psychologists typically have extensive formal training and professional certifica-
tion, most managers must face these challenges with little or no
training. For example, a social worker trainee is assigned one or
more clients with whom to practice techniques learned in the
classroom. Audiotapes and videotapes of the intern's sessions are
reviewed with the training supervisor. Doctors serve as interns
in hospitals, and lawyers practice prosecuting and defending in
mock court. In contrast, management trainees learn about the
value of performance reviews, giving feedback, and setting goals
but have little opportunity to practice under supervision or to
receive feedback. Even MBAs, who are schooled in the latest
theories, have little actual hands-on training in managing people.
In the business organization, there is far too little applied training.

POOR SELF-MANAGEMENT

Many people dampen their own motivation by managing themselves poorly. Perfectionists are good examples. Perfectionists
set standards that are nearly impossible to achieve and consider
themselves successful only if they perform at a near-perfect
level. The perfectionist, although he works hard, get few wins
and a lot of self-imposed losses because his thinking represents
the critical boss internalized. Working is not fun because it is
fraught with frustration and failure. Besides setting unreasonable
standards, perfectionists give little self-acknowledgment and little self-reward. Self-acknowledgment is important. It is central
to self-starting and self-motivation.

Goal setting is another important self-management skill. Poor
self-managers set vague goals, and this makes it difficult to determine in what direction to move or what action to take. And
when goals are vague, it is difficult to judge progress or accomplishment. Consequently, we can never be sure if or when we
are winning.

Good self-managers break goals down into small, easily attainable, concrete steps, whereas poor self-managers demand everything all at once. The sure route to success is to move small step by small step. We'll talk more about this in Chapter 4.

Poor management, whether self-imposed or from above, can diminish motivation. But worse, it can set a vicious cycle in motion. When people are poorly managed, performance suffers. Drops in performance bring criticism and lowered self-esteem, which tends to adversely affect motivation. And as motivation wanes, we tend to lower our sights and restrict our dreams. We strive less, achieve less, tackle less, learn less, and become less.

Career feudalism promotes an environment that erodes feelings of control in those who work within it. People are promoted up through the management hierarchy on a basis of adherence to the Company Way rather than demonstrated management ability. The problem of inadequate management skill is exacerbated by an organizational tendency to neglect the training function and the hierarchical system of control. The result is that employees develop feelings of helplessness and vulnerability to job burnout. Costs to individuals, to organizations, and to our society are immeasurable.

Innovation doesn't occur spontaneously in a vacuum. Power over one's work, a feeling that one can make an impact, is an important catalyst. When employees feel powerless, they plod along, performing adequately at best, but rarely innovating. A sense of ownership motivates employees to invest the energy required to birth new ways of doing things. Career feudalism, work in which employees feel beholden to the Company Way that they are powerless to influence, destroys motivation to perform excellently. To sustain high levels of motivation and promote innovation, employees must feel they have the power to affect their work.

EMPOWERING EMPLOYEES

Empowerment of employees can be tackled in two ways. First, as an individual, you must develop a sense of personal power or a feeling of I-can-do that you can act to control your work. Companies, on the other hand, empower by providing "good work"—work in which employees feel they have some measure of control and can accomplish their assignments.

Paths to Personal Power

> Why, then the world's mine oyster,
> which I with sword will open.
> —Shakespeare

Self-Knowledge

There are many paths to personal power, but they all start
with self-knowledge. You can have little control over what happens to you if you don't know how you function physically, intellectually, and emotionally. When you understand how you
work, how events impact on you, what increases or decreases
your motivation, what you like and don't like, you have the keys
to personal power. (Self-knowledge is discussed in more detail
in Chapter 4.)

Stress Management

As you learn more about how your body and psyche function
and what situations trigger responses, your ability to self-com-
mand increases because you can use this understanding to raise
and lower tension level as needed. Personal power comes in
knowing that, although you may not like difficult situations, you
can handle them. Such feelings of command enable you to rise
to the occasion rather than avoid problem situations. Consequently, you are more likely to handle difficulties skillfully.
(Stress management is discussed in greater detail in Chapter 6.)

Decision Making

The ability to make sound decisions is another component of
personal power. When you know how to get pertinent information, you are able to withstand the inevitable uncertainty while
weighing the pros and cons; and if you are able to commit yourself to a plan, you will have more confidence when faced with
change or endowed with new responsibility. If, on the other
hand, you avoid decisions, thereby making them by default, or
if you let others decide, your personal power is greatly reduced.
For it is through the decisions you make that you shape your life.

Skill Building

Inevitably, you will encounter situations requiring skills you've not yet developed. But when you know how to arrange learning situations for yourself, you'll have the confidence you need to tackle challenges, handle the unexpected, and move into the unknown. You'll have freedom of movement.

Thought Control and Mood Management

Many people feel that, at times, their thoughts have lives of their own, and they feel out of control in the face of their emotions. It's as if they fall victim to run-away thinking and obsessive ruminations over unhappy experiences. Not knowing how to curb their thoughts, they respond to every red flag waved before them. Such knee-jerk reactions render them predictable and easy to maneuver. *Ronin* samurai, on the other hand, increased their power and formidability with the mental discipline of Zen. By emptying their minds of chatter, they were able to be more attentive. And it was the calmness afforded by mental discipline that enabled them to take the fractional side steps to avoid an unexpected sword's blow.

CHOPSTICKS NOT SWORDS

A *ronin* samurai went to the *bushi* Master, who said, "You have made little progress since I saw you last." Dismayed, the *ronin* cried, "What do you mean? I'm the fiercest samurai on this island. I've lost to no one's sword." And the Master replied, "Yes, but you have lost to your own sword. The highest skill is not to draw your sword at all." "But how can I win without drawing my sword?!" the *ronin* protested, "I will be killed!"

Later, while eating at the inn, three cocky young samurai taunted the *ronin*, anxious to test their skill. Eyeing them while brushing away a pestering fly, the *ronin* remembered the words of the Master: "The highest skill is not to draw your sword at all." Wondering how to win without a sword, the *ronin* suddenly drew his chopsticks and with them plucked the annoying fly from the air. Astonished, the three other pests made respectful bows and quickly withdrew.

Detached Concern

Detached concern is a higher-order level of mental control in which control is gained by letting go. It is attachment to our notions about how things are and ought to be that imprison us in the dilemma of the paradox. With detached concern, opportunities can be made out of paradox. As with the Chinese finger puzzle, it's only when you stop pulling that you can break loose.

Four Promoters of Good Work

Companies empower by providing "good work." Good work is being able to get the ball, run with it, and score. Good work is work we can win at, where we can accomplish our goals and carry out our responsibilities. Good work builds esteem. We feel like good people. Good work provides meaning and purpose. "Bad work," on the other hand, requires that we roll up the hill the rock that always rolls back down. When work is bad, we cannot succeed, cannot accomplish what is demanded of us. Bad work is soulless. Our motivation, drive, and spirit stifle and die.

The four ingredients of good work are goals, feedback, participation, and acknowledgment.

Goals

Setting an achievable goal immediately yields more control and power in any situation because it provides a target to shoot for, something to aim at. A goal serves as a beacon that helps us get our bearings and navigate through decisions.

Feedback

Feedback on progress toward the goal is the second essential ingredient. Suppose, for example, you were learning archery and you shot an arrow toward the target but didn't get to see where the arrow went. How fast would you learn? You probably wouldn't. The results from the shot help determine what adjustments to make for the next attempt to hit the bull's-eye. Without that feedback, you can't tell if you should shoot higher or lower, more to the left or to the right. Suppose you shoot an arrow and six months later during the annual performance review you are told, "Remember that arrow you shot the day you were read-

ing *The Way of the Ronin?* Well, it went into the second rung."
If this happened, your mastery of archery would probably be
slow and tedious, if you ever did master it. The sooner the feedback, the more potent it is in keeping us motivated, and the faster
we learn. For example, if you touch a very hot object, your fingers
burn and you learn quickly not to do it again.

Participation

Industrial research has shown that, when employees participate in setting goals for their own work, both high-level employees, such as scientists and engineers, as well as those working at lower levels set higher goals and achieve them more often
than when they do not participate.' This translates into money
for the company. Participation in determining the parameters of
one's own work also promotes a feeling of ownership and control.

Acknowledgment

Reward, reinforcement, I prefer to call it acknowledgment,
for good work is the final ingredient. To maintain motivation at
a high level, we need to believe that we will win, that something
we desire will occur as a result of what we are doing. Acknowledgment of good work helps build self-esteem, because what we
have accomplished is recognized as having value.

Of course, there's nothing startling about the four ingredients
of good work. They are at the core of management philosophy—
practically clichés. It is one thing, however, to talk about setting
goals, giving feedback, eliciting participation, and acknowledging work well done and quite another thing to do so. As with any
skill, these are easy to talk about but difficult to actually do. It
is easy to read a book or talk about skiing, for example; that
doesn't mean you can get down a slope with any form or grace!

In Chapter 7, "Corporate Ronin," you'll find a practical step-
by-step procedure, TASC+, for integrating the essential ingredients for good work into your routine management day.

MIDLIFE CRISIS OR MIDLIFE FLOWERING?

The notion that the midlife crisis is a virtually inescapable stage
of male development is widely accepted. Beginning around age

40, men must confront unpleasant realities. Decline in physical and sexual prowess, mortality, the goal gap—the discrepancy between what he had hoped to do and what he has done—having to step aside so that younger men can step into the fast lane, and boredom are the most commonly cited catalysts.

The finger of blame is pointed at the restrictive male role that limits men's acceptable range of activities and expression. What is overlooked is that the notion of acceptable male behavior has been defined largely by the needs of career feudalism. Men have been duped into becoming society's drones—the worker bees. By comparison, experts claim that women are much less likely to experience a crisis at midlife, and they handle it with less trauma when they do. I predict that this will change as women enter the executive suites and boardrooms of corporate America.

The feudal career system, with the straight-line track and specialization, is a setup for a crisis at midlife whether the person be male or female. By midlife, the worker is so invested in one direction that other alternatives, although not impossible to follow, require a tremendous sacrifice. Worse, in the process of specializing, a person develops only a small part of his or her abilities, and this results in a skewed personality, with some aspects exaggerated while others are dormant. Midlife is a time when many hope to move into middle management. And it is at middle management that the crunch comes, because the pyramid narrows rather dramatically. Feeling unable to move up and unable to change, the linear strategist at midlife is a prime candidate for burnout—another casualty of career feudalism. What a waste of the precious human resource!

> Statistics show that only a handful of highly educated men will continue to move up the ladder after forty, while the majority will merely hold on to whatever rung they have already reached. And some, usually the least educated, will start to slip down. This is the reality in America today.
>
> —Nancy Mayer
> *The Male Mid-Life Crisis*[8]

People on the specialized linear track tend to be successful in the beginning, when they are young. Promotions come fast, and they move ahead quickly. By comparison, in the early stages the Ronin strategy often appears to be unfocused. Promotions are sacrificed for lateral and nonlinear moves, as Ronin follow their interests rather than specializing. Ronin believe that the quality of the journey along the path is what is important, not making it to the next rung on the ladder. Consequently, they are often criticized for making little progress.

But for Ronin, midlife is an entirely different experience. Ronin are less likely than career feudalists to regret the paths not taken or to feel their lives lack meaning, challenge, or adventure. At midlife, those who have followed a linear track find that advancement slows, perhaps stops. And this is doubly difficult for the fast-trackers, who have come to expect rapid advancement and have learned to define themselves in these terms For Ronin, on the other hand, midlife is a time of flowering. At midlife, Ronin come into their own. A variety of skills forged from a range of experiences are drawn upon in unique ways. Rather than feeling locked into an unfulfilling job, at midlife Ronin experience success, often quite dramatic. It is a time of maximum influence, of being able to participate fully and creatively in the World Game.

Notes

1. New York: Random House, 1970, pp. 130–131.
2. Abraham Zaleznik, Manfred Kets de Vries, and John Howard, "Stress Reactions in Organizations: Symptoms, Causes, and Consequences," *Behavioral Science*, Vol. 22 (1977), pp. 151–162.
3. Ibid. p. 160.
4. Thomas J. Peters and Robert H. Waterman, Jr., *In Search of Excellence: Lessons from America's Best-Run Companies* (New York: Harper & Row, 1982).
5. *Helplessness: On Depression, Development, and Death* (San Francisco: Freeman, 1975).
6. The discussion here is not a report of any one particular study. Rather, it is a synopsis of several studies and their results.
7. Gary P. Latham and Sydney B. Kinne, "Improving Job Performance Through Training in Goal-Setting," *Journal of Applied Psychology*, Vol. 59, No. 2 (1974), pp. 187–191.
8. *The Male Mid-Life Crisis: Fresh Starts after 40* (New York: New American Library, 1978), p. 56.

3

The Way of the Ronin

The most reputable martial arts masters ... have claimed that *bujutsu* [is] something more than merely a variety of practical and effective methods of combat. They indicate that these arts are "ways" or disciplines of moral advancement intended to further the formation of a mature, balanced, and integrated personality, of a man at peace with himself and in harmony with his social as well as his natural environment.

They refer, therefore, to a system of ethics, of morality, which motivates and inspires the practice (*jutsu*) from within and leads it towards the achievement of ultimate, remote goals far beyond the immediate and narrow confines of the world of combat. ... This system is usually referred to ... as

budo—a term formed by the combination of . . . *bu*
(which . . . denotes the military dimension . . .) with
. . . *do* . . . [which] is generally translated either as
"way" (. . . the way of seeing, of understanding,
and of motivating behavior in the philosophical . . .
sense) or as "doctrine" (. . . the principles taught
and accepted by a body of adherents to a philosophy
. . .). As such, *do* denotes belief rather than technique, insight rather than execution, motivation
rather than action
                              —Oscar Ratti and Adele Westbrook
                              Secrets of the Samurai[1]

SELF-DIRECTION AND SOCIETY

We come into the world capable of many ways of being, but we
don't stay that way for long. Socialization begins immediately as
we learn to conform to the society in which we live. When adept
in acting properly, we become socializing agents ourselves
through our responses; by punishing or rewarding others' actions, we shape their behavior. And so the world around us becomes predictable, and people can move from one situation to
the next, as seemingly independent individuals.

David Riesman, in his classic work *The Lonely Crowd*, analyzed the way in which people in different eras learned to conform, as shown in the accompanying diagram. When social order
is relatively unchanging, for example, the conforming of the individual tends to be directed by traditions that reflect membership in a particular age-grade, clan, or caste. Important relationships are controlled by rigid etiquette, and individual choices of
life-style and goals are minimal. This socially implanted self-
directing mechanism can be likened to a map or template that
indicates how, when, and where to act. Orientation is toward
standards set by ancestors. Failing to meet these standards, the
tradition-directed person is filled with shame. As with other
areas of life in the unchanging society, work also is determined
largely by tradition. Occupation is rarely chosen but is an insep-
arable part of the station of one's birth. Likewise, when to work
and when to play is determined by custom, not individual style.

By comparison, in preindustrial or developing societies, the
map is inadequate as a directing mechanism. There are too many

MODES OF CONFORMITY

	TRADITION	INNER	OTHER	AUTONOMOUS
Predominant Era	Middle Ages Feudalism	Renaissance Reformation	Postwar growth era	Information era
Directing Mechanism	Map or template	Gyroscope	Radar	Omni
Standard	Etiquette Custom	Belief system	Peer group	Excellence
Goal	Belonging	Achievement	Approval	Actualization
Failure Emotion	Shame	Guilt	Anxiety	Anomie
Success Emotion	Honor	Pride	Security	Fulfillment

Some of the information in this table is adapted from David Riesman, *The Lonely Crowd* (New Haven, Conn.: Yale University Press, 1969).

unpredictables. People are more mobile and come into contact with competing traditions. In expanding societies, socialization involves internalizing a "psychological gyroscope." This inner directing mechanism ensures conformity while allowing individuality.

The gyroscope, once it is set by parents or other authorities, keeps the *inner-directed* person on course, providing for the maintenance of a delicate balance between the demands of individual goals and the requirements of society. But the gyroscope is not selected or shaped by the individual. It is inner in the sense that it is implanted by elders early in life and directed toward personalized but nevertheless inescapably destined goals, revolving around duties, production, and achievement. In fact, inner-directed people often tend to become workcoholics, working longer hours and living with less leisure time than would have been deemed possible by traditional standards. Inner-directed people can be driven because they are willing to

drive themselves. When efforts to meet their internalized standards fail, the inner-directed are racked with guilt.

An outstanding asset of the inner-directed is the ability to stay
on course in unsupportive, even antagonistic or alien situations.
But this apparent independence is actually, according to Riesman, conformity to a rigid belief system set in place by early
socializers. In fact, when confronted with dramatic change, the
gyroscope becomes a liability because it is not flexible enough
for the rapid adaptations required.

Industrialized society, with its centralization and bureaucracies, imposes yet different requirements upon those populating
it. There is little room (and little tolerance) for the rugged in-
dividualist. Instead, getting along with others assumes primary
importance. In such a society, socialization involves learning
how to coexist closely with others, which means the individual
must develop a heightened sensitivity to the actions and wishes
of others. Consequently, peers rather than ancestors or parents
become the primary source of direction.

This is the *other-directed* person. The other-directed develop
a self-controlling mechanism similiar to a "psychological radar"
that senses what others deem appropriate and determines how
closely they are meeting that standard. Approval rather than belonging or achievement is the primary goal, and when withheld
anxiety is experienced. As a result, other-directed people develop exceptional social skills that allow them to move easily
among new associates, quickly and almost automatically sensing
what is expected and adjusting their actions accordingly. The
negative side of this process is that tempers, moodiness, and
other demonstrations of negative emotions are ostracized by the
peer group and idiosyncracies tend to be muted if not eliminated
entirely.

On the face of it, other-directed people appear to be shallow
conformists virtually devoid of selves. Yet, they do have an invaluable asset. Heightened sensitivity to others enables the
other-directed to change with relative ease. Unlike the tradition-
and inner-directed, the other-directed are not fixed, they are
adaptable. Like chameleons, they change with the times to reflect the prevailing norms. In fact, one could draw a persuasive
argument that the other-directed are preautonomous, ready to
develop the self-controlling mechanism of the fourth character
type.

Modern society is undergoing a dramatic transformation from industrialization, with its conglomerates and centralization, to a new and as yet undefined form, the information society, which futurists claim will be characterized by decentralization, diversity, and shockingly rapid change. The future that is unfolding promises to follow new rules. Those who are to survive and thrive must cut paths into the unknown, following the old rules when they work and making new ones when they don't. Alvin Toffler in *Future Shock* predicts that in the information era bureaucracies will give way to the "ad-hocracy," groups formed for a particular goal that, once the goal is achieved, disband. If his predictions are accurate, the survivors must be able both to work cooperatively with others and to go it alone. Yonji Masada[2] asserts that in the information era society will function around the axis of information values rather than material values. Although there is a danger that these will evolve into an "automated state," he believes there is much potential for the evolution of a "computopia" (computer utopia), in which independence of the individual will be enhanced.

> The development of information productive power will liberate man by reducing dependence on subsistence labor, with rapidly increasing material productive power as the result of automation, thus increasing the amount of free time one can use. There will also be an expanded ability [for the individual] to solve problems and pursue new possibilities, and then to bring such possibilities into reality.[3]

In other words, as computers enable us to be more productive in shorter periods of time, society will encourage individuals to pursue and satisfy the need for self-fulfillment. Masada envisions the evolution of diverse volunteer communities that come together around the formation and accomplishment of mutually shared goals and predicts that, as individuals pursue their own goals, they will "work synergistically as a group to achieve a shared goal, and all [will] exercise self-restraint so that there will be no interference with the social activities of others."[4] If Masada's predictions are accurate, socialization in the future will involve the development of self-determination and self-discipline.

Out of this turmoil of change, a new type of person is emerging, the *autonomous-directed* person. This the modern Ronin, a person capable of conforming to the norms of society, yet one who has an ability to choose when to conform and when not to conform. The directing mechanism of the autonomous is like the

aircraft omni that determines position independently without reliance on input from others. Ronin have the self-directing ca-
pacities of the three other types, yet go beyond them. Tradition
is not thrown out, rather it is followed when deemed appropriate.
Like the inner-directed, Ronin are achievement oriented but not
bound by it. And like the other-directed, Ronin have useful social
skills and are sensitive to others but not enslaved by needing
their approval.

The Ronin's primary concern is with self-development and
self-fulfillment. Ronin strive to achieve excellence in all areas,
personal as well as vocational. When efforts to meet self-defined
standards fail, Ronin experience anomie, a loss of self, and hope-
lessness.

SEEKING EXCELLENCE

Ronin are people struggling to break out of the confines of socialization in order to actualize personal potentials and to live
the fullest possible lives. Central to this process is becoming
autonomous. Although complete autonomy can be only an ideal,
the process of struggling toward it is the Way of the Ronin, a path
one follows through the twists and turns of life. To explain this
Way, I will draw upon the philosophy of Aristotle.

You might wonder at the need for calling upon a man who
lived before Christ for clues to handling modern dilemmas.
There are a number of reasons for doing so. First, Aristotle's
philosophy has had an immeasurable impact upon the values of
Western civilization and therefore have indirectly found their
way into our own psyches. Second, were you to read *The Nicomachean Ethics*,[5] you would find guidelines for the development of autonomy. Aristotle believed that no one set of absolute standards can serve as principles governing actions in
every situation, because each situation is unique. This means
that the tradition-, inner-, and other-directed are all limited because their internalized self-controlling mechanisms do not allow
a full range of choice. Ronin, by comparision, strive to perform
the right action in each situation. In *The Ethics* Aristotle describes how to determine right actions. Finally, Aristotle himself
was a Ronin. He founded several fields of study, including biology, psychology, logic, and politics, and educated Alexander
the Great, for example. There were times when he was embraced

by his fellows and other times when he had to stand alone because he was considered persona non grata.

Let's look at what he had to say. By ethics, Aristotle meant character. He believed that it is inappropriate to answer the question "What kind of person is he or she?" by saying "He is talented" or "She is intelligent." Such qualities are incidental to the question. Aristotle believed that we reveal what we are by what we do.

> The creation and the destruction of any virtue are effected by identical causes and identical means. . . . It is as a result of playing the harp that harpers become good or bad in their art. The same is true of builders and all other craftsmen. Men will become good builders as a result of building well, and bad builders as a result of building badly. . . . Now this holds also of the virtues. It is in the course of our dealings with our fellow-men that we become just or unjust. It is our behavior in a crisis and our habitual reactions to danger that make us brave or cowardly, as it may be. So with our desires and passions. Some men are made temperate and gentle, other profligate and passionate, the former by conducting themselves in one way, the latter by conducting themselves in another, in situations in which their feelings are involved. We may sum it all up in the generalization, "Like activities produce like dispositions."
>
> —Aristotle[6]

Aristotle also believed that all productions of nature have an innate tendency in the direction of the best condition of which they are capable. That is, an acorn, for example, grows into the best oak tree possible given its genetic makeup and the conditions of the soil and climate. The best possible condition of humans is happiness. But happiness is not the accumulation of material goods, having fun, or winning acclaim. Although we all have the potential for happiness, it does not come automatically. Aristotle says, "Fortune can supply the happy man with the means, and create for him the conditions, of his happiness; it cannot create his happiness."[7] Happiness, as we all know, cannot be purchased or given. It depends upon ourselves—how we act. Happiness comes from actualizing potential by developing into

the best possible self that we can be. To do this, we must strive
for and achieve what he called goodness or excellence. Excellence is not a grade or a ranking; it is the way in which we handle
daily situations, the tests of life. We pass the tests when we carry
out the right or excellent action. For each situation, which is
unique, there is a right way to act at the right time and to the
right degree. This "right way" is excellence.

But Aristotle was not alone in emphasizing the importance of
striving for excellence. Don Juan, in showing Carlos the Way of
the Warrior, stressed excellence, or living impeccably as he
called it. Consider this story: Don Juan and Carlos were walking
through a steep ravine when a huge boulder came thundering
down and landed several feet in front of them. Don Juan used
the event to teach Carlos a lesson in living impeccably. He posed
the following dilemma: Suppose you had stopped to tie your
shoelaces and by doing so you had gained a precious moment
that saved you from being crushed by that boulder? Or suppose,
on another day in another ravine, you stopped to tie your shoelaces and by doing so you lost a precious moment and were
crushed by the boulder? What should you do? Flustered, Carlos
didn't know what to answer. Don Juan answered that the only
possible freedom in that ravine consisted in tying your shoelaces
impeccably.[8]

How do we determine the excellent action? Aristotle offers a
flexible standard for determining excellence: the golden mean.

The Golden Mean

It is in the nature of moral qualities
that they can be destroyed by deficiency
on the one hand and excess on the other.
We can see this in the instances of bodily health and strength. Physical strength
is destroyed by too much and also by
too little exercise. Similarly health is ruined by eating or drinking either too
much or too little, while is is produced,
increased, and preserved by taking the
right quantity of drink and victuals.

Well, it is the same with temperance,
courage, and the other virtues. The man
who shuns and fears everything and can

stand up to nothing becomes a coward. The man who is afraid of nothing at all, but marches up to every danger, becomes foolhardy. In the same way the man who indulges in every pleasure without refraining from a single one becomes incontinent. If, on the other hand, a man behaves like the Boor in comedy and turns his back on every pleasure, he will find his sensibilities becoming blunted. So also temperance and courage are destroyed both by excess and by deficiency, and they are kept alive by observance of the mean. . . .

By "goodness" [in this passage read goodness as excellence] I mean goodness of moral character, since it is moral goodness that deals with feelings and actions, and it is in them that we find excess, deficiency, and the mean. It is possible, for example, to experience fear, boldness, desire, anger, pity, and pleasures and pain generally, too much or too little or to the right amount. If we feel them too much or too little, we are wrong. But to have these feelings at the right times on the right occasions towards the right people for the right motive and in the right way is to have them in the right measure, that is, somewhere between the extremes; and this is what characterizes goodness.

—Aristotle[9]

In any situation, there is a continuum of possible actions between two extremes. Excellence is that action somewhere in the middle that is the right way to feel, the right way to act with this person at this time under these circumstances. As Archimedes said, "Give me a fulcrum upon which to place a lever and I shall move the world." The golden mean is the fulcrum in human action and, when found, yields great power: excellence. For the samurai, the excellent blow is the right moment to strike the opponent in the right way.

You can see how this standard differs from the type of standard used by the tradition-, the inner-, and the other-directed. The other-directed don't make these judgments. Instead they look to others to determine the right way to act. The tradition-directed look to rules and etiquette. But etiquette does not vary with the nuances of situations. It's a grid or template laid over all situations. The inner-directed, on the other hand, look inward to a fixed value standard that is also limiting. Any value can be dangerous if one takes it as the sole determinant of action rather than weighing the particulars of the situation. There comes a point beyond which any value, no matter how noble, can become tyrannical if it is followed exclusively. For example, "Always think twice" can immobilize one with indecision if it is taken to an extreme because there are times when one must act immediately. The person striving to be autonomous by following the Way of the Ronin has the challenge of making the right choice between extreme courses of action. Excellence is determined by applying the right principle to the particular situation. The accompanying chart shows examples of extremes and means.

Let's consider a couple. Wrestling with assertiveness is a problem for many, especially women. Typically socialized to be passive, with few assertive models to emulate, women often go to the other extreme, becoming aggressive in misguided attempts to be assertive. Some rigidly adhere to a hard line, pouncing on any and all remarks or actions that might be construed as put-downs. Although there are many times when a woman should confront demeaning behavior, an all-or-nothing rule is rarely an effective means. Too often it is overkill, in which she wins the battle and loses the war. Instead, each situation should be responded to on its particulars. There are times when another's action is a put-down, but it's to her long-run benefit to let it pass without response; other times she may be being hypersensitive, seeing what is not there; and sometimes it is imperative that she speak out. But judging *when* to act is only part of the challenge. She must also determine *how* to act. Should she confront the offender? Leave the situation? Report the affront? Or quietly change the parameters of the situation? An excellent action demands many considerations.

Men, on the other hand, have their struggles with the ex-

EXCELLENCE

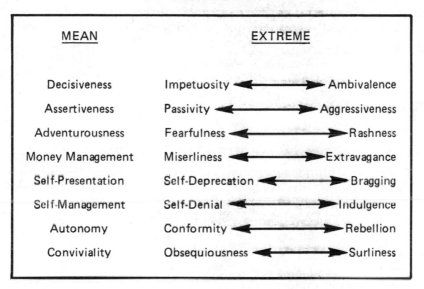

MEAN	EXTREME	
Decisiveness	Impetuosity ◄————► Ambivalence	
Assertiveness	Passivity ◄————► Aggressiveness	
Adventurousness	Fearfulness ◄————► Rashness	
Money Management	Miserliness ◄————► Extravagance	
Self-Presentation	Self-Deprecation ◄————► Bragging	
Self-Management	Self-Denial ◄————► Indulgence	
Autonomy	Conformity ◄————► Rebellion	
Conviviality	Obsequiousness ◄————► Surliness	

tremes of reason and emotion. Socialized to think and not feel, many men have difficulty finding a mean in which they are both sensitive and masculine. Or consider self-managing, an ongoing challenge for most of us. Although some have had the fortune of acquiring good self-management skills from their parents, few of us have ever had any direct training. In fact, many take self-management (self-control, self-discipline) to mean withholding pleasure and other forms of punishing oneself. But self-denial is just as much an extreme as is overindulgence. Being able to motivate ourselves to do things that we don't care to do; knowing when and where and to what degree to pleasure ourselves; knowing when to work and when to play are all prerequisites for autonomy. We simply cannot become autonomous if we can't manage ourselves. Good self-managers can work in unstructured and unrewarding situations by creating their own goals and rewards. They can self-start and keep themselves going. Poor self-managers, on the other hand, depend on others to start them, to set their goals, and to dole out their rewards.

Judicious money management is another challenge. Executives who pinch every penny by meeting clients in the office rather than spending allotted expense accounts or by saving paper clips and scraps of paper are as bad as those who constantly go over budget or authorize needless expenditures. Each day presents many opportunities to tackle the challenge of the golden mean, determining the excellent action. We can never completely master the challenge of excellence but can hope only to become increasingly proficient. The Way of the Ronin is a life-long path.

Freedom

Freedom is a key issue. We cannot be autonomous if our actions and attitudes are bound by external constraints. In traditional societies, for example, one is not free to make life-style and vocational choices because they are virtually set by the station of one's birth. Autonomy requires that a range of alternatives be available. And given that sufficient alternatives exist, we must be able to choose freely among them. The inner-directed and other-directed have many alternatives available, but their freedom of choice is limited by internalized socialization: a rigid adherence to a belief system or the tyranny of others' opinions and approval. Thus, the first issue in freedom is achieving freedom from constraints, both external as well as internal.

> A *positive decision* is one in which you choose among alternatives to maximize your happiness.
> A *negative decision* is one in which you choose among alternatives to minimize your unhappiness.
> —Harry Browne
> *How I Found Freedom in an Unfree World*[10]

In the 1960s the issue of "freedom from" came to the foreground. In experimentation with drugs, sexual expression, and alternative living arrangements, the flower children sought freedom from societal and governmental constraint. They chanted, "Turn on, tune in, and drop out." Turn on to life and all its possibilities; tune in to yourself and all your potentialities; and drop out of the constricting system. Break out of others' definitions of who you should be, and find out who you really are. If you're angry, yell; if you're sad, cry; if you want, indulge. Discover your authentic self! The "Me" decade of the 1970s followed.

Idealism faded, however, as "authenticity" revealed itself to be narcissism in disguise. Capricious and whimsical indulgence and fits of pique did not lead to actualization at all. The golden mean had been missed, and a whole generation found itself enslaved in "freedom from."

> Arbitrariness is the Achilles's heel of individualism. Pursued to its extreme the freedom from all determinants turns into an indeterminancy so total that one has no reason for choosing anything at all. The cost of total liberty is nihilism. If nothing constrains the will then nothing justifies the will. The fiction of total freedom from all constraints leaves one with no more volition than the rock released from the constraint of the hand that held it. Its *motion* is hardly equivalent to *action*.
>   —James Ogilvy
>   *Many Dimensional Man*[11]

Freedom is not individual license. Yet thinking it is leads to reactive rebellion against every structure and guideline. Freedom is responsibility. "Response-ability" is being able to do something, to make an affirmative choice. Freedom is not just putting one's heels in the dirt, and saying "No!" but also the ability to say "Yes!" And so, although autonomy requires first freedom from binds, we must not go to the extreme of rebellion or dropping out. Find the mean, "freedom to": freedom to reason, to imagine, and to develop and follow goals; freedom to become all that you can become. To become autonomous, to embark upon the Way of the Ronin, we must find the golden mean somewhere between always saying no and always saying yes; somewhere between always rebelling and always conforming.

> It is by refraining from pleasures that we become temperate, and it is when we become temperate that we are most able to abstain from pleasures. Or take courage. It is by habituating ourselves to make light of alarming situations and to confront them that we become brave, and it is when we have become brave that we shall be most able to face alarming situations.
>   Aristotle[12]

Through seeking excellence in daily activities, we develop our ability to be free to, which requires the development of discipline not just breaking out of constraints. Musicians, for example, cannot improvise creatively until they have disciplined their fingers and ears through practice. Likewise, as we become increasingly adept at performing excellently, we become freer to do what we choose to do. Soon our actions feel natural rather than forced.

Wisdom

How do we determine the golden mean or excellent action? The faculty required is wisdom. Aristotle, in his discourses, identified two types of wisdom, theoretical and practical. We must develop and utilize each to actualize our potential.

Theoretical Wisdom

Theoretical wisdom is the formal knowledge we acquire from education—what we learn in school, from the media, from books, and from experts. These are the facts that we know to be true, or at least believe to be true. Knowing that a balanced diet is essential for health is theoretical wisdom, for example. Similarly, knowing we must be decisive rather than ambivalent or impetuous when faced with a decision is theoretical wisdom. Theoretical wisdom is what we ordinarily think of as intellectual knowledge. But it is not limited solely to facts we are told or have read in a book.

Theoretical wisdom comes also from intuitive reasoning, which is that part of our intelligence that enables us to grasp fundamental principles. For example, we are engaging in intuitive reasoning when, after experiencing a given number of instances, we suddenly catch on to the truth that is present in those examples. Intuitive reasoning is that part of our intelligence that enables us to figure things out for ourselves, the "aha" experience. For example, by observing the behavior of falling objects, Newton grasped the law of gravitation. Or if from watching others interact we gain the insight that others tend to like us when we show interest in them, we are using our intuitive reasoning powers. This insight about people then is added to our theoretical wisdom.

Theoretical wisdom is general information and universal truths we draw upon when we contemplate ends or goals and our strategies for achieving them. Theoretical wisdom tells us that happiness is an actualized life, for example, and that we actualize our potential through excellent actions. But theoretical wisdom doesn't help with the particulars. How do we show interest in this particular person so that he or she will like us? What is too obsequious? Too surly? Where is the golden mean? For these answers, we need practical wisdom.

Practical Wisdom

Practical wisdom is sound judgment in practical situations. It is prudence, the capacity or habit of deliberating well about what is good and advantageous to oneself. Practical wisdom involves carefully attending to all circumstances that may relate to an action. Good deliberation, however, does not depend on a long process of reasoning. It is the product of applying theoretical wisdom or general principles to particular circumstances. It is the habit of correctly sizing up the situation, of evaluating the problem at hand in terms of its general characteristics, and then deciding the way it is to be handled and the time it is to be done. Practical wisdom is the direct appraisal of the situation and of the excellent action. In sum, whereas theoretical wisdom is developed through education, practical wisdom comes from experience. Theoretical wisdom helps us understand universal principles and situations in the abstract; practical wisdom helps us determine how to act in particular situations.

The primary obstacle to practical wisdom is what the Eastern philosophers call "being asleep" or going through our daily lives reacting to situations with our minds elsewhere. Practical wisdom requires that we be conscious, pay attention. To the samurai, being fully alert and paying attention while assessing the circumstances meant the difference between a long or short life. At any moment, there could be a razor sharp sword chop from an unexpected opponent. The martial arts master trained the student to pay attention to everything in the moment by unexpectedly jumping out and applying a painful whack to any exposed area and admonishing the student to "be here now!" Be alert, use your practical wisdom here in this situation, now, rather than letting your mind wander elsewhere or reacting emotionally without deliberation.

THE WHACK

He was carrying the last of two brimming buckets up the mountain path. The blow came from behind and landed squarely across his right ear. The tremendous pain was like looking into the sun. He blinked and found himself on the ground. The buckets were rolling happily back down the mountain and the Old Man was looking down at him with great satisfaction. . . .

There were three more attacks before supper. By then, the boy was so jumpy that he decided against eating. Ordered to come in, however, he obeyed. . . .

They ate in their usual silence then the Old Man said to him through the twilight, "An animal will jump at every sound, a leaf in the wind, a falling cone. A disciplined man will move only when it is necessary." There was a ruminative pause, then the addendum: "The moment *before* it is necessary. . . ."

Thereafter, he never turned his back on the Old Man again. He might be carrying a load of wood, reading a sutra or helpless in the bathing barrel, but part of his mind was always alert for that vicious stick of bamboo. . . .

Yet in time he found it possible to duck instead of dive, to veer and not drop the wood, the water or the book. He was almost surprised to find it was possible to move with caution and still get all of his chores done in good time. . . .

Then no longer did he merely pass through a door thinking of something else. It became an act of dangerous importance. Nor did he round a corner unthinkingly, approach the top of a hill blithely, nor pass closely by a tree. Reverie was replaced by exquisite attention to what he was doing. Each act called for total concentration if he was to avoid pain, a fall of pride and the tattoo of a bruise. So, to avoid hurt, he learned to perceive Everything that is Now.

—William Dale Jennings
The Ronin[13]

THE FIVE ENEMIES

The Way of the Ronin is far from trouble free. Five natural enemies lie in wait. They are much like the three demons that the Hindus warn keep us tied to the cycle of reincarnation, doomed to relive our unlearned lessons. So too, the enemies threaten to detour the Ronin, making full actualization improbable. Only with the first enemy, fear, is an encounter obvious. The others stalk us in ways we do not notice until too late. In fact, realizing that the enemy is near is half the challenge. All are dangerous, tempting us to forget the Way. If we ignore these formidable enemies, we will be enslaved. Yet once mastered, each becomes a faithful ally.

Fear

Fear, the first natural enemy, stops us from taking risks. Without risking, we can meet few challenges, pursue few dreams, and learn little. Attempting to avoid or escape what we fear is a natural response. But if we give in to this tendency, we will never be free. Fear will grow stronger and spread until it becomes the master.

Fear's capability to enslave is much like that of the magic Ring of Power that Bilbo Baggins stole from the evil hobbit, Gollum, in the popular hobbit fantasy tales.[14] When wearing the ring, Bilbo became invisible, easily escaping goblins and other enemies. But there was a dark side to the ring. There was something seductively alluring in the security of invisibility. Bilbo discovered that, each time he gave in to the desire to hide, the compelling urge to slip that ring on again increased tenfold. The evil hobbit cannibal, Gollum, hiding in the dank cave's murky waters in the heart of Misty Mountain, was a living testimony of the Ring's power to enslave a hobbit's soul.

> *About the Ring, the wizard Gandalf warns:*
> It is far more powerful than I ever dared to think at first, so powerful that in the end it would utterly overcome anyone of mortal race who possessed it. It would possess him.
> A mortal . . . who keeps one of the Great Rings, does not die, but he does not grow or obtain more life, he merely continues, until at last every minute is a weariness. And if he often uses the Ring to make himself invisible, he *fades*: he becomes in the end invisible permanently, and walks in the twilight under the eye of the dark power that rules the Rings. Yes, sooner or later—later, if he is strong or well-meaning to begin with, but

neither strength nor good purpose will last—sooner or
later the dark power will devour him.
                                    —J. R. R. Tolkien
                                    The Fellowship of the Ring[15]

Fear can never be conquered by running from it or trying to
be invisible. For each time we try to get away from it, fear becomes more powerful until soon it is so terrifying that we cannot
help but run from it. To master fear, we must hold our ground
and face it down.

> Don Juan: "Fear! A terrible enemy—treacherous, and
> difficult to overcome. It remains concealed at every turn
> of the way, prowling, waiting. And if the man, terrified in
> its presence, runs away, his enemy will have put an end
> to his quest."
> Carlos: "What will happen to the man if he runs away
> in fear?"
> Don Juan: "Nothing happens to him except that he
> will never learn. He will never become a man of knowl-
> edge. He will perhaps be a bully, or a harmless, scared
> man; at any rate, he will be a defeated man. His first
> enemy will have put an end to his craving."
> Carlos: "And what can he do to overcome his fear?"
> Don Juan: "The answer is very simple. He must not
> run away. He must defy his fear, and in spite of it he must
> take the next step in learning, and the next, and the next.
> He must be fully afraid, and yet he must not stop. That
> is the rule! And a moment will come when his first enemy
> retreats. The man begins to feel sure of himself. His intent
> becomes stronger. Learning is no longer a terrifying
> task."
> —Carlos Castaneda
> The Teachings of Don Juan[16]

Identify and confront your fears one by one. Fear of speaking
up in a group, for example, can be a shackle on maneuverability
in the work world. Those who give in to this fear avoid jobs and
projects that could offer the adventure of experience and learning
simply because it might require that they speak before a group.
They have allowed fear to limit them and have strayed from the
Way of the Ronin. Instead of running away, confront and defy

fear. But fear cannot be mastered by ignoring it or by acting rashly. Instead, make fear an ally. Like the boy in "The Whack," use the alertness that comes with fear to be observant, noticing Everything that is Now. Then, deliberate well and act. Soon you will feel sure of yourself where once you were fearful.

Confidence

When fear has been vanquished we gain a great sense of freedom. But in its place we acquire confidence, the second natural enemy. Confidence makes us feel strong—we believe in ourselves. Although confidence releases us from fear, it also blinds. We forget to listen to our ally fear; forget to observe, forget to deliberate well. Instead, we may act boldly when we should have exercised caution; we speak up when we should have listened, we improvise when we should have prepared.

Confidence makes us forget our ignorance. We begin to believe we know what we do not know and can do what we cannot do. Shunning good counsel, we reject helpful suggestions. If we succumb to confidence, we stop learning, swagger about, and feel invincible instead.

To defeat this second enemy, we must do what we did with fear—defy it. We must harness confidence to push ourselves forward, yet never forget to heed our ally fear. Be alert, wait patiently, and deliberate carefully before taking new steps. Mastered, confidence becomes self-trust. We can rely on ourselves to move forward in the right measure at the right time.

Power

Power, the third natural enemy, is the strongest of all because it is so innately satisfying and delicious. The danger it poses is that seeking power becomes an end instead of a means. The easiest thing to do is to give in to power. Prowling in many disguises, it is upon us before we know it. Authority, license to command others, is the easiest to recognize. Power is subtle, circling slowly without our noticing until one day we discover others view us as capricious or cruel rule makers—or worse!

With fear and confidence in check, opportunities at work multiply. As we meet the challenges of opportunity, our ability and experience grow. As we become more valuable, money comes. And so does power, the power to have things, to go places, and to buy others' service and allegience. Power beckons us to work for money, setting aside the Way of the Ronin. Day by day, we make compromises. The pursuit of money, instead of excellence, becomes the goal.

But most insidious is power disguised as persuasion, the ability to influence others' lives. At first, we give advice with the noblest of intentions. We seek only to help and guide. Soon, however, being able to shape and move others seduces. Persuasion becomes an end in itself. Forgotten is the other's freedom and welfare.

When we work for power, whatever the form, we are lost. Ronin must grapple with power and master it. Refusing power is not the solution. Without power we can effect nothing, we cannot play the World Game. Following the Way of the Ronin, we naturally gain more power—more authority, more money, more charisma, and more ability to create and effect goals. These are the tools we need to play the World Game—to create and to effect. Power is necessary but must be mastered. And it is mastered by mastering ourselves: knowing our desires and motives well and satisfying them through excellent action. When we hold ourselves in check, power is an ally—the ability to influence and effect according to intention.

> Carlos: "How can he defeat his third enemy, Don Juan?"
> Don Juan: "He has to defy it, deliberately. He has to come to realize the power he has seemingly conquered is in reality never his. He must keep himself in line at all times, handling carefully and faithfully all that he has learned. And if he can see that [confidence] and power, without his control over himself, are worse than mistakes, he will reach a point where everything is held in check. He will know then when and how to use his power. And thus he will have defeated his third enemy.
>
> —Carlos Castaneda
> *The Teachings of Don Juan*[17]

Complacency

The fourth enemy is the subtlest and most difficult to defeat. Having mastered such formidable enemies as fear, confidence, and power, we feel strong, able to defy any foe. Then complacency creeps in, unnoticed, on cat's feet as self-satisfaction lulling us into smugness.

Assisted by its sister, tiredness, complacency makes us grow weary of challenges and long to hang loose and coast instead. But we must not give in to complacency because it leads to stagnation and the midlife crisis. As with the other enemies, we must defy it. We must be alert, watching ourselves, keeping the other enemies in check. For as soon as we drop our guard, they will attack again. Defy complacency by seeking out challenges and looking for barriers to surmount, new goals to strive for. It may even be necessary to create some degree of discomfort in order to shake complacency.

When tamed, complacency becomes an ally in the form of fulfillment and renewal. Whereas complacency seduces us into remaining in the comfort of the known, expending little effort, fulfillment is both satisfaction with completion and a prompt to begin again.

The Shadow

The fifth natural enemy can take many forms. It is always there at our side, yet we rarely notice it—our shadow. The shadow is our habitual extreme. We usually have more than one. Many people are generalists, for example, following nonlinear paths. Yet they do not grow because, instead of seeking excellence, they are driven by their shadows. Perhaps it is dilettantism—sticking a toe in here and there but being unable to make a commitment. Or perhaps it's fascination with new sensations for their own sake, like a drug pursued for the thrill, rather than the ability to enjoy sensations as the side benefit of development and self-expansion.

The shadow is our personal weaknesses. We can never rid ourselves of the shadow by suppressing it, pretending it is not there. To do so only makes the shadow stronger—lurking, waiting to sabotage us. We must defy the shadow, resisting its enticement, not by suppression, guilt, or criticism, but by self-knowledge. We can defeat the shadow and put it into its rightful place by the simple task of observing ourselves. Get to know what you do, how you do it, and when you do it. Learn your tendencies. Then use this self-knowledge and practical wisdom to determine the excellent action when the shadow tempts you with a familiar extreme. As the accompanying chart shows, the shadow can be a terrible foe. But it can also be a great ally. For as an ally, the shadow represents consciousness or awareness, being alert and alive in the moment, and seeking excellence.

COMMON RONIN SHADOWS

ENEMY	ALLY
Noncommitment Lack of follow-through; excessive interest in starting projects but leaves follow–through to others	**Detachment** Ability to let go of the old and move on to the new; not clinging
Arbitrariness Being whimsical, capricious, flighty, and unpredictable; inclined to change abruptly without warning	**Adaptability** Being flexible, open; adjusting to change easily
Lack of focus Inability to accept structure, scattered, insistence on the ad hoc	**Creativity** Acceptance of uncertainty; productive in vaguely defined situations
"Meism" Narcissism, excessive self-interest, dwelling on one's importance, abilities, and projects	**Assertiveness** Favorable presentation of one's ideas, abilities, and projects; attentive to one's self-interests
Dilettantism Dabbling, superficial involvement, jumping from one project to another	**Generalism** Acquiring knowledge and skills in many fields; wide range of experience
"Sensationism" Using personal style or language to shock others; excessive attraction to the sensational; constantly seeking stimulation	**Adventurousness** Taking calculated risks; enjoying change and venturing into the unknown
Opportunism Adapting actions and thoughts to circumstances in order to further immediate interests without regard for excellence or eventual consequences	**Decisiveness** Evaluating an opportunity and carrying out the excellent action without ambivalence
Irresponsibility Refusing to be accountable for one's actions	**Self-Acceptance** Bouncing back from failure without excessive regret over wrong actions
Cleverness Using right means for wrong ends; giving opportunism the appearance of excellence	**Ingenuity** Originality, resourcefulness, and inventiveness
Glibness Having smooth, easy manner and fluent, offhanded speech; acting extemporaneously	**Confidence** Projecting self-assurance and self-sufficiency; preparedness; carrying out actions with aplomb

Don Juan: "An impeccable stalker can turn anything into prey. . . . We can even stalk our own weaknesses. . . . You figure out your routines until you know all the doing of your weaknesses and then you come upon them and pick them up like rabbits inside a cage."
—Carlos Castaneda
The Second Ring of Power[18]

SCHOOLS

The primary function of school is to socialize youth to function well within society and its institutions. Hans Gerth and C. Wright Mills[19] in *Character and Social Structure: The Psychology of Social Institutions* say, "Education is a deliberate attempt to transmit skills and loyalties, as well as forms of inner cultivation and conventional deportment required by status group membership." William Scott and David Hart[20] in *Organizational America* agree: "The major responsibility for the development of the requisite character belongs to the educational system, and it has accepted this responsibility with enormous gusto, at all levels." In other words, most of us have been molded in school to fit into the organizational world of bureaucracies.

In his cynical dissertation, *The Student as Nigger*, Jerry Farber described the process by which schools train us in the appropriate behavior. He says, "For most of your school life, it doesn't make that much difference what subject you're taught. The real lesson is the method. The medium in school truly is the message. And the medium is, above all, coercive. . . . And throughout, you're bullied into docility and submission."[21] In short, education for conformity has been more highly prized than creativity or independent thought and action.

> When they've tortured and scared you for 20 odd years
> Then they expect you to pick a career
> When you can't really function you're so full of fear
> A working class here is somthing to be
> A working class here is something to be
> —John Lennon
> Stanza from "Working Class Hero"[22]

Educating for Conformity

Let's take a closer look. Each degree that we earn indicates the extent of our socialization. With advanced education, we gain more power to play the World Game.

> Because of the steady increase of educational requirements for an increasing range of specialized occupations, the opportunities to climb the ladder of occupational success become more and more dependent upon education.
> —Hans Gerth and C. Wright Mills
> Character and Social Structure[23]

Acquiring the first degree, the high school diploma, determines whether we are allowed to play the World Game or not. Those who do not earn a high school diploma are virtually excluded from positions of authority and power in our society, relegated instead to the lowest status and least skilled jobs. Yet high school dropouts as a group are not, as many think, less intelligent than those who graduate. In fact, according to Louis Bright, director of research for the U.S. Office of Education, high school dropouts in large cities where figures are available have higher IQs than do high school graduates.[24]

Often problems in school lie, not in an inability to do the work, but in an inability to conform to the system. These students are the "behavior problems," who act in the wrong way or who say the wrong thing. Many students who show independence of thought are penalized by teachers with low or failing grades and thereby are restricted from participation in the World Game. For example, one creative boy attending a Catholic School heard a nun say, "You should love Jesus and hate the devil," and reasoned, "If everyone hates the devil, no wonder he is so bad and evil. I will love the devil, instead." Foolishly, he expressed this notion and was labeled a bad and rebellious boy and given a failing grade.

The fact is it doesn't take 12 years to learn what is taught at the secondary level. Recall Farber's contention that how we are taught is more important than what we are taught. During secondary education, students learn to stand in line, sit quietly at their desks, raise their hands, speak respectfully to teachers, and stay in study hall on beautiful days when they might rather be out exploring the world and having adventures. The high school diploma indicates that the graduate successfully made it through the secondary system. He or she has accepted authority and can abide by it, at least to a minimum. Those who cannot are not granted the degree.

Next comes the bachelor's degree. What is required to obtain a B.A.? Students, typically living away from home, are free of the constant parental overseer who prompts them to get up in the morning or to do their homework. Instead, they must prompt themselves. The B.A. degree indicates that a person has successfully made it though four years of college, with five courses a semester. This entails attending each class under one's own direction, feeding back on tests and in class discussions what was transmitted in lectures and books, studying rather than playing on evenings and weekends, writing laborious papers, and memorizing for tests innumerable facts of questionable usefulness. It is no wonder that the new college graduate is the prime candidate for management trainee! Holding a B.A. degree indicates one is malleable and can follow directives on one's own.

> I emerged from school to discover I was empty of enthusiasm. I had a profession but nothing to profess, knowledge but no wisdom, ideas but few feelings, rich in techniques but poor in convictions, I'd gotten an education but lost an identity.
>
> —Sam Keen[25]

Next comes the master's degree. In many ways, this is the easiest degree to obtain. The course of study is shorter, typically nine months, and in an area of the student's interest and ability. Instructors are more likely to take other academic commitments into consideration. Finally, the classes interlock so that material from one augments what is presented in others. On graduation, one is annointed with the label "professional" and allowed a larger measure of respect, freedom, and power in the World Game. One is often freed from punching the time clock, and there is usually a substantial increase in earning potential.

The final degree is the doctorate. The first two years of doctoral training are perhaps the easiest of all years spent in post-high school education. By this time, students are skilled at studying. Able to extract vital information from lectures and texts, they have the intellectual capabilities to analyze ideas and the writing and speaking skills to communicate them. They know how to get the grades and how to impress the professors. The critical test comes with the dissertation. Up to this point, the student followed the authority of teachers, feeding back what they said, studying what they assigned, taking required courses, and meeting the teacher-set deadlines. But with the dissertation, the ground rules change. No longer can the student rely on teachers for direction, structure, or feedback.

To pass the test of the dissertation, the candidate must do two things. The first requirement is an original scholarly study or quality research project. This is the easy part. By the time candidates have gotton to this point, they are thoroughly acquainted with their fields. Thinking of something no one has done before is easy. The difficulty is deciding which of the many possibilities to choose. The second and critical requirement of the dissertation is that the student do the original work completely independently. Gone are the deadlines of tests and papers assigned by teachers. Students can literally go for weeks, sometimes months or even years floundering around, not knowing how to proceed and making little progress. No one prompts, no one threatens, and few encourage the candidate to work. After 18 or more years of being directed by teachers, the student must find self-direction. Although the work must be original, it must at the same time adhere to rigorous parameters of intellectual discourse or research design. Many are unable to meet this standard and drop out with what is commonly called the "ABD degree"—all but dissertation.

Completion of the dissertation and subsequent awarding of this highest degree indicates that acceptable intellectual behavior and values have been internalized to the extent that the graduates impose them on themselves. And the reward for this feat of socialization? The label "expert" and, as college teacher or researcher, being allowed to pursue one's work independently, with little or no supervision. Although many believe that the Ph.D. is highly creative and no less than brillant, this is often not the case. At every step along the educational process, those who venture outside of the acceptable parameters of thought are given failing marks and not allowed to pass to the next step. Innovative thought is not safe. Thus, the highly creative are precluded from having too much power in the World Game. Only those who are safe, who are appropriately socialized are given enough power to push the frontiers forward.

Fortunately, schools have not functioned perfectly. A few of the innovative do succeed in finding their ways through the psychological labyrinth. These are the Ronin. Knowing when to conform and when to be innovative, when to speak out and when to maintain a low profile, like Bilbo Baggins, they sneak into the dragon's lair and steal the jewels without being devoured. For within the ivory towers of our educational institutions lie the keys to the knowledge, intellectual discipline, and technical skill needed to play the World Game. The trick is to obtain these while retaining a sense of one's self and one's creativity.

Educating for Autonomy

Until recently our schools have functioned well in shaping the other-directed people needed to fit into the feudal bureaucracies. Organizations find creativity and idiosyncratic behavior threatening. It's disruptive. Acceptance in organizations requires conformity and loyalty, and doesn't allow questioning or doing things in new ways. This process functioned to help bring about industrialization and our modern world, but things are changing. All indications suggest that the future will require more autonomous and self-directed people.

Those who survive the rigors and constraints of our present linear system are not necessarily the best and the brightest, but rather those who have become most wily

in the art of bureaucratic survival—careful not to be
overly creative and bright, more concerned with appear-
ance than substance, never rocking the boat.
                                           —John Oliver Wilson
                                           After Affluence[26]

Education no longer guarantees a sure route to economic security and social status. Because of blocks in climbing up the
ladder—the shrinking pyramid, economic problems, technological change, too many baby-boomers for too few jobs—we need
to break out of our narrow and rigid career patterns. Rather than
following a linear career pattern, we need to develop more flexibility. When blocked in an existing job because there's no place
for advancement, we need to move laterally. But to do this, we
must be generalists with more latitude in our career choices. Yet
our schools are preparing millions of young Americans for career
feudalism—to climb an occupational ladder that narrows dramatically at the top, thus ensuring rising frustration and increasing dissaffection.

John Oliver Wilson in *After Affluence*[27] offers advice for the
education of flexible and autonomous people. He says that education should include programs in three major areas—basic
skills, flexibility and alternatives, and wonder. The course in
basic skills should provide the tools to earn a living. These should
include both technical skills (such as accounting, engineering,
or management) and basic communication skills (reading, writing, and speaking). To these essentials, I would add self-managing skills, knowing how to set goals and how to motivate oneself to attain them. The primary aim should not be to prepare for
a single vocation but to equip the graduate for many careers.
Whereas technical skills can quickly become obsolete, basic
communication and self-management skills provide the flexibility needed for the world of the future.

The course in flexibilty and alternatives should teach how to
live in the world of change. Familiarity with alternative life-
styles and experience in radically different jobs is essential. Wilson believes we must learn to create whole lives from our many
varied experiences.

Finally, Wilson suggests a course in wonder to prepare graduates to develop what he calls "our inner silence, to cultivate
the ability to let things happens, to welcome, to listen, to
allow."[28]

Notes

1. *Secrets of the Samurai: A Survey of the Martial Arts of Feudal Japan* (Tokyo, Japan: Charles E. Tuttle Co., Inc., 1973), p. 445.
2. *The Information Society of Postindustrial Society* (Tokyo: World of Future, 1980).
3. Ibid., p. 149.
4. Ibid, p. 151.
5. *The Ethics of Aristotle: The Nicomachean Ethics*, trans. J. A. K. Thomson (London: Penguin Classics, 1953). Text references to *The Ethics*, to *The Nicomachean Ethics*, and to *The Ethics of Aristotle* are used interchangeably and all refer to this book.
6. Ibid., p. 56.
7. Ibid., p. 43.
8. Carlos Castaneda, *The Second Ring of Power* (New York: Simon & Schuster, 1977), p. 274.
9. *The Ethics*, pp. 58, 65.
10. New York: Avon, 1973, p. 30.
11. *Many Dimensional Man: Decentralizing Self, Society, and the Sacred* (New York: Colophon Books, 1979), p. 64.
12. *The Ethics*, pp. 58–59.
13. *The Ronin: A Novel Based on a Zen Myth* (Tokyo, Japan: Charles E. Tuttle Co., Inc., 1968), pp. 103–107.
14. J. R. R. Tolkien, *The Fellowship of the Ring* (New York: Ballantine Books, 1965).
15. p. 76.
16. *The Teachings of Don Juan: A Yaqui Way of Knowledge* (New York: Pocket Books, 1974), p. 84.
17. p. 87.
18. New York: Simon & Schuster, 1977, p. 221.
19. New York: Harcourt Brace Jovanovich, 1964, p. 251.
20. Boston: Houghton Mifflin, 1980, p. 153.
21. New York: Pocket Books, 1970, pp. 19–20.
22. Copyright 1970 Northern Songs Ltd. All rights for the United States and Mexico controlled by Maclen Music Inc., % ATD Music Corp. Used by permission. All rights reserved.
23. *Character and Social Structure: The Psychology of Social Institutions* (New York: Harcourt Brace Jovanovich, 1964), p. 253.
24. Cited in George B. Leonard, *Education and Ecstasy* (New York: Delta, 1968), p. 11.
25. Cited in John Oliver Wilson, *After Affluence: Economics to Meet Human Needs* (New York: Harper & Row, 1980), p. 196.
26. p. 204.
27. pp. 204–205.
28. Ibid., p. 205.

Have Skills Will Travel

Self-reverence, self-knowledge, self-control,
these three alone lead to sovereign power.
　　　　　　　　　—Alfred Lord Tennyson

As mentioned earlier, a Ronin television character widely known
in America is the frontier gunfighter Palladin, played by Richard
Boone. Palladin's business card depicted a knight chess piece
and carried the motto "Have Gun Will Travel." The motto informed prospective clients that his martial skills were available
by contract. The knight denoted that he was not merely a hired
gun, but a sophisticated multidimensional strategist.

Like Palladin, modern Ronin use their skills as a ticket to ride.
Career feudalism encouraged unidirectional travel—climbing
the ladder up. Increasingly, however, the ladder is overcrowded.
Talented and ambitious feudalists are stuck midlevel. In some
cases, they are pushed down a step or knocked off the ladder

altogether. Ronin avoid ladders and tracks. Instead, they use their skills to move around the corporate arena. Travel does not necessarily mean moving from one company to another. Ronin often move within an organization, from department to department, team to team, or even one job to another within the same office. And they look sideways for opportunity and adventure, not always up.

Generic skills, those essential in all fields, are the most powerful. Self-managing, self-knowing, deciding, transforming, and communicating are skills of adaptability and ongoing development. And it is these skills that Ronin constantly practice and refine.

MANAGE THYSELF

The discipline of the Japanese samurai is legendary. Faced with life-or-death situations, the samurai operated under an unwavering will, unswayed by distractions. But the samurai was indentured, working under the direction of his feudal lord. Those who were thrown on the waves of fate with no master, the *ronin*, faced life's supreme challenge. *Doing ronin* meant struggling to become one's own master, to direct one's self.

For many of us, discussion of discipline or self-control triggers images of denial, withholding, and coercion, and not too surprisingly, we resist. Actually, discipline is a process of management in which you are both manager and managed. Critical, threatening bosses can extract reluctant, resentful performances, whereas the manager who employs a positive approach gets consistent quality output. The same holds with managing ourselves. Luckily, self-management is a cluster of skills and habits that can be learned and perfected. Managing thyself is requisite to pursuing excellence.

Motivation

> The name of the game is action. Doing.
> Overcoming your inertia and *acting* will
> give you a whole new lease on being
> creatively alive.
> —Wayne W. Dyer
> *Pulling Your Own Strings*[1]

How do you motivate yourself? Do you work for positives or to avoid negatives? As with managing others, effective self-management requires knowledge and skill. But most of us have acquired our self-managing skills informally, usually from parents, teachers, and friends. Few have had guided training and practice. Consequently, many of us manage ourselves in ways that sabotage our interests or that we rebel against.

Clearly, "working for" motivation is most desirable. With our focus on positives we want to achieve, "working for" promotes self-starting and finishing. We can increase "working for" by becoming more skillful. Self-mastery skills are assets in any endeavor. They are transferable, enabling you to move in any direction you choose.

Goals

Without a goal, we are but a ship without a sextant, going around and around with no direction. A goal provides a target, something to shoot for. It guides efforts, especially at points of decision, helping us to decide which path to take. Poor self-managers resist setting goals in much the same way that they resist external management, feeling locked in, obligated, unfree, and forced to do something.

Keep in mind that goals are but tools, meant to be used in our service, not to enslave us. Good self-managers know that having something desirable just out of reach, something to strive for, is motivating. And they use this to move themselves in directions they want to go. Reaching the goal is not the point. In fact, more often than not, once a long sought after goal is achieved, we feel let down and motivation wanes. Why? We no longer have something to work for.

GUIDELINES FOR SETTING GOALS

1. State what you want to do, not what you think you should do.
2. Translate what you want to avoid into what you want to occur.
3. Use action phrases—that is, such verbs as get, develop, ask, explore, give.
4. Focus on what you can influence.
5. Be specific: State what, when, where, how, and to what degree.
6. Reevaluate and reform periodically.

Small Steps

The first step is the hardest.
—Marie De Vichy-Charmond

The surest way to reach a goal is to break it into achievable small steps. We climb the mountain step by step. Poor self-man-

agers sabotage themselves by demanding enormous steps. Consider this principle from physics: The law of inertia says a body at rest will tend to stay at rest and a body in motion will tend to stay in motion. Just as it requires a tremendous effort to overcome a large rock's inertia before it will move, the same is true of yourself. Moving yourself toward a goal will require a large effort in the beginning. The easiest way to get yourself in motion is through small steps, each requiring you to travel only a short distance. Climbing the first step brings a feeling of success. And success begets success. Avoid the macho approach of demanding huge steps, of forcing yourself to strain through difficulty. Not

THE FIRST STEP

The young poet Eumenes
complained one day to Theocritus:
"I have been writing for two years now
and I have done only one idyll.
It is my only finished work.
Alas, it is steep, I see it,
the stairway of Poetry is so steep;
and from the first step where now I stand,
poor me, I shall never ascend."
"These words," Theocritus said,
"are unbecoming and blasphemous.
And if you are on the first step,
you ought to be proud and pleased.
Coming as far as this is not little;
what you have achieved is great glory.
For even this first step
is far distant from the common herd.
To set your foot upon this step
you must rightfully be a citizen
of the city of ideas.
And in that city it is hard
and rare to be naturalized.
In her market place you find Lawmakers
whom no adventurer can dupe.
Coming as far as this is not little;
what you have achieved is great glory."

—C. P. Cavafy
Rae Dalven, Translator[2]

only is the large-step approach painful, it is a setup to fail. Good self-managers set themselves up to succeed by demanding only very small steps. When a step is too large or too difficult, divide it into smaller ones to get motion going.

Self-Acknowledgment

Self-acknowledgment, focusing on what was done well, provides the wins necessary to climb the small steps. Poor self-managers tend to do just the opposite. Focusing on the failures, they criticize what has been done poorly. Self-criticism tends to set up a vicious cycle of "working to avoid," whereas self-acknowledgment promotes "working for."

Self-acknowledgment is similar to positive thinking but is more refined, going beyond "In every day and every way, I'm getting better and better." Instead, self-acknowledgment zeros in on the specific aspects of our performance that we have done well. Acknowledgment can be expressed by giving ourselves things we want, by allowing ourselves to participate in activities we enjoy, or by giving ourselves praise.

We all like to enjoy ourselves and experience pleasure. But many undermine their enjoyment. These poor self-managers feel guilty or anxious when they could be having fun. They worry about what they should have done, what they should be doing instead, or what they must get back to. In contrast, good self-managers are "contingent indulgers"—they reward themselves for making small steps.

One technique that is very popular and quite effective is using a want list. If you've never tried this before, you might do so now, just as an experiment. Then notice what happens to your motivation.

Exercise: Using a Want List

Make a list of things you want. Write this down. Include activities and social encounters you enjoy, and things you do a lot and want to continue doing. Next break your work up into small units. Finally, each time you complete a small unit of work, acknowledge or reward yourself with an item from the want list. It may be as little as a cup of coffee or looking at a magazine. At the top of the next page are some examples:

Want List

What I do a lot	Things I like	Activities I like
Open mail	New outfits	Lunch with friend
Talk on phone	Stereo cassettes	Go to theater
Photocopy	Sheepskin covers	Hike after work
Drink coffee	Magazines	Sunbathe
Read trade journals		

Chances are that if you try this you will discover that you accomplish more—and that both working and indulging will be more pleasurable. No guilt trips, no negative feelings. These are pleasures you have earned! There are many ways to tailor this motivational technique to your situation. Experiment with the strategies given here, and maybe create some of your own. It's a tool for developing "working for" motivation. When you're facing an unpleasant task or a work block, try this method. If it doesn't work, break the task into even smaller pieces. Some people feel that this is self-bribery. But even if it is, does it matter? Remember, the object is to get that body in motion!

Exercise: Task Management

You can increase your productivity by managing your work. Here are two strategies.

Strategy 1

Break your work down into tasks or units and divide into two categories: those tasks you do right away or like more and those tasks you put off or like less. To increase motivation, productivity, and a sense of control, re-arrange the sequencing of your work. First, complete a work unit you like less or tend to put off, then follow it with a work unit or task you like more or tend to do right away. Periodically acknowledge your productivity with items from your want list. Remember: To complete a big project with ease, break it into small steps!

Strategy 2

There are many work activities that are necessary for keeping up with your profession or preparing for a promotion. This is "later" work. The problem is that later

work often has no definite deadline and gets put off in
favor of "now" work—work with daily or weekly deadlines. You can increase the amount of later work accomplished by first doing a little later work, then a little now
work. Periodically acknowledge your accomplishments
with items from your want list.

If you make a habit of motivating yourself in this manner, you
will have discovered the secret of "intrinsic motivation." Eventually, you won't notice that you work for your wants. You'll be
too busy enjoying working, living, and learning. And others will
marvel at your discipline, drive, and commitment. They will call
you Ronin. But more important, autonomy increases as you master self-motivating with contingent indulgences in which you
award yourself goodies for completing small steps. You will have
gained one degree of freedom. If there are few or no external
rewards, you can "work for" anyway. The ability to self-reward
reduces dependence on others for reward and increases personal
power.

Avoid Perfectionism

Perfectionists are among the poorest self-managers. And contrary to popular opinion, they rarely perform perfectly. In fact,
overall their track record often falls short. First, they set unreal-
istic criteria for success. For the perfectionist, nothing less than
99.9 percent is acceptable. The realist, on the other hand, sets a
high but achievable standard. Suppose, for example, both the
perfectionist and the realist, who uses a 90 percent standard for
success, are each preparing a customer presentation. Who is
likely to make their presentation first? While the perfectionist
labors away on refinement after refinement, the realist has gone
on to give the presentation to a second, perhaps a third customer.
Because perfectionists set unrealistically stringent standards,
they continually experience failure. The realist, in contrast, frequently wins. Perfectionists tend to self-criticize, because anything less than 99.9 percent is considered inadequate. Realists,
on the other hand, demand less of themselves and applaud what
they do well.

Perfectionism is a management approach that destroys motivation. To perform, perfectionists must use guilt and punitive
techniques to coerce themselves to work to avoid their own

wrath. Because they make performing such a negative experience, perfectionists tend to avoid working until the latest possible time. The resulting procrastination combined with the perfectionist's critical orientation exacerbates the problem, creating a vicious cycle of procrastination and self-flagellation. By setting high but realistic standards, realists get themselves into motion, and by focusing on what they have done well, they provide a steady stream of wins that fuel motivation, leading to more success. Ninety percent is an A, after all. And think about this: If you do *everything* at 90 percent (or even 85, which is a B+), you are doing very well, indeed! When you set your criteria for acceptable performance at realistic levels, you will get more done, achieve more success, and enjoy yourself more.

Incremental Commitment

Using the New Year's type resolution is another way many people sabotage themselves. Those employing this all-or-nothing approach to commitment resolve *never* again to do whatever it is that they want to stop doing or *always* to do something instead. One transgression and they have failed. It's an impossible standard to meet. We can build commitment in small increments with the use of a self-contract.

SELF-CONTRACT

I will _____
_____
                    (small step)
When I complete this, I will _____
                                (item from want list)

_____
    (contract term)
_____   _____
        (date)   (signature)

Looking at the accompanying example, you'll see that you specify only one small step toward a goal and define exactly what you will do. Another notable feature is the time frame. There is a finite term to the commitment, which should be no longer than what you can adhere to successfully. The contract states what win will be forthcoming when the agreement is completed. Success is built in. Finally, it is written down, signed, and witnessed when possible, to emphasize the importance of the agreement.

The contract is a tool for moving through the small steps. Write a contract for only as much change as you know you can accomplish, and be sure the time frame is short enough so that you *know* you can stick to your resolve. This is important. When the contract is fulfilled, move to the next step. Increase the amount, intensity, or quality of the performance or the term of the contract. Successfully completed contracts are wins that fuel motivation. Remember, the contract is a tool to get in motion and to keep in motion. It's a way of teaching yourself to "work for" and to develop enthusiasm for work.

Creating Your Own Structure

As you master yourself, you will become more adept at structuring your work. You'll be increasingly able to handle free-flowing, vaguely defined projects—the creative work. This requires setting long-range goals and short-term action objectives, then dividing each into small daily, even hourly steps. Handling creative work often means performing in a reward–recognition vacuum for long periods. To maintain enthusiasm, you must "work for" and self-acknowledge. Once this is mastered, you'll be a true Ronin, able to live by your wits and will. Chances are you will never want to return to the confines of the clearly defined, closely monitored work life.

KNOW THYSELF

> Man ignorant of self, creates his own
> unhappiness. The world masters him,
> when he was born to master the world.
> —Paul Brunton
> *The Secret Path*[3]

Finding compatible work, whether it's part-time, a short-term fill-in, or a long-term position, without having first analyzed your occupational temperament is chancy. An ill-fitting job, like the pinch of wrong-size shoes, detracts from the pleasure of working and living. Being able to articulate who you are is an essential step in becoming self-determining and in actualizing potential. When you know your needs and rhythm, it is easier to make decisions about which positions to accept and when to stay in or leave a job.

Be leery of the tendency to use ability as the measure in making career choices. There's a danger in using what you can do as the sole determinant of what you ought to do. For example, test results indicated that Wilma had an aptitude for electronics. Blinded by the optimistic economic forecast for the industry, she neglected to look at herself and at what she needed in order to thrive before undertaking expensive, specialized training. Although she excelled, graduating at the head of her class, her first job was a disappointment and so were the several that followed. Electronics work required intense concentration and working alone. But to stay sane, Wilma needed frequent interactions with others. Because she ignored temperament and looked solely at ability, the investment of time and money left Wilma sidetracked and discouraged. Don't concern yourself with skills while conducting an inventory of your occupational temperament. Acquiring the necessary skills is easy when you enjoy what you're doing.

Positive feelings are a divining rod that can guide you to your best-fitting work. Study situations in which you feel good. Fond memories of enjoyable activities provide mental pictures that will help you draw a clear portrait of your occupational temperament.

The most effective analysis is a scientific one. Observation and data collection are central. To delineate accurately who you are, watch yourself. Recording what you see helps maintain objectivity. Keep a diary or journal. Like your appointment calendar, a personal journal is an excellent self-management tool. If you've never tried it, why not do so now? Any kind of notebook will do. You'll have to experiment to discover what packaging you prefer. The journal is somewhat like a diary because you can use it to express your desires, doubts, and struggles. Later, this material proves fascinating to study. But the journal is also a place to save ideas, post reminders, work out priorities, write goals, record progress data, and give praise. Filled with lists, charts, and notes, the journal is a working tool for studying and directing your "self."

Occupational Temperament Inventory

Occupational temperament is composed of six factors: The *medium* most conducive to expressing your creativity; the *mode* or that part of yourself you enjoy using most; *personal style*; *satisfiers*; optimal *managerial climate*; and optimal work *environment*. Each is described in The Occupational Temperament Inventory that follows. It is meant to give you a quick sketch of your occupational temperament.

OCCUPATIONAL TEMPERAMENT INVENTORY

Part One

Instructions: For each of the temperament factors, order the items from "least characteristic of me" to "most characteristic of me."

MEDIUMS

The medium is the arena that feels most comfortable and conducive to success. Stated differently, it is the material of self-expression. Just as artists work in their favorite mediums (such as poetry, sculpture, film, or dance), so too must we discover which mediums to use to actualize our selves.

_____ *Interactions*. I enjoy using an understanding of people's feelings, problems, and aspirations to facilitate productive interactions. Cooperating with others and developing productive relationships is a challenge I seek out. My creativity is expressed in the way I relate to others.

_____ *Things*. I enjoy using tools or machines to create, repair, test, or move things. Striving to be exact is a challenge I like to tackle. My creativity is expressed in concrete form: making something that can be used, looked at, listened to, or touched.

_____ *Abstractions*. I enjoy putting together ideas and information to understand, explain, plan, and organize. Synthesizing divergent elements to find a new perspective is a challenge I enjoy. I express my creativity by developing new ideas and new ways of doing things.

_____ *Authority*. I enjoy determining situations and overseeing projects. Influencing others and having an impact on their lives is my challenge. I seek out responsibility and express my creativity by orchestrating people's efforts to accomplish a goal.

MODES

Modes are the tools we use to implement our impact and to express our power.

_____ *Body: Movement.* I feel best when engaged in physical activity. My hands and coordinated movements are my favorite tools.

_____ *Mind: Words and Images.* I approach the world through my intellect and enjoy concentrating. Words and images are my favorite tools.

_____ *Heart: Feelings.* I approach the world through feelings. Intuition, perceptiveness, and empathy are my favorite tools.

PERSONAL STYLES

Style is the way you express yourself, the strategies you employ in making your moves.

_____ *Controlled.* I avoid taking risks, take a lot of time when making decisions, and solve problems by gathering and analyzing all available facts. I am generally calm and speak with a consistent tone of voice, using few gestures. I tend to be somewhat distant.

_____ *Expressive.* I take risks, make decisions quickly, and solve problems by taking action and doing something. I am excitable and speak with emphasis, using many gestures. I tend to express emotions.

SATISFIERS

Satisfiers are what you strive for and what brings meaning. They are your wins.

_____ *Prestige.* Being looked up to and respected; having eminence, notoriety, or fame.

_____ *Security.* Having peace of mind; feeling settled, safe, and established.

_____ *Self-Actualization.* Acquiring knowledge and skills; developing potential and meeting challenges.

_____ *Adventure.* Expending energy and being bold in the face of hazard; being stimulated; experiencing something new; winning at gamesmanship.

_____ *Service.* Feeling useful; giving succor and assistance; ameliorating pain and suffering.

_____ *Spiritual Awareness*. Developing wisdom and making ethical choices; striving for excellence.

_____ *Achievement*. Accomplishing goals; having expertise, proficiency, or adeptness.

_____ *Power*. Determining situations; commanding, exercising authority, and having privilege.

_____ *Social*. Enjoying companionship and convivial interactions; feeling that I belong and in harmony with others.

_____ *Wealth*. Enjoying material comfort; feeling affluent and having access to fine things.

Part Two

Instructions: For each of the following pairs, circle the asterisk that indicates what fosters your peak performance. Circle the middle asterisk if you are indifferent.

MANAGERIAL CLIMATE

Managerial climate refers to the style of management most effective in controlling and mobilizing your performance.

Structured	*	*	*	*	*	*	*	*Unstructured*
What I do, when, and how are clearly defined.								What I do, when, and how are loosely defined.

Monitored	*	*	*	*	*	*	*	*Unmonitored*
Frequent supervision, feedback, and opportunities to ask questions.								Infrequent supervision, feedback, and opportunities to ask questions.

Directed	*	*	*	*	*	*	*	*Undirected*
My goals are set by others.								I set my goals.

ENVIRONMENT

Environment refers to the structure of the setting where you feel most capable.

Indoor	*	*	*	*	*	*	*	*Outdoor*
Alone	*	*	*	*	*	*	*	*Peopled*
Slow Paced	*	*	*	*	*	*	*	*Fast Paced*

Part Three

OCCUPATIONAL TEMPERAMENT PORTRAIT

Instructions: Select the items that you rated as most like you, and fill in the Occupational Temperament Portrait.

I tend to be _____ and I like to work in
                      (personal style)

settings that are _____ where I am
                      (environment)

_____ while using
           (managerial climate)

my _____ with _____ in
      (mode)   (medium)

order to gain _____ .
             (satisfiers)

The Occupational Temperament Portrait is useful in interviews and social events where you are expected to talk about yourself. And it helps identify imbalance and undeveloped potential. For an in-depth portrait of your occupational temperament, try the following activities.

Using Memories of the Past

Call up a time in the past when you were feeling good, fully alive, involved in what you were doing, and effective. While rerunning the memory in your "fantasy theater," making it as vivid as possible, step back like a scientist and objectively observe what you were doing. Notice the medium through which you expressed yourself, your mode and style, what was satisfying, the management climate, and the environment. Take time and observe thoroughly; record your observations in your journal. Look for patterns in the data to identify compatibilities. Repeat this process with several memories. If you feel up to it, review past scenarios in which you felt frustrated, perhaps even failed. The data you collect in this mildly painful exercise help identify incompatibilities.

Analyzing What You Like to Do

In your journal write the heading "What I like to do" and list 15 or 20 activities you enjoy. Avoid searching and struggling for things you feel you ought to like to do or you should write down. Just write what comes to mind first. Analyze each activity in terms of the six occupational temperament factors. Record the results.

Analyze Your Data

Carefully review the data you collected, looking for trends and commonalities. Write a summary statement for each occupational temperament factor. The combination of these summaries is your self-portrait. Return to your fantasy theater, and project yourself into a typical day at work. How does the "you" in your job compare with the "you" in your portrait? If the match is good, you are well on your way. If, on the other hand, you feel stifled, work for satisfiers you don't value, have to do things you dislike, or have little opportunity to express and develop yourself, it's time to find a job that offers a better fit.

Analyze Your Skills

At the top of a clean journal page, write the headings "Activities/Tasks/Responsibilities" and "Skills Used." List your most frequent activities, tasks, and responsibilities. Include the avocational, personal, and social as well as those you used frequently in the past. This list can be quite long. Next, review each job you tried out in your fantasy theater and identify the skills you used. For example, selecting vendors could be staffing; looking up material in the library could be researching; intervening between angry co-workers might be mediating; and getting several people together to work on a project might be team building.

A PARADOX

The higher a skill level you can legitimately claim, the more likely you are to find a job. Just the opposite of what the typical job-hunter or second careerist starts out believing.

—Richard Bolles
What Color Is Your Parachute?[4]

If you get stuck and find skill identification difficult, try the checklist "Your Functional/Transferable Skills" in *What Color Is Your Parachute?*[5]

Finding Work That Fits

The next step is to identify a variety of occupations that might fit your occupational temperament. A good starting point is *Matching Personal and Job Characteristics*, which you can order by phone or mail from the U.S. Government Printing Office in Washington, D.C. There is a table in this helpful pamphlet that matches 23 occupational characteristics and requirements similar to the ones we've been discussing here with 281 occupations. It can assist in identifying several occupations that might fit you.

Next go to *The Occupational Outlook Handbook*, another government publication and probably available in your local library. The handbook provides sketches of 800 popular occupations, with specifics on the educational and training requirements, the skills needed, the nature of the work and environment, the projected number of positions available as well as where to go for further information. Another excellent source of job descriptions is *132 Ways to Earn a Living Without Working (For Someone Else)*, by Ed Rosenthal and Ron Lichty.[6] This book describes off-beat and out-of-the-way work.

You don't need reference books to identify possible occupations. Novels, movies, and television offer a myriad of possibilities. Everywhere you go and everywhere you look, people are working. Notice those around you working, and in your fantasy theater, project yourself into their lives. Ask others about their work. This is easy. People like to talk about their work. And as they talk, try it on in your fantasy theater.

> The American dream is alive and well—and found in unexpected places. The Sixties counterculture has spawned a new mini-capitalism rich in economic opportunities . . . if you can . . .
> · Speed-read, walk dogs, panhandle
> · Screen movies, weld, bake a pie
> · Gamble, sew, shoe a horse
> · Garden, babysit, refinish a floor
> · Iron, write a grant, clean
> · Lecture, model, start a religion
> · Make juice, tutor, prospect for gold
> · Type, counsel, or any of (hundreds of) other often overlooked or under-rated activities.
> —Ed Rosenthal and Ron Lichty
> *132 Ways to Earn a Living Without Working (For Someone Else)*[7]

Look up occupations that you've identified as potentials. After reading each sketch, retreat into your fantasy theater to try it on. Notice how it fits. Notice ways in which it binds or limits. Notice where and how it feels good. Jot down in your journal what you learn. When you have narrowed your investigation to a small number of potential occupations, it is time to start interviewing.

Explore Alternatives

Locate and interview several people in each occupation under investigation. Your goal is to find out as much as you can about the nature of their work so that you can try it on later in your fantasy theater. Imagining that you're an investigative reporter while you do this helps and makes it fun. Don't be shy; most people will be flattered to help. Discuss what you learned about your occupational temperament, and find out from the person you're interviewing how well suited he or she thinks the work is for you. Don't rush through the process of exploration. The care you invest now will repay itself in challenging and satisfying work, work that provides an opportunity to develop.

When you have identified what work best fits you (for now), it is time to deal with the practical issues of finding or creating a specific job. Three helpful books—Richard Bolles's *What Color Is Your Parachute?*, Betty Michelezzi's *Coming Alive from Nine to Five: The Career Search Handbook*,[8] as well as my book *Beating Job Burnout*[9]—give guidelines for analyzing your skills, determining a job search plan, developing a resume, and preparing for job interviews.

Assessing occupational temperament should not be a one-time activity but an ongoing process of self-observation. Update your self-portrait as you travel through life, gathering experiences and developing skills. Keep your journal active.

TRANSFORM DISSATISFACTION

> For of all sad words of tongue or pen,
> The saddest are these: "It might have
>   been!"
> —John Greenleaf Whittier
> *Maud Muller*

Work that is unsatisfying, that leads to nothing, that provides little opportunity to develop new skills or to expand responsibilities is dead-end. Ronin do not accept such work; they transform it. The following transformations serve as starting points. As you read, if you are an emerging Ronin, you will think of other transformations, perhaps ones you have used successfully. When you do, jot them down in your journal. Later use your intellectual and analytical skills to refine the fleeting ideas and recollections that will occur. They provide clues to the keys you can use, purposefully and powerfully, to transform unsatisfying work into satisfying work.

Make It a Game

Thinking about work as a game will change your perspective, feelings, and eventually even your performance. But don't make the mistake of concluding that, because you call it a game, work is frivolous or unimportant. The Super Bowl is a game, but it certainly isn't frivolous. Hundreds of thousands of dollars are involved in preparing, playing, and televising it. Thinking of work as a game creates a degree of detachment that brings a broader perspective, enabling you to make better decisions.

What does "work is a game" mean? First associations bring to mind play, sport, or amusement. Use these images as a reminder to see ways to derive pleasure and fun from work. Game also suggests competition of some sort, where there is a winner or a goal to be achieved. That is, a game is a test of skill. Use this image as a reminder that it is at work that you test your skill. Finally, a game involves an element of risk. Use this as a reminder to keep alert and to remember that in risk there is also adventure.

Seek Challenges

"Only as a warrior can one withstand the path of knowledge," [Don Juan] said. "A warrior cannot complain or regret anything. His life is an endless challenge, and challenges cannot possibly be good or bad. Challenges are simply challenges.

"The basic difference between an ordinary man and a warrior is that a warrior
takes everything as a challenge," he
went on, "while an ordinary man takes
everything either as a blessing or as a
curse."
                              —Carlos Castaneda
                                Tales of Power[10]

We excel and grow by stretching our capabilities. Challenges
and high goals are the technology. Don't play it safe, always
doing only what you do well. Although you may get better and
better, becoming better than those around you, deep down you'll
know you are not going anywhere, not learning anything new.
Instead seek challenges.

KANJI SECRET

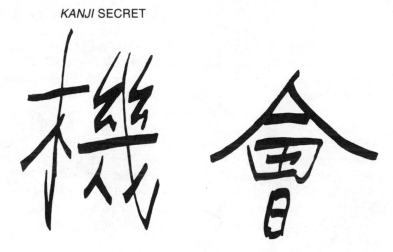

In Japanese and Chinese, whole words are written
with a symbol, or *kanji*. Often two completely unlike *kanji*,
when put together, have a meaning different from either
of their two separate components. These two *kanji* stand
for "*trouble*" and "*gathering crisis*." When combined,
they mean "opportunity."

Volunteer for assignments you've never done before. If there
is an area in which you feel weak and uncapable, seek out ways
at work and at play to develop the needed skills. For example,

if you fear speaking in front of a group, challenge yourself to find situations that'll require you to speak up. Don't let the first enemy, fear, hold you back. Challenges are the keys for opening doors to new vistas.

Compete with Yourself

Competition is healthy. It motivates, spurring us on to reach new heights, to stretch our capabilities and limits. In the process, we feel enthusiastic and develop confidence. But competition can become oppressive and downright stressful when it means competing with others to avoid losing. Competition with others, when the stakes are high and losses severe, encourages focusing on the gap between ourselves and our competitors, and dwelling on all the ways we don't match up. In organizations, such detrimental competition can go to extremes, with people sabotaging one another by withholding information, being uncooperative, or back stabbing. Avoid this type of competition. Instead, use your own past performance as the measure to surpass. Healthy competition is fun and invigorating.

Use the Next-Time Rule

Watch yourself. Pay attention to your actions, to your work, to your performance. When you've performed poorly, stop and evaluate. What was good about it? Acknowledge yourself for that good performance. What could be improved? Don't criticize yourself, use the "next-time rule."[11] Determine what you will do next time. Rehearse the next-time plan in your fantasy theater. The next-time rule uses criticism and feedback positively to push you forward. When your performance is less than you hoped, consider it a challenge to overcome and a competitive standard to exceed. What will you do next time?

Find a Need and Fill It

In the cliché "Find a need and fill it" lies the secret of the next transformation. When unsatisfied at work, we tend to develop a negative focus, zeroing in on problems and bummers, quickly being seduced into a vicious cycle of negativity. Focusing on difficulties, we feel worse, our performance drops, and the problems become ever more oppressive.

> All with whom we are associated can become our co-operators (without knowing it!). For instance, a domineering superior or an exacting partner becomes, as it were, the mental parallel bars on which our will . . . can develop its force and proficiency. . . . Talkative friends or time-wasters give us the chance to control speech; they teach us the art of courteous but firm refusal to engage in unnecessary conversation. To be able to say "no" is a difficult but useful discipline. So the Buddhist saying goes: "An enemy is as useful as a Buddha."
>
> —Robert Assigioli
> *The Act of Will*[12]

Problems signal that something is out of sync. Hidden in every problem is a need to be filled. Think of dissonant events as challenges to overcome, needs to be discovered and filled, rather than as bummers to be tolerated. By filling a need, you increase your visibility, feel more in control, expand job responsibilities, and become more valuable to those who need your skills.

> *Consider Joan:*
> Early in my career I worked as a social worker with inmates in the county jail. Very quickly I discovered a tremendous need. There simply was no referral network. So I started an information referral system myself, though I didn't realize it at the time. Each morning I looked through the newspaper and clipped out pertinent items and wrote the information down on index cards. It wasn't long before I had an enormous file. Not only was everyone else in the office coming to *me* for information and referrals for various kinds of services, but I began getting calls from other agencies as well. Eventually I became identified as the "referral agent." When I left the job, maintaining the referral service was an official part of the job for the person who took my place.

Identify Needs

Be alert. Open your eyes and look around. What problems do you encounter at work? Focus on those touching you directly.

These are the ones you are most likely able to have an impact on. Note observations in your journal. Periodically review the list of problems and convert each one into a statement of need.

Assess Your Skills

What do you know how to do? Which needs require your skills? Brainstorm. Write down all ideas, however fanciful they may seem at first.

> Job market diagrams never include
> jobs for which no vacancy exists.
>
>   It rarely occurs [to the job hunter] that if, instead [of looking for vacancies] he selects the organizations or companies that interest him, and does enough research to unearth their problems (and how he can help solve them) that they will be perfectly willing to create a new job, for which no vacancy exists just because they will ultimately save money by doing so. (Problems always cost a lot more.)
>   —Richard Bolles
>   *What Color Is Your Parachute?*[13]

Consider Your Interests

Consider each skill—need match. Which tickle your fancy? Which provide a satisfying challenge or a stepping-stone to your goals? Zero in on these. Devise a plan of action. For those requiring authorization, prepare a formal proposal for how you will fill that need. Often, however, you can simply proceed with your plan, as Joan did with the referral service. All jobs have at least some leeway. Shape yours to fit you. Don't wait for permission or to be directed. Take the initiative. Use your personal power; command your work.

Make Friends at Work

Any work, no matter how routine, monotonous, or stressful, can be transformed by doing it with friends, people you feel good about, share parts of yourself with, and have fun with.

A number of years ago, a friend of mine invited me to a "Spring House Cleaning Party and Barbecue." I was amused by the idea and went because I felt like socializing. I hadn't realized, however, the seriousness of her intention to clean house. For an hour, we all labored away with a lot of enthusiasm, making jokes and laughing while cleaning the house from top to bottom. Afterward we drank beer and had a grand feast of barbecued hamburgers and franks. I, somehow, was assigned to the bathroom. I never did like cleaning bathrooms, and I never knew anyone else who did either. As I scrubbed away at the toilet with an ammonia-filled sponge, wearing the rubber gloves she provided, I wondered, "What am I doing *here* cleaning this other person's toilet? Why aren't I home cleaning my own?" The answer was simple: there I'd be doing something dreary, alone with no friends to transform it into fun.

Make friends at work. Stop demanding that others always share your likes and dislikes. Instead, see what ways you resonate with co-workers. With this approach, you can have a workable and enjoyable friendship with practically any person. When you look forward to going to work to see friends, working will be transformed.

Create Balance

Aristotle and Confucius alike professed striving for balance. Extremes disrupt balance, and disharmony results. Industrialization and its demand for specialization created the imbalanced work style and environment we have come to consider standard. Indeed, balance seems impossible, if not abnormal. This is the world of the workcoholic, devoting herself to work at the expense of all else. This is the world of the specialist, who cannot communicate with anyone not intimately acquainted with his esoteric knowledge. This is the world of repetitive work. This is the world of career feudalism.

How do we know when we are losing our balance? There are two indicators: what others say and how we feel. We each live inside our own reality. What we do, how we act, how we think, what we like, or what we don't like all make perfect sense to us. We cannot escape our minds. It interprets everything in terms of a personal reality. We can never get outside, never see ourselves as others do.

Feedback from those around us is a mirror. Criticism and compliments are the reflection. Reflection from others is a valuable gem—a gift. Reflection offers a check of where you are and how you stand: Are you succeeding or failing? Are you acceptable or unacceptable? Many reject the gift of feedback by punishing the giver with defensiveness, attacks, and ignoring. Foolish! Why should someone continue to give gifts? Don't do this. You need reflections from the world, especially in times of change. Don't close it off. Instead, listen to what others say. Encourage them. Ask questions, and actively seek feedback. Listening to others does not mean you must accept what they say. But you can't decide if what they say is valid or invalid unless you first listen. You need not have a knee-jerk reaction, shutting it all out. Be autonomous instead. Take what is useful; discard the rest.

If others say in jest or in seriousness that you're working excessively, for example, or goofing off or spending too much money, or being too stubborn, or drinking a lot, listen. Feedback is also the lighthouse beacon. Look to see if you are getting close to the rocks.

The second balance indicator is feelings of satisfaction or dissatisfaction. Dissatisfaction is a warning that something is wrong. There is imbalance. You are not receiving something you need; you are doing something too much. Dissatisfaction is your psychological tummy saying, "I'm hungry. Feed me. Feed me." There is no one feeling, no one thought to watch for. Record all your feelings and thoughts in your journal. When you have many, review them. Go to the meta-level, and look beyond the specific thoughts or feelings for a pattern of balance or imbalance.

The Occupational Temperament Inventory we looked at earlier is a useful tool. Use the categories as aids in considering actions you might take to restore balance. Consider "mediums," for example. Are you a social worker advising clients and interacting with staff all day? Working with things or with abstractions might restore balance. Volunteer to write a funding proposal that would require working with abstractions, for example. Michael, a big-city police officer, found the imbalance of so much authority overwhelming. He saw himself as the bearer of bad news and was disturbed by his increasing tendency to be suspicious of others, even when off duty. Michael counterbalanced by delivering flowers for a florist on the weekends. He brought others beautiful things and shared their triumphs and tragedies.

When you were a child first struggling to ride a two-wheeler, you quickly learned to avoid extreme shifts and to make many rapid counterbalancing adjustments instead. By mastering balance on the physical level, you learned to ride at high speeds on two thin wheels and were no longer restricted to walking. There are many more secrets of balance to be learned and transformations to be uncovered. Each time you experience dissatisfaction or receive disturbing feedback, remember it is an opportunity to learn more about the magic of balance, just as each fall from your two-wheeler taught you more about how to ride.

Change Your Thinking

How you think determines emotional responses, including satisfaction or dissatisfaction. You can control your thinking. Thoughts are like the software that runs the computer. Change the program, and the computer acts differently. Our thoughts have a similar impact on how we act and feel. Transform dissatisfaction by changing thought programs.

Develop an I-Can-Do Attitude

Thinking that you are helpless, that there is nothing you can do, is guaranteed to provoke feelings of dissatisfaction, anxiety, and depression. Helpless thinking is dangerous. When we feel there is nothing we can do, we stop doing. Helpless thinking puts us in the role of victim. We give our power away, expecting others to do while we wait passively.

The I-can-do attitude has the opposite effect. It evokes feelings of potency, determination, hopefulness, and enthusiasm. I-can-do is the Ronin's mental sword that cuts through fears and hurtles, bringing triumph in the end.

Develop a habit of focusing on what you can do rather than on what you did wrong or what you should have done. I-can-do is personal power: ability to direct, to propel, and to transform yourself.

Think of Today's Job as a Stepping-Stone

There's one thing you know with certainty: You won't be in this job doing this work forever. Today's work is a stepping-stone to where you'll be tomorrow. Resist thinking that this job is the end of the line for you. Instead, think of it as one step in your journey along life's path. While on this step, make the most of it. What can you learn? What skills can you develop? What knowledge can you gain? What allies can you make? Don't overlook negative lessons. Today's job may be an opportunity to learn to transform dissatisfaction. Since you're here, you may as well get the most from it. Simultaneously, focus on the next stepping-stone. Where does today's job lead? What opportunities does it open? Remember, look sideways, not always up. Climbing the ladder is not the only path.

Work for Yourself

This is your work, your life. Think of yourself as your own boss. If you have a full-time position, think of yourself as a private contractor, a vendor, or a consultant with a long-term contract. Thinking of your relationship with your employer in this way increases your personal power. A contract is a two-way relationship. Considering it as such reminds you that there is a two-way agreement between you and your company, with commitments and responsibilities on both sides.

Break out of career feudalism. Don't be indentured. Become your own master, a corporate Ronin. You're in command of your life and destiny. Set personal and professional goals, and find ways to meet them by working toward the company goals. The company is an arena for playing the World Game. If you want to develop managerial skills, take advantage of the company training program; if you want to improve writing skills, find ways to contribute to company publications; if you want to shape up consulting skills, find ways to consult in the course of your work.

Take command. Use your skills to move around the corporate arena. Break free of the track mentality. Like Palladin, the frontier Ronin, you can use your skills as a ticket to ride: "Have skills will travel."

Use Power

The samurai's power and credibility flowed from the *daimyo* who retained him. The *ronin*, who were not indentured, had no formal or institutional power. The *ronin's* power was in the way he handled himself. Likewise, the challenge for modern Ronin is using personal power to perform excellently: to take the right action at the right time with the right person in the right measure.

Whether working in an organization or on your own, you must work with and through others at least part of the time. Working through others is often disdainfully called "office politicking." Indeed, to get work done and move toward your goals, you need alliances and the cooperation of others whom you enlist with your personal power.

Exercising power involves knowing and using your knowledge of what others want. People want attention, to feel like winners, to fulfill needs and meet goals, and to be understood. The ways in which you do and don't satisfy the wants of the others are the ways in which you use your power. Ronin do not trust unconscious and uncontrolled actions; instead they acknowledge and use their power.

The Power of Attention

The desire to be noticed and to feel that you belong is natural. Everyone wants attention. It is not something to be put down; it is normal. Attention is a response from the world, a connection. Attention is powerful. We can influence, make allies of enemies, enlist cooperation, or create hassle with our attention.

What do you pay attention to in others? The faults, the mistakes, the ways they don't make the mark? Or the progress and successes? Are you exercising the power of your attention positively or negatively? Chances are if you tend to focus on others' shortcomings, you give negative, critical attention, communicating to the person "You're a loser." Instead, when noticing faults in others or when encountering irritating behaviors, make a practice of first identifying exactly what it is you don't like. What do they do? Say? How do they do it or say it? When? Under what conditions? Next, translate what you don't want into what you do want. What do you want these people to do instead? How should they do it or say it? When? Third, watch for instances when they do do what you want, and pay attention to these behaviors. This type of attention is likely to be positive and reaffirming, communicating "You're a winner." When you use your attention positively, others will do more of what you want and less of what you don't want.

The Power of Understanding

We all want to be seen as unique and to feel understood. Use this theoretical wisdom. When others feel that you see things from their perspective, you'll gain their loyalty and support as well as a great deal of power. For with understanding comes the knowledge of what others want and what they abhor. And in that knowledge is the power to reward and punish.

The rule of thumb for gaining and communicating understanding is: Ask questions. Don't assume you know how others see things and feel, or why they react. Instead, ask them. Draw others out, and encourage them to describe their feelings, ideas, and motivations. Don't analyze with "You're silly" or "You're overreacting." Such statements impede understanding. Don't tell others how they feel, "You feel angry, don't you," ask instead "How do you feel?" Resist the tendency to jump in and complete others' sentences and thoughts. By asking, you communicate interest and a desire to understand. By asking, you gain the information needed to understand.

Asking questions is a valuable tool to use when under attack or confronted with a difficult person. The best way to defuse an angry person is to ask questions. The person is upset and wants to be understood. By asking questions, you allow the angry person to express frustration and discharge anger, while giving yourself an opportunity to gather your wits and to think about how to respond. "What's an example of that?" "How have I done that?" "What do you expect?" "What do you suggest?" When attacked, don't defend; ask instead. If you don't know what to do after asking everything appropriate to ask, you can always excuse yourself with "I will consider what you said and get back to you in an hour." Then you can consult with allies and meditate on the excellent action.

The Power of Making Others Winners

You exercise power when you help others meet their goals and fulfill their needs. All of us have this power, but most don't realize it. We focus instead on what others can, can't, or won't do for us. When others' actions help us get what we want, we're rewarded; when their actions frustrate us, we're punished. Turned around, this means that your actions are someone else's rewards and punishments.

How do you use your power? Positively? Or negatively? Do you give others what they want? Do you let others know they're winners? Are you encouraging? Do you make the small effort it takes to clue someone in or to make a helpful connection? Or do you withhold, even put barriers in the way? Do you act like you don't know someone instead of saying "Hi!"? Do you hold back critical information when you could easily share it? Do you nag and wag your finger at flaws, demanding nothing short of perfection? If your actions help others win, those others will be positively disposed toward you.

Use this guideline: When your boss or a co-worker does what you want (such as stating expectations clearly, keeping a commitment, or being on time), respond in such a way that he or she wins. Make sure others win when they help you win. The win doesn't have to be big. Timing and sincerity are more important. Sound Machiavellian? Well, in the truest sense, it is. It is using personal power to influence. Yet, we do this all the time anyway. Is an unconscious stimulus—response interaction preferable?

Obviously power, our most potent enemy, must be leashed with strong character and personal control. The challenge is to always strive for the golden mean, the excellent action: The right action, with the right person, at the right time, to the right degree. Without this meta-level control, you will have strayed from the Way.

Notes

1. New York: Thomas Y. Crowell, 1978, p. 213.
2. *The Complete Poems of Cavafy*, trans. Rae Dalven (New York: Harcourt, Brace & World, 1961), p. 6.
3. *The Secret Path: A Technique of Spiritual Self Discovery for the Modern World* (New York: Dutton, 1935), p. 117.
4. Berkeley, Calif.: Ten Speed Press, 1978, p. 82.
5. Ibid., pp. 206–224.
6. New York: St Martin's Press, 1978.
7. Back cover.
8. Palo Alto, Calif.: Mayfield Publishing, 1980.
9. New York: Ace Business Library, 1983.
10. New York: Simon & Schuster, 1974, pp. 108–109.

11. This technique was suggested by motivational speaker James New-
     man in a speech given to members of the National Speaker's As-
     sociation in San Francisco on March 5, 1983.
12. Cited in Michael Korda, *Power! How to Get It, How to Use It* (New
     York: Random House, 1975), p. 15.
13. Berkeley, Calif.: Ten Speed Press, 1978, p. 121.

5

Career Strategies

The *Book of Changes (I Ching)* is often considered the Oriental apotheosis of adaptation, of flexibility. . . . The theme of this work is that everything in existence can be a source of conflict, of danger, . . . if confronted directly at the point of its maximum strength. . . . By the same token, any and every occurrence can be dealt with by approaching it from the right angle and in the proper manner— that is, at its source, before it can develop full power, or from the sides (the vulnerable "flanks of a tiger"). If by chance, the frontal impact of events should overtake a man, the *I Ching* advises him to avoid any direct opposition and adopt an attitude of "riding along" or "flowing" with the tide of events (a boxer might say "rolling with the punches"), thus

keeping slightly ahead of or on top of that massive
force which, like any other concentrated force in
creation, will inevitably exhaust itself once its concentration has been dissipated.
                    —Oscar Ratti and Adele Westbrook
                    Secrets of the Samurai[1]

Most of us have been so indoctrinated into climbing the promotional ladder that we often aren't even aware that it's a strategy. Few realize there are alternatives. In the postwar growth
era of the 1950s and 1960s, the linear strategy was a winning one.
The economy and companies everywhere were booming and expanding. There was plenty of room at the top. All an aspiring
careerist needed to do was to get in on the ground floor and find
a winning track to ride up the hierarchy. Promotions and pay
raises came quickly and easily to the talented.

Industrialization and expansion has ended. Now the linear
strategy is perilous, filled with cul-de-sacs, as shown in the accompanying diagram. The bulging number of baby-boomers entering midlife and midmanagement are facing a squeeze. No
longer is there plenty of room at the top. Instead, the majority of
these eager, highly trained, and ambitious careerists risk becoming underemployed, blocked, even derailed.

Economic uncertainty compounds the problem. The 1980s
witnessed massive layoffs, with whole industries struggling to
survive and unemployment reaching an all-time high. During
such periods of uncertainty, organizations respond by tightening
up, becoming more centralized, and demanding conformity from
employees.

Adding to these problems is the increasing speed of technological advancement. Many are finding themselves entering
the information era with skill obsolescence, unable to make the
transition. Future shock is here. In the midst of increasing
change, motivated and talented specialists are facing reduced
options and feeling trapped, Unable to adapt, many become vic-
tims of job burnout and the midlife crisis.

From every corner of the nation, in every field, Ronin are
emerging out of this chaos and uncertainty. They do not subscribe to the traditional linear-track game plan. Instead, Ronin
follow a new game plan, one optimal for the 1980s and beyond:
a strategy that opens rather than closes opportunities, that allows
for the development of one's whole personality and the pursuit

LINEAR CAREER STRATEGY: THE CORPORATE LADDER

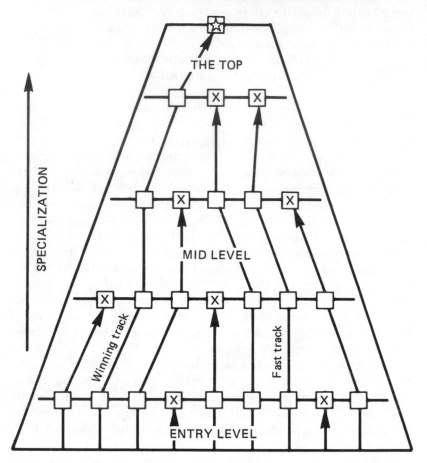

of self-fulfillment. Ronin strategies foster adaptability, individuality, creativity, and diversity.

GREGORY BATESON[2]

Gregory Bateson, one of the greatest thinkers of our time, leaped into the World Game with a degree in anthropology when he went to New Guinea to do fieldwork. In the years that followed, he married and divorced Margaret Mead and zigzagged in and out of anthropology, genetics, biology, and psychiatry. He was, for example, a professor of anthropology at Harvard; he worked with dolphins at the Oceanographic Institute in Hawaii; he was a research associate at Langley Porter Neuropsychiatric Institute. But Bateson not only moved across disciplines, he made significant contributions in each as well. To psychiatry, for example, Bateson added the double-bind theory of schizophrenia and is considered one of the fathers of the family therapy movement. Conjoint family therapy and neurolinguistic programming trace their lineage back to Bateson's double-bind work.

When Bateson crossed over into a new field, he brought the old one with him and applied it in a new way. One secret of his creativity is that he applied patterns he identified in one area to the new endeavor. For example, while struggling with questions regarding the arrangement of facilities and functions in a New Guinea village, he recalled a biological organizational pattern he'd studied in the claw of a crab and suddenly realized that this biological pattern was useful in understanding the village pattern.

Let's take a closer look. For our alternative to the linear-track game plan, we'll use the ancient Chinese game *Wei Chi,* or *Go,* as it is more commonly called. Like chess, Go is a game of strategy, but more complex and sophisticated. The object is to surround or capture territory. Attempting to gain control over territory or to expand one's sphere of influence is also a pervasive, but unstated, goal in the workplace. Your sphere of influence may be an area of expertise. For example, by writing the book *Beating Job Burnout,* I became an identified "expert" on how to prevent and overcome work malaise. I increased my sphere of influence, capturing new territory. Spheres of influence can be based on status, authority, knowledge, or wealth.

STRATEGY: MOVE INDIRECTLY

In the accompanying illustration of the Go gameboard, Black uses the linear strategy. Step by step, he places his stones in a straight line, with the objective of surrounding the area in the upper-right corner. White, on the other hand, uses a nonlinear strategy. At first, her moves seem disconnected as she proceeds indirectly toward her goal. If the players continue with their re-

NONLINEAR STRATEGY: GO GAMEBOARD

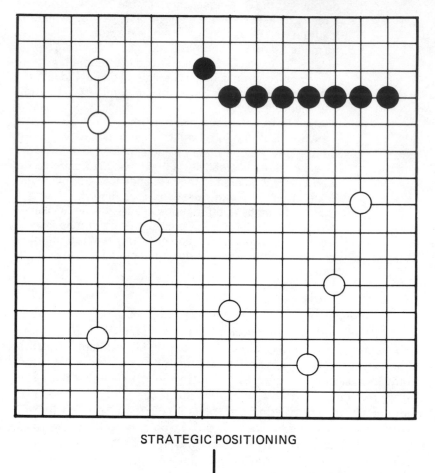

STRATEGIC POSITIONING

ENHANCED SPHERE OF INFLUENCE

spective strategies, who is going to win this game? In all probability, White will win.

Black employs the strategy of the specialist. Scientists, for example, can devote an entire career to a succession of replicative studies, exploring variations of a hypothesis or refinements of a model, systematically filling in each square or small corner of knowledge. This strategy has reliable success to the degree that the scientist will in time certainly acquire influence over the corner. White is not likely to challenge. But Black's influence, although secure, is limited to the corner. When at the end of the game points are tallied, Black gets a low score. Similarly, the aspiring executive who hopes to climb the corporate ladder step by linear step to the top is assured of several easy moves in the beginning, winning a limited degree of influence. But the executive is unlikely to get past the middle-management moves. Instead, he finds himself blocked in, unable to move anywhere. Ronin, on the other hand, bypass roadblocks by indirect moves, moves that appear sideways, occasionally even backward, on the linear-track game board.

The "frontage road" tactic is another way to conceptualize moving indirectly. Freeway traffic jams can be bypassed by exiting from the freeway onto the frontage road, which follows alongside. While others inch along the highway, Ronin zip ahead. Likewise, many prefer when traveling to take country back roads in lieu of the direct, four-lane highway. Often arrival time is the same by either route, but even when the freeway is decidedly faster, traveling the side roads makes for a more adventuresome journey. We still arrive at the same destination, the end of our travels. The difference lies in the quality of our lives. Traveling on the less populated side roads, moving indirectly toward our goals, not only opens options but allows for an individually tailored work and life experience.

Tactics for Moving Indirectly

Find an Understaffed Organization[3]

An understaffed organization is one in which there aren't enough people to do everything that needs doing. This means opportunity—opportunity to gain essential hands-on experience, often without having the standard prerequisite training and education; opportunity to change your job classification, often dramatically; opportunity to experiment and showcase your accomplishments. Let's take a closer look.

Consider a simple example. Bill wants to play on the high school football team. Although quick to learn and well coordinated, Bill is an average player. Although he couldn't be considered big by most standards—5'11", 175 pounds—he's one of the biggest guys in his class of 100 students. John, Bill's identical twin, attends a different school, where there are 1,000 kids in his class. John, too, aspires to be on the football team. Both Bill and John are somewhat shy and feel self-conscious as they try out for the teams. One makes it; the other doesn't. Who makes the team, Bill or John?

Bill makes the team. Why? The competition is much less in the small school. Bill's coach doesn't have a lot of boys from whom to choose, so the acceptance criteria are lower. To the coach in the small school, Bill looks like a good candidate. He's big, he's smart, and he's motivated. In fact, there's a good chance that, if Bill hadn't tried out, the coach would have tried to persuade him to do so. In contrast, John hardly gets a moment's consideration from the big-school coach. There's nothing outstanding about John, and there are many boys to pick from, all eager to play ball. The big-school coach can be picky. He can raise his acceptance criteria. John is rejected. His football career ends before ever starting.

For Bill, on the other hand, it's just the beginning. Being accepted for the team builds Bill's confidence. He throws himself into practice, and he learns fast. Since Bill's coach can't afford to lose him, he gives Bill a lot of attention and encouragement. Success breeds success. Bill excels. Girls think he's a hunk, while his twin, John, watches with pride and envy. Bill refines his skills, he stands out. He is the area all-star. At graduation, Bill looks forward to college football and an athletic scholarship, something he never dreamed possible that day, so long ago, when he tried out for the team.

Because Bill's small school was an understaffed organization, Bill had an opportunity to play football on the team. In the process, he had a chance to develop his skills, to build confidence, and to learn to take risks. On the other hand, John not only experienced failure at the tryout, but he did not have the opportunity Bill had to build confidence. Bill graduated with an I-can-do identity; John graduated with an I'm-nothing-special identity. Bill is likely to take risks in the future because he's learned he can rise to the challenge and is confident that he can succeed.

Understaffed organizations are more fluid than are organizations in which every job and task is adequately filled. Also distinctions between jobs are blurred. Often a situation will arise in which there is a deadline and not enough staff to do everything. This is an opportunity. If you have some skill in performing the needed task, you are quickly recruited. You're an able body, and bodies are needed. In an understaffed organization, you'll have a chance to learn and refine your skills. If you lack sufficient experience or the required education, look for the understaffed organization. It can be your big break!

Because the linear strategy of climbing the corporate ladder is so all-pervasively accepted, we often get trapped on a track, unable to get off. We are labeled with a job classification. And once we have that label, it sticks and restricts. One of the hardest labels to shake, for example, is secretary. As soon as the personnel officer, employment counselor, or prospective boss sees "secretary" on a resume, the applicant is categorized and slotted, not considered for anything but a secretarial position. If you want to switch tracks, to change your job label, position yourself in an understaffed organization.

Consider Tracy:

When I went to work as a receptionist for a toy manufacturer, I had a lot of ambition and drive but little training or experience. Receptionist was nowhere, but it was a toe hold, a start. I decided I'd be the best receptionist I could, and it paid off. In the course of answering phones and taking messages, I developed a "phone relationship" with most of the accounts. After a few months, they needed someone to process orders. I was a natural choice since I knew the accounts. And in less than a year, I was promoted again, this time to assistant sales manager because I was the only one who knew all the accounts and who ordered what.

And consider Dan:

I'd been knocking around in publishing for a couple of years when I joined a small press as a free-lance editor. In a matter of months, I was on the payroll as a full-time editor. At that time, there was no in-house promotion. I knew next to nothing about it. But then no one else did either. So I began doing promotion for our books.

Well, I got good at it, and I discovered I liked promotion. And I developed a good reputation for myself. Two and a half years later, I took the position of marketing director for a large prestigious specialty publishing house. Now that's on-the-job training!

Understaffed organizations have another positive feature: People in such organizations are typically more accepting of differences. People in overstaffed organizations are often cliquish, with in-groups and out-groups. If you want to feel like you belong, that you're an essential member of the team, look for an understaffed organization. But there is a dark side as well. Understaffed organizations tend to be stressful environments in a constant state of change and chaos. You must be comfortable with change and masterful at handling tension and frustration to excel in an understaffed organization.

The Vaguely Defined Job: A Window of Opportunity

The position that allows the maximum leeway is the one that is vaguely defined. Clearly defined jobs have parameters, guidelines, and standards. Accountability is built in. Clear definitions of what is expected provide rulers for measuring your performance. You know what you are to do and so does your employer. Clarity of job description provides an objective basis for evaluation and acknowledgment. Clearly defining jobs is good management, but when the definition focuses on how functions are to be performed instead of what is to be achieved, definitions can become constrictions.

Before accepting any position or assignment, Ronin are cautious in looking over job descriptions. They favor those that specify what is to be produced and avoid those that spell out how. Because Ronin are capable self-managers and comfortable with ambiguity, they seek out vaguely defined jobs in key positions. The absence of limits, definitions, and standards of evaluation is a window of opportunity allowing you to make the definitions, to set the limits, to determine the standards of evaluation, and to move into new territory.

The vaguely defined job has its perils. But its virtue is that you can make it into what you want. You can define it and redefine it.

Expand Your Responsibility Domain

You rise in a feudal organization by leaving your present job and taking on another at the next level within the company or by changing companies. In either case, upward progress is made one step at a time.

EXPAND, DON'T CLIMB

> The promotion ladder only exists as long as people believe in it, and are willing to trudge up it. . . . Each step taken . . . [in your rise in the hierarchy] . . . means abandoning the one below it, just as you have to take your foot off rung A of a ladder to place it on rung B. This kind of promotion requires a great deal of time, and the competition for each rung is severe. Worse, you have to abandon what you have in order to reach for what you want, thus increasing your risk of falling off and landing back on the heap, at the foot of the ladder. And you are planning your career in terms of an existing and rigid structure, which means you're playing according to someone else's rules.
>
> —Michael Korda
> *Power! How to Get It, How to Use It*[4]

You can bypass the ladder by using the expansion tactic, in which responsibilities are extended by gradually enveloping people and functions. The strategy in expansion is to retain control of the old responsibilities while simultaneously adding to your titles and responsibilities.

Don't think in terms of rungs. Instead, take over the boring or difficult projects, those no one else wants. Expand into areas that require liaison and communication between departments. Look for territories that are central to the operations of the corporation, such as sales in a manufacturing company or loans in a bank. Stay close to the flow of money. For example, becoming a line manager of a profit center opens up more territory than becoming a higher-paid staff administrator.

Analyze your formal job description. Can you make a legitimate claim to the function you are eyeing? If so, you might be able to assume it de facto. If the function is currently performed by someone else, review your job description with your boss and ask that the function be transferred to your direction. Don't move precipitously, however. First, assess your competitive strength and prepare your case.

If the expansion area lies outside of your job description, begin by establishing a presence. Place a stone in the area by working as a collaborator on a project within someone else's responsibility. It is smart to assign members of your staff to projects under others' jurisdiction. They will serve as extensions of your influence within the corporation. Using this expansion tactic, you can identify gaps in no-man's-land. Then assign your people to work on the unassigned and vaguely defined functions.

Periodically, link up the functions you have acquired into a coherent project tied into your job description. Connect disconnected functions into a territory, and formalize authority over the territory. At the appropriate time, you might consolidate your acquisition by asking for an offical appointment of title and duties.

If someone makes a strong inroad into your sphere of influence, it is best not to confront the spearhead directly. Instead, like a martial arts master, use the momentum of the invader's trust to throw him off balance. Fall back to a solid position that is well integrated into your main function and tied to a core interest of the company. Draw the invader into your sphere of influence. When the invader is extended well beyond his designated functions, take your case to the common boss, requesting a transfer of tasks, projects, personnel, and resources to your jurisdiction. And ask that your job description clarify your authority over the disputed territory.

STRATEGY: CONCENTRATED DISPERSION

The game of Chinese baseball is almost identical to American baseball—the same players, same field, same bats and balls, same method of keeping score, and so on. . . . There is only one difference. And that is: after the ball leaves the pitcher's hand and as long as the ball is in the air, anyone can move any of the bases anywhere.

In other words, everything is continually changing—not only the events themselves, but also the very rules governing the judgments of those events and the criteria of value. This kind of situation is alien to the scientific tradition of fixed boundary conditions, clearly defined variables, objective assessments,

and rational consistency within a closed
system. In the ball game of power, everything is flux and all systems are open.
There is no such thing as a challenge,
which can be met and put away for all
times. . . .

The secret of Chinese baseball is not
only keeping your eye on the ball alone
but also on the bases, and doing some
fancy-footed kicking of the bases around
yourself.

—R. G. H. Sui
The Craft of Power[5]

Consider the game board again. You'll recall that Black set out
to capture the corner by proceeding to surround it step by step.
Black's direct strategy has made him vulnerable because all his
stones are in one basket. Should research funds dry up, for example, Black's sphere of influence could be seriously threatened.
White, on the other hand, employed indirection. She proceeded
in a defused fashion toward the objective of capturing territory.
White optimized the impact of each stone by concentrated dispersion. Instead of focusing solely on one area, she established
footings on several fronts. She positioned herself so that she has
many options and many arenas in which to move. With a single
stone, carefully placed, she gains de facto influence over a corner.
Should Black challenge, White has the advantage of a stronghold.
White can play calmly because the threat of losing a corner is
not overwhelming; she has strongholds in two other corners as
well as in much of the territory in between. Later, White may
even choose to sacrifice a corner to consolidate her position elsewhere.

Tactics for Concentrated Dispersion

Diversify: Have Many Hats

We are moving from the specialist
who will soon be obsolete to the generalist who can adapt.

—John Naisbitt
Megatrends[6]

Our world is changing; things are no longer predictable. Futurists say we are at one of those points we read about in history books: the transition from one era to another. Computers, acting both as catalyst and as means, are transforming our world into an information society that promises to be vastly different from the industrial society of our youth. This is no time to put all your stones in one corner, as Black did. At best, specialization wins us a small niche that once meant professional and economic security, but no longer. Now specialization can mean obsolesence. In uncertain times, diversify. That's the rule of thumb.

The ability to adapt to the coming changes is the key to survival, success, and fulfillment. Limited in range of knowledge and skill, the specialist is inflexible, hence vulnerable. What, for example, does a professor of Latin and Sanskrit do when college enrollment drops and along with it the demand for classics professors? Even if your current position is in the mainstream now, you cannot expect to remain in the same job or profession for life. Instead of specializing, prepare for an uncertain future by being a generalist with specialities.

Versatility, having many skills and many areas of knowledge, is a prerequisite of adaptability. It provides the maximum advantage when confronted with puzzles of change. The Japanese *ronin* did not stare fixedly at one small spot on his opponent, but used instead a soft, diffuse focus, taking in all of his opponent. He was ready to counter a blow from any direction.

THE ARRIVERS AND THE DERAILED COMPARED

In the first place, derailed executives had a series of successes, but usually in similar kinds of situations. They had turned two businesses around, or managed progressively larger jobs in the same function. By contrast, the arrivers had more diversity in their successes—they had turned a business around *and* successfully moved from line to staff and back, or started a new business from scratch *and* completed a special assignment with distinction. They built plants in the wilderness and the Amazonian Jungle, salvaged disastrous operations, resolved all-out wars between corporate divisions without bloodshed. One even built a town.

—Morgan W. McCall, Jr., and Michale M. Lombardo
"What Makes a Top Executive," *Psychology Today*[7]

Modern-day Ronin have many hats and are masterful in generalizable skills that they can apply across specialities to a wide range of endeavors. The most generalizable skills include people skills of communicating, negotiating, interviewing, organizing, motivating, teaching, and directing; problem-solving skills of observing, researching, analyzing, and evaluating; thinking skills of inductive and deductive logic and categorizing as well as many others. These are like the many ways to cut that the Japanese *ronin* practiced and perfected. *Ronin,* as professional warriors, specialized in more than one weapon. For any particular battle, they could choose to use the long sword or the short sword or both.

But the *ronin's* expertise was not limited to fighting. Trained as samurai, they were skilled in brush painting and composing poetry, educated in the philosophy of their time, and disciplined in meditation. While *doing ronin,* some became writers, Confucian scholars, or schoolteachers; some taught swordsmanship or other military arts; others traded on their ability with their weapons and hired themselves out as bodyguards and troubleshooters for rich merchants.

Similarly, modern Ronin are multiskilled, having a variety of hats to wear. They often operate within a broad professional field, such as law, psychology, business, or publishing, but resist narrowing into one speciality. Being secure in their ability to adapt, Ronin welcome change as an opportunity to learn and create. For Ronin, flexibility means security.

Whenever contemplating any move, always consider the strategic degrees of freedom[8] such a move will provide. That is, how many opportunities or paths to your goal are opened by this move?

Find the Intersection of Your Specialities

> The vacational vocation is the vocational vacation.
>
> So and So[9]

As the game of Go progresses, if the players continue their original strategies, Black will strengthen the hold on his corner while White's influence expands and arenas that once seemed divergent converge. By the end of the game, White will dominate most of the board and win.

By employing the dual strategies of indirection and concentrated dispersion in our career planning, we can often merge two or more specialities. The point where our specialities, including avocational interests, intersect is an area of strength and advantage. Not only do we have a broad foundation and the mystique of being different, we also have the advantages of a broader perspective and reduced competition.

Max in the accompanying monologue did this with law and engineering, for example. Although there are thousands of engineers and thousands of legal researchers, relatively few are knowledgeable and skilled in both. Max put himself at the head of the competition and elevated himself from the status of average by intersecting his specialities.

Consider Max:

After 10 years in engineering, I was burned out. I couldn't relate to my colleagues because they had such a limited view of everything. I felt socially cut off. So after my divorce, I quit my job and dropped out. At first I withdrew and did nothing for a while. A friend who volunteered for a neighborhood legal assistance center convinced me to volunteer, too. It was fascinating and I enjoyed it. And I discovered I could use a number of my engineering skills in the legal research: logical thinking, how to use the library, how to solve problems, how to make an argument. Before long, I was the No. 1 volunteer legal researcher. Eventually there was an opening for a paid position and I got it even though I had no formal training in law at all. I worked for the center for about three years, and although I couldn't go to court, I did do some legal counseling. I liked the involvement with people.

I had made enough contacts and had developed enough skill and confidence that I was able to become a free-lance legal research consultant. So I left the center. During the next two years, I built up a substantial clientele. I did O.K. But it was a feast or famine situation. So when a large prestigious law firm in the city approached me with an offer, I jumped at it. They needed someone with expertise in both engineering and law. Well, I got the job. Now I have what I like about engineering and what I like about law and I make a lot more money, too. The smartest thing I ever did was listening to my inner voice and leaving engineering.

Composite Careers

Doing the same general activity 40 hours a week for years numbs, thwarting development. You can break out of this rut with a composite career, in which you perform different functions for different employers. The composite career is, in essence, an array of part-time positions. This strategy offers variety, a breath of fresh air to those whose full-time classification is restricted to one function. A composite is often made up of modules of one limited function, such as accounting and bookkeeping, performed in one work environment and another limited function, such as selling software packages, performed in another work environment. Of composite careerists, William Bridges, who is researching the phenomenon and is the author of *Transitions*, says, "They actually represent a social phenomenon of great importance. They are vocational pathfinders of a new sort. They represent a new work ethic and the vanguard of a new work force."[10]

If you choose a composite career, it will serve as a buffer, making you less vulnerable. In economic hard times, you will have a broad, strong foundation; your stones will not all be in one corner. Just as capital investors and corporations diversify their portfolios, you too can increase security by diversifying job involvements. Even if one or more pieces of your composite are lost, you still have others for support.

An equally important benefit is the enhanced feelings of personal power and control over your work life. Should one of the jobs turn sour, threatening to become a burnout situation, you can leave with relative ease. You are not faced with an all-or-nothing situation, forced to choose between putting up with the intolerable or standing in the unemployment line.

> Even if you don't operate a business, you're in a better position if you act as a supplier of a service rather than as an employee. You can contract with companies to perform specific services for them at specific prices. In addition to the tax benefits, you can choose your own working hours, usually make more money, and have more free time.
> —Harry Browne
> *How I Found Freedom in an Unfree World*[11]

Composite careers can also serve as a transition and exploration step, a way of ferreting out the intersection of your specialities. Starting off with a part-time commitment in one speciality, another in another speciality, perhaps yet another in a third area of interest, you may be able to bring the divergent activities together into a hybrid of your specialities in which you offer a unique and sought-after service or product. Using this modular strategy of being on the payroll of more than one company can be the beginning of a transition into becoming an entrepreneur, never again an employee. Composite careers offer freedom and flexibility in activities and scheduling as well as an opportunity for balance.

Consider Ramona:

There are four things that are of vital interest to me: dancing, religion, children, and being a mother. And I've managed to work them all into my career in a very satisfying way by having more than one job. I earn most of my money three nights a week as a professional showgirl dancing in one of the big clubs. It's a lot of fun. I love the glamour, the glitter, and the audience. And they love me.

My second job is the one that surprises most. Every Sunday I teach a Bible class for preschoolers. Some think it's odd, my being a showgirl and all. But there's nothing immoral about being a dancer. I've had no problems with the parents, either. In fact, a lot of them have come to see me dance. And the kids love me.

In the afternoons twice a week, I teach dance to sixth graders in one of the local schools. That leaves most of my days free, allowing me to be with my own little girl. It's important to me to be a good mother. As I said, I'm very happy with my combination of jobs. It allows me to satisfy all of my needs. I don't feel that I have to sacrifice anything.

STRATEGY: MAINTAIN THE INITIATIVE

Those who desire *personal* power are very different. Instead of controlling a portion of the existing world, they set out to create their own.
—Michael Korda
*Power! How to Get It,
How to Use It*[12]

In Go, *sente* refers to certain carefully placed offensive moves by one player that demand a defensive response from the opponent. For example, suppose Black has heavily invested in a group in one corner but has not yet secured it, and White places a stone two squares away, threatening to jump in underneath Black. This forces Black to use his next turn to defend against White's offensive move. White maintains the initiative because on her next turn she can decide to continue the offensive on Black's group or to place a stone elsewhere instead.

Rather than waiting to be directed to develop a certain area, for example, Ronin take the initiative. Sophie, an editor, noted the software explosion. She also noted many bookstores were starting to carry limited lines of software. The indicators suggested that electronic publishing is the wave of the future. Rather than waiting until her boss told her to investigate the feasibility of expanding into software publishing and distributing, she took the initiative. Sophie educated herself by going to computer conventions, reading computer trade magazines, and talking to distributors and bookstores as well as to other publishers. She then put together and presented the board of directors with a strong proposal, arguing the benefits of expanding into software distribution in bookstores. After much debate and consideration, a new department was formed headed by Sophie.

Maintain the initiative in your career and on your job. Position yourself so that you can act rather than react. Endeavor to be the cause of events, not at the mercy of their effect.

STRATEGY: CONCENTRATE ON THE KEY FACTORS FOR SUCCESS[13]

Following a track in the same way as others competing for positions in your field yields no competitive edge. Instead, if you can identify those areas that are decisive for success in your particular line of work and add the right combination of skills and experience, you may be able to put yourself in a position of real competitive superiority. But first, you must identify the key factors for success. Then devise a plan to invest your resources and efforts in a way most likely to develop superior strength in the key areas.

Tactics for Identifying the Key Factors for Success

Conduct a Product Analysis

Categorizing the market is preliminary to deciding where to concentrate your major efforts. The easiest way to do this is to make a product–market matrix. List your products down the side of a sheet of blank paper. Your products are what you offer: skills you have, results you can deliver, or services you can provide. Next, divide the market into categories and list them across the top of the paper. Your market categories might be the different users of your service, or organizational needs.

Cheryl Lynn had been running the flea market for a local community college for several years. Her mother, in the course of fund raising for the Junior League, had coordinated many events. The pair got along well and decided to give a joint venture a try. They wanted to put on some kind of fair but were not sure what. They started by making a product–market matrix, as shown in the accompanying diagram. On the vertical axis they listed the kinds of events they could produce, and on the horizontal axis they listed their target markets.

A computer software trade show for career women interested them the most and seemed to have the greatest potential for making money. Alternatively, they thought a technical trade show

PRODUCT–MARKET MATRIX

Markets

	Professionals	Laypeople	Special Interest
Sale of used items	Office equipment recycle sale	Flea market	Photography swap meet
Computer trade show	Software trade show for business women	Computer games trade show	Display of technological aids for handicapped
Craft or cultural show	Office art display	Street crafts fair	Art show by handicapped artists

Products: Skills and Services

focused on the needs of the handicapped might be a winner because they lived in an area with a high population of independently living handicapped people. Having identified these two
potential ventures, Cheryl Lynn and her mother began researching the needs of the market.

Compare Winners and Losers

Another method of identifying where to concentrate your efforts is to compare people who have achieved a goal similar to
yours and those who have tried but failed. What is different about
these two groups and what is similar? What did winners do that
losers failed to do?

Greg, for example, was a systems analyst for a small mid-
western city and wanted to move to the fast-paced Silicon Valley.
So did a lot of others. The competition was stiff, and Greg had
trouble getting interviews. He began calling companies where
he had sent resumes and asking about the qualifications of people
who were hired. He learned that those most often brought in
from out of state had IBM mainframe experience. Based on this
knowledge, Greg made a lateral transfer to a local company that
was using IBM mainframes. Two years later, he landed a position
as a systems analyst in a fast-growing Santa Clara company.

STRATEGY: RIDE TRENDS; AVOID FADS

Forecasting trends or the general nature and direction of the
course of events is as important in determining where to place
our career stones as it is in deciding which of thousands of issues
in the stock market to purchase. Obviously, we want to move into
areas with the most opportunity and growth potential.

Accepting a job position or undertaking training in a speciality
that turns out to be a fad can result in serious losses or setbacks.
In the early 1980s, for example, the price of silver shot up almost
500 percent in a matter of a few months. But to the despair of
most of the investors, it was a fad that ended abruptly when the
price dropped to the prefad level within a couple of days. By
contrast, those who invested in selected software issues profited

by riding a trend. By 1983 software had become the fastest growing industry in the world.

> Trends, like horses, are easier to ride in the direction
> they are already going.
> —John Naisbitt
> *Megatrends*[14]

Clearly, the ability to distinguish between a fad and a trend
is essential in planning career moves. But what do we look for?
First, as the examples illustrate, fads are short term. Like a comet,
they dazzle for a moment only. True, money can be made and
quick advancement achieved by riding fads, but it's risky. The
stakes are high. To capitalize on a fad, you must call it right as
well as be in the right place at the right time. Although fads take
off fast, only those in on the first wave profit. Fads are almost
always get-rich schemes where most get fleeced instead.

The Circles of Gold, which drew so much attention in 1978,
was one such fad. On the basis of the pyramiding or chain letter
concept, groups of people, meeting in secret, paid the player at
the top of the list $100–$1,000 in cash on the promise that they'd
get back thousands when their names came up and new members
of the circle made their "investments." Only those who were in
on the fad from the start and who got out early profited, while
the latecomers paid for that profit.

Trends, on the other hand, build momentum slowly. Timing
is important but not urgent. Being in on the beginning of a trend
is not usually the best position. Trends allow you time to analyze,
consider, and plan optimal moves. As the trend expands and
speeds up, opportunities multiply. Even if you delay until after
the peak, you are still likely to profit from your invested efforts.
Trends plateau, whereas fads dive.

Typically, fads originate from one source. The Hunt brothers,
for example, created the Silver Rush of 1980. Opportunists
started Circles of Gold in suburban hideouts. Trends, on the
other hand, come from many sources, beginning in many places
at the same time, like grass roots. There is no one root, no one
master mind, no one catalyst behind the software industry, for
example.

Tactic for Riding Trends

Look for the Interface

> Every problem you can solve means
> more money for you. A problem is a mar-
> ket for a solution. Be sensitive to the
> problems of everyone you do business
> with.
> —Harry Browne
> *How I Found Freedom in
> an Unfree World*[15]

The point at which two industries or two vital functions converge is the interface. That convergence often means friction. It
can also mean opportunity. If you can devise a way to mesh gears
of divergent concerns smoothly, to provide a clutch so to speak,
you have a shot at dominating a whole new territory. You'll gain
a lot of freedom and probably a lot of money as well. At the
interface, there are opportunities for both entrepreneurs and
"intrapreneurs" (see Chapter 7) to develop new services or products, to add new territory to the game board, and to increase
autonomy.

There are infinite possible interfaces. Some are more fertile
and have more potential than others. The optimal interfaces are
to be found at the conjunction of two (or more) initially divergent
components of a trend. Here is an interface that has long-term
potential. If the trend is a strong one, there is potential for the
interface to expand into a full-fledged industry.

The personal computer for professionals, for example, was
simultaneously a godsend and a nightmare. The machine was
great; the software a marvel. But learning to use it was an ordeal.
The manuals were incomprehensible. Software writers spoke
computerese, not English. What the hell were DOS, RAM, CPM,
and CPU? Fortunes were to be made in that interface. And Ronin
were quick to move in with user-friendly software manuals and
informational workshops, for example.

Another example of a thriving interface is the mailing list industry, which interfaces between mail order retailers and buyers.
Those selling mailing lists are in the position to move into a new
interface: the link between the electronic cottage (see Chapter
1) and an international marketplace. In fact, as we move into the

information era, sales of information will become an increasingly profitable venture. So find the interface, it means opportunity.

STRATEGY: GET VISIBILITY

By now, most of us realize that good work alone may bring a few promotions or merit raises but is not likely to win much influence in the World Game. Being seen is essential if you want to expand your sphere of influence. The modest strategy of waiting for merit to be noticed more often than not leads to invisibility. Visibility does not come by chance; it is a direct result of how people present themselves. Some are shy. Others find the notion of self-presentation distasteful; it sounds like selling yourself. But self-presentation need not be forced or repugnant. And the fact is we are presenting ourselves all the time anyway. No matter what we do or how we act, others make judgments that can aid or hinder our career progress.

Tactics for Getting Visibility

Articulate Your Skills

Amazing as it may seem, many people cannot state their skills clearly and concisely. When asked, they describe jobs they've held, projects they've completed, and tasks they've performed. That is, they describe ways they've used their skills, but the skills themselves are only implied. This leaves to the listener the task of distilling the skills from the list of functions performed. The danger is that the listener may not be clever enough or interested enough to identify the skills. Don't give up your power in this way. Articulate your skills and do so within the listener's frame of reference. That is, translate your skills into the listener's language, one that resonates with the listener's needs.

Demonstrate Your Skills

Seeing is believing, and one of the most effective ways to present your best self is to show rather than tell. Seek out situations in which you can show others what you can do. At work, remember that you are not merely performing a function, not merely earning money, you are also demonstrating what you can do. Embrace every task, no matter how routine or how mundane, as an opportunity to demonstrate your excellence!

Serve Associations

Think of some association meetings you've attended. Who stands out? What people do you remember? Chances are it's the officers. By serving associations as a committee member or officer you create an opportunity to demonstrate what you can do—to show off your skills. At the same time you have an opportunity to learn and refine new skills, such as negotiating, organizing, delegating, and motivating others. In short, by serving associations you can create a learning lab in which to teach yourself how to lead.

Showcase Accomplishments

> To be a great leader is to be a shaman. You must be seasoned in the art of using images to instill an unshaken belief among your followers that you will always succeed in whatever you undertake.
> —R. G. H. Siu
> *The Craft of Power*[16]

Modesty is admirable in many situations, but some people take it to an extreme, literally hiding accomplishments. Don't do that! That's like passing your turn in Go, and putting no stones at all on the board. Those who are overly modest subscribe to the erroneous belief that worthy accomplishments automatically bring deserved recognition.

Consider Ralph:
A big investment outfit wanted to put in a shopping center near here. Well, a bunch of us got upset and formed an ad hoc committee to study the environmental impact. We were going to take it to the county. It took months. I ended up doing most of it—interviews, collecting articles, doing research in the library, gathering stats. I put most the report together, too. I wrote about

> 80 percent of the articles and did all of the layout and typing. You could say I was the force behind it all. But everyone who worked on it got credit—even if their contribution was small. I saw to that. I listed in alphabetical order all their names, mine, too. And we succeeded in blocking the shopping center. I'm really proud of that report. The experience turned my head around. I think I would like to get into local politics though I don't know how to start.

Ralph in the preceding example hid his accomplishment. By being overly modest, you can sabotage your motivation, putting roadblocks on your own path, closing off your opportunities.

Don't give your power to others who are expected to notice and acknowledge but don't. Find a way to showcase your accomplishments. Whenever possible, make sure that your name is on any product you produce and associated with any services you provide. Speak up and tell others about your accomplishments. Send a "news release" to the public relations people. They may run it in the company paper or even place a story in a local paper. Inform the secretary of your professional association. Perhaps he or she will place a notice about your accomplishment in the association newsletter. Be creative. Seek out ways to bring your accomplishments to center stage. Showcasing your accomplishments makes your company look good, too.

Publish

Publishing is a powerful way to present yourself and your accomplishments. Your name, as author, in print will increase your self-confidence and your credibility in the eyes of colleagues, giving you the aura of "expert." If you publish a lot, soon your name will be associated with a bit of territory. You will have enlarged your sphere of influence.

Teach

Opportunities to teach abound. Continuing education for adults is the frontier of education, and growing rapidly. Virtually every community college and university has an extended education program offering practical one-day and evening courses. Assess your skills. What can you do? Make a list of possible skills you could teach. Check the offerings in your local college catalog. What can you teach that's not listed? Prepare a course proposal, and sell it to the college's program director. It's easier than you imagine, and the benefits you'll reap can be many. In addition to the satisfaction of teaching and what you learn from the experience, you'll make vital contacts from a position of expert. Teaching brings visibility. Your course, name, and bio will be printed in the college catalog, which is sent typically to thousands of people and often to hundreds of company personnel departments.

But colleges are not the only market for courses. There are high school adult education programs, community centers, and associations. If your course is free, practical, and focused on a vital topic, you'll get a lot of takers. Eventually, you can get paid—sometimes quite handsomely. This can provide a nice financial buffer, add variety to your work, as well as make a nonlinear career move possible. You can place your white stone in a new territory!

If you have material pertaining to management, training, or career development, investigate the American Society for Training and Development (ASTD).[17] ASTD is a very active and motivated national organization with chapters in most metropolitan areas. Look for them in the Yellow Pages under "Associations." They can provide a receptive audience for workshops. If you've never taught a workshop, those ASTD sponsors can serve as a training lab.

Give Speeches

The list of associations in the Yellow Pages is also a source of possible speaking engagements. If you live in a metropolitan area, that list probably covers more than a full page, and the majority of these associations are continually seeking speakers for their meetings.

Look at your game board. What territory of expertise have you captured? What do you know about? What can you do? Chances are there are a lot of people who need that information or skill.

Whether a beginner or seasoned speaker, you'll probably want to join the National Speakers Association.[18] The format of their meetings provides an opportunity to observe several speakers of varying skills, to learn valuable speaking tips, as well as to speak before the group yourself.

Job	Possible Presentation
Mechanic	Ten-point checklist for evaluating a used car *before* you buy.
Bank Clerk	Ten ways a safe-deposit box can save you money and inconvenience.
Doctor	How to use your doctor effectively to cut medical bills while staying healthy.
Lawyer	Cut your lawyer fees in half by using the law library.
Firefighter	Eight common household firetraps.

If you've worked or done *anything*, you have skills. With creativity and boldness, you could catapult yourself into a whole new territory. Teaching, speaking, and publishing are ways of drawing opportunities to you. When you showcase your skills, prospective buyers get to window-shop. There's no hard sell. And it's an avenue for obtaining individual clients and project contracts. If you're especially charismatic and persistent, and provide quality material, your talk could be a first step toward a consulting practice.

STRATEGY: CONNECTING

We gain access to new territory in the World Game through other people. Others hire you, buy your services, publish your papers, back you up, invite you to join. It is others who teach you and inspire you. If you want to expand your sphere of influence beyond yourself, it behooves you to connect with other people. Through connecting, we develop relationships and satisfy our social longing to belong. These relationships can be stimulating, intimate, and supportive; they can open closed doors; they can even be erotic. Let's look at some strategies for connecting.

Tactics for Connecting

The first step on the path of power is the assembling of a well-knit cadre, backed by followers beyond that. . . . In general, the magnitude of power in your hands is a direct function of the size of

> your constituency. . . . Until you have
> developed this necessary base, do not
> dream of going anywhere. Conversely,
> do not reach for power beyond the
> strength of the platform you have con-
> structed.
>
> —R. G. H. Siu
> *The Craft of Power*[19]

Network

Networking is a process that, although only recently defined, has been going on for centuries. Networking is what you do when you meet others at association meetings: share stories, offer advice, give support, and make referrals. Networks provide a community, an in-group to which to belong. Seeking connections through a professional or social network is a time-tested strategy for locating the best prospects for a nonlinear move. All other things being equal, people will naturally select those they know for job appointments and consultation contracts.

Networking within your profession is good, but networking outside is a tactic of the astute. Often you can expand your sphere of influence by connecting with people outside your area of expertise. Because you are unique, people notice and remember you. And you will learn valuable information about practices, problems, and trends in other specialities that may be helpful in your current work in unexpected ways. As a rule of thumb, when you want to make a job change or move into a new field but don't know where to start, start by networking. Before you know it, opportunities will appear. Will you be open to them?

Show Belonging

It's not enough to simply place yourself in a setting. If you want to connect, you must do more. You must take the initiative. Consider the following situation. Imagine you are a guest at a party. What does a guest do? Guests stand around waiting to be introduced, feeling shy, and not knowing what to do. What does a host do? The host is expected to approach newcomers, introduce them to others, and help guests feel as if they belong.[20]

The secret to effective connecting is to act as if you're a host even though you are a guest—at association meetings, company parties, and other social affairs. It doesn't have to be your party. Everyone will like you and remember you. Act as if you already belong. Don't wait until someone says you belong. That's the passive role.

Build Alliances

The way to get results in any organization is through alliances. Allies support you. They speak up, saying "That's a good idea," when you present a proposal, for example. Allies remove road-blocks. Then you get results. Of course, it's essential to remember that an alliance is a two-way commitment. Allies will expect you to help them around roadblocks, too. Don't let them down. If you take too much from an ally for too long, you'll soon have an adversary.

One common strategy is to develop a "front-runner." For example, imbue an ally with your idea and encourage him or her to bring it up in planning. Then you function as the supporter. When two people are behind an idea, it has a greater chance of being actualized. Building alliances is the essence of teamwork.

You can develop allies in your immediate work group and in other sections of the organization as well. Some of the best allies are to be found among secretaries. They can clue you in to important gossip; they can make sure your work is completed accurately and on time; they can get you an audience with the boss.

Become a Mentor

You've probably heard a lot about the importance of having a mentor, an advisor more seasoned than you who knows the ropes. A mentor can alert you to the unstated do's and don'ts in your organization or profession and advise you on the most effective strategy to reach your goals. A mentor can mention your name in the right places, opening many doors.

But with so much emphasis on finding a mentor, we often neglect thinking about becoming mentors ourselves. Mentoring has many rewards. Much satisfaction is to be gained in guiding a junior, especially when our gems of wisdom are applied and succeed. When a protégé excels, you as mentor share the credit. You'll feel good and look good. Not only can a protégé bring enthusiasm, helping to revitalize your own, but often the junior has new ideas, new visions, and information about the latest technology and developments. Finally, being a mentor builds strong alliances that may be beneficial in unanticipated ways.

Notes

1. *Secrets of the Samurai: A Survey of the Martial Arts of Feudal Japan* (Tokyo, Japan: Charles E. Tuttle Co., Inc., 1973), pp. 430–431.
2. Information from Bateson, *Steps to an Ecology of Mind* (New York: Ballantine Books, 1972); *Mind and Nature: A Necessary Unity* (New York: Dutton, 1979).
3. For the results of an extensive research project on the characteristics of an understaffed environment, see Allan W. Wicker, *An Introduction to Ecological Psychology* (Monterey, Calif.: Brooks/Cole, 1979).
4. New York: Random House, 1975, pp. 120–125.
5. New York: Wiley, © 1979, pp. 178–179. By permission.
6. *Megatrends: Ten New Directions Transforming Our Lives* (New York: Warner Books, 1982), p. 37.
7. February 1983, p. 30.
8. For more information on the strategic degrees of freedom, see Kenichi Ohmae, *The Mind of the Strategist: The Art of Japanese Business* (New York: McGraw-Hill, 1982).
9. In Statis Suspensionicus, *Therapeutic Imperatives and/or Edifying Tautologies,* ed. Sebastian Orfali (Berkeley, Calif.: Sebastian Orfali, 1968).
10. From a lecture given by William Bridges to the Santa Clara chapter of the American Society for Training and Development at the University of Santa Clara (Calif.) in January 1983.
11. New York: Avon, 1973, p. 259.
12. New York: Random House, 1975, p. 42.
13. For more information on identifying the key factors for success, see Ohmae, *The Mind of the Strategist: The Art of Japanese Business* (New York: McGraw-Hill, 1982).
14. p. 9.
15. New York: Avon, 1973, p. 279.
16. New York: Wiley, © 1979, p. 157. By permission.
17. The national headquarters of ASTD are located at 600 Maryland Ave., S.W., Washington, D.C. 20024.
18. The national headquarters of the National Speakers Association are located at 5201 N. 7th St., Suite 200, Phoenix, Arizona 85014.
19. New York: Wiley, © 1979, p. 113. By permission.
20. The term *showing belonging* and the host/guest story are based on the work of Adele M. Scheele, *Skills for Success: A Guide to the Top* (New York: Morrow, 1979), pp. 87–97.

6

Doing Ronin: Riding
The Waves of Change

The word "ronin" means literally *"wave-man."* It implies that the unattached warrior was tossed helplessly upon the seas of a cruel destiny. Roughly, this is comparable to looking on a tiger as a victim of his environment.

—William Dale Jennings
The Ronin[1]

Change is inevitable. Something we all know but often forget. No situation is permanent. Time moves on. People are born, grow up, become old, and eventually die. Jobs, even the most routine and seemingly fixed, are fluid and changing. When the pace of change was slow, stretching over generations, society and individuals were able to adapt slowly. But change is no longer stretched over generations. Reflect for a moment on how things were when you were a child. Picture your telephone. What did it look like? It had a dial, not push buttons. Picture your family car. What type of features did that car have? Certainly no electronic ignition or cassette stereo. Remember propeller-powered airplanes? There was no flying from coast-to-coast in a few hours. Since we were children, we've seen spaceships fly around Saturn and the space shuttle launched and retrieved. Soon, perhaps, we'll be commuting to the moon. Sound like sci-fi? Well, much of what we now take for granted while moving through our daily lives was sci-fi not long ago.

As computers proliferate and expand their capabilities, we transit from the industrial to the information era. The pace of change is speeding up, and it will continue to speed up. Buckminster Fuller, Alvin Toffler, and others have pointed out that technology advances exponentially, that the rate of change follows the law of acceleration. For example, Toffler claims there were more scientists alive in the 1970s than in all previous history added together. According to visionary Robert Anton Wilson, this means our generation should witness more scientific and technological breakthroughs than all previous generations combined![2] Technology is transforming our personal and our work lives. As whole fields of endeavor are made obsolete, sometimes almost overnight, new fields are opening simultaneously. There will be more opportunities and more changes. Will you be prepared? The fact is we are going to have to handle change whether we like it or not. We cannot hide from it.

Most people are ill prepared for change, especially when it's unexpected and constant. We grew up expecting to find a comfortable niche in life: a cozy home in the suburbs, a lifelong mate, a secure and successful career. We were told and believed that, by focusing our interests and climbing onto the fast track, we'd live the good life. To make the American Dream ours, all we had to do was to select a speciality, go to school, get good grades, work hard, and cleverly play corporate or professional politics. Our schools, our institutions, our mores prepared us for stability, not change. While the indicators were apparent long before, it came as a shock to most when, in the late 1970s and early 1980s, millions were confronted with unemployment, dead-end careers, and a seemingly shrinking job market.

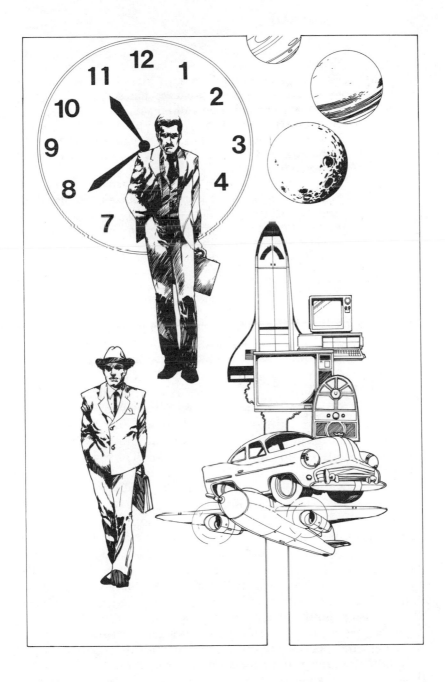

DOING RONIN

> It is preposterous to feel upset when you are offered
> to be ronin. Those people who served in the reign of Lord
> Katsushige never failed to say, "You cannot be real sa-
> murais until you do ronin seven times. You must have
> seven falls and stand up eight times.
>
> Hyogo Narutomi, I hear, actually became a ronin seven
> times. You must understand yourself as a Dharma (self-
> righting) doll. A Lord ought to give leave to his samurais
> for ronin trial.
>
> A samurai once said, "Samurai fear becoming ronin
> because it involves thousands of troubles and miseries.
> So they become very depressed when they are told to do
> ronin. But once you actually do ronin, you will not find
> it as difficult as you expected; quite different from your
> fearful anticipation. I personally want to do ronin again.
> —Tsunetomo Yamamoto (1659–1719)
> *Bushido: The Way of the Samurai*[3]

Uncertainty and feelings of loss of control are threatening. In the face of such uncertainty, most people dig in, entrenching themselves in an attempt to regain control and make life predictable again. It's a natural tendency at such times to cling tenaciously like a barnacle to the known. A prevailing attitude in the early 1980s was "I'm lucky to have a job even if it is dead-end (or boring, or not utilizing my skills, or a burnout situation)." Yet, opportunities abounded and jobs went empty because traditional careerists didn't see the possibilities. They were focused on the next rung on the ladder to the top or so overly specialized that they moved through their work lives wearing blinders.

When faced with change, Ronin dramatically differ from other careerists. Ronin do not fear change, running from it or clinging to the past. Ronin thrive on change. They seek and create change in their lives. Change provides new challenges, which when embraced rather than avoided, result in the acquisition of new skills and the refinement of old ones. For Ronin, change is an opportunity to grow, to expand. Viewing change as adventure rather than disaster, Ronin find it stimulating and exciting.

Most people realize that negative changes bring apprehension, fear, and anxiety, but few realize that positive changes, such as graduation, receiving a long-sought promotion, buying a new house, or getting married, are also stressful. No matter what the nature of the change, it is accompanied by uncertainty and the necessity of adapting to new circumstances. We have a tendency to try to race back into the known, to the predictable, even when it's a negative situation.

Making a change requires a time of being in limbo. If we are to move forward to new things, we must be able to get through the uncertain period. Fortunately, there are a number of techniques or actions we can take to minimize apprehension and increase the sense of control during the transition through the unknown. With practice, changing becomes easier.

MANAGING STRESS

> When Heaven is about to confer
> A great office upon a man,
> It first exercises his mind with suffering,
> And his sinews and bones with toil;
> It exposes him to poverty
> And confounds all his undertakings.
> Then it is seen if he is ready.
>
> Moshe[4]

The word *stress*, as we know it, was first used by Hans Selye to refer to physiological responses (including increased heart rate and adrenaline level, muscle tension, quickening of breath) he called the "general adaptation syndrome."[5] This pattern is considered a general syndrome because the same changes occur in response to a wide variety of events. The events do, however, have one thing in common: an element of threat. The physiological changes occurring during the stress response are in preparation either to fight the threat or to flee from it. The stress response is adaptive because it helps us to survive. If we fail to fight or flee, negative consequences can ensue; when we succeed in overcoming or avoiding the threat, we survive.

It is not possible to eliminate stress, nor is it desirable to attempt to do so. Selye emphasized that stress is a beneficial and essential life process. It is intimately involved in physical development and in learning. The stress response is an all-stops-pulled state of readiness, preparing us to move quickly and forcefully. Problems occur, however, when we remain in this state of physiological arousal too long. That is, when we do not succeed

STRESS: THE GENERAL ADAPTATION SYNDROME

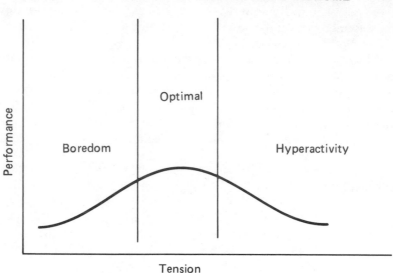

in defeating or in getting away from the threat or when there is an overwhelming number of threats (changes) to confront. Our bodies are not constructed to tolerate this state of readiness for long periods of time. Resources and defenses wear down, leading to detrimental health and psychological dysfunctions.

If you look at the accompanying figure, you'll see that the relationship between stress and performance is curvilinear, not linear. Notice when levels of tension (or stress) are low, performance tends to be low as well. There is too little stimulation to be able to keep attention on what is at hand. This is commonly considered to be boredom, understimulation, or depression. At high levels of stress, performance is also low, because the stress impairs physical and intellectual functioning. This state is often experienced as spinning our wheels. High stress interferes with creative performance and may be manifested by hyperactivity, forgetfulness, frequent mistakes, lack of concentration, and irritability. Because of the complexity of the modern world and the difficulties that many encounter at work, as well as the increasing pace of change in our lives, most of us experience chronic high stress.

The objective of stress management is to keep stress or tension levels within the optimal range for performance, health, and well-being. That is, when bored or depressed, we should increase tension levels. Listening to upbeat music, taking a cold shower, jogging, working in peopled areas such as the cafeteria, or even eating hot spicy foods are all stimulating activities that increase tension levels.[6]

Because most of us experience chronically high stress levels and will have to cope with increasing change, it behooves us to know a number of ways to bring the stress level down into the optimal range. It's a mistake to attempt to reduce stress by avoiding change. Although a natural tendency, avoidance is not acting in our best interest. If we are to grow and move forward as we navigate the limbo between the old and the new, we must be able to tolerate a certain degree of stress. There are four stress buffers: feeling that you are in control, relaxation, a strong social support group, and having fun.

Be Prepared

Personal power is the most potent buffer. It is the ability to influence what happens to us, which significantly reduces the detrimental consequences of stress. An effective method of increasing such feelings of power and control is to be prepared for change.

Consider All Possibilities

The most frightening aspect of change is the unknown. When we make the unknown known, much of the stress of change is dispelled. The first step is research or gathering information. Find out as much as you can about what others consider to be the possibilities. What ideas do they have for handling change? Talk to friends and associates; attend lectures; read periodicals, books, and newspapers. The objective of the initial research is not to terrify yourself with dire possibilities but to become aware of what might be so that you can develop a plan of action should the possibility become a reality.

Many possibilities can be discovered by using your imagination. Go back to your fantasy theater where you can view the drama of possible future selves. Try this now by doing the following exercise.

Exercise: Using Your Fantasy Theater

Find a comfortable place where you won't be disturbed. With eyes closed, imagine being in the audience of a theater with a large screen. Project one possible future situation onto the screen. Observe the drama in a detached manner. Simply allow it to unfold, and notice what happens. Think of yourself as a scientist, objectively collecting data on how possibilities could influence you. If at the conclusion of this drama you feel somewhat anxious, and you probably will, relax once again. Then jot down what you observed in a journal. Now repeat the process with another possibility. This technique is useful for pre-experiencing several alternative options you are considering to resolve a problem, for example. Some of the scenarios may seem very far-fetched; ignore these. Concentrate on those possibilities that have a high probability of actualizing or that have dramatic consequences, positive or negative, for you or others in your life.

The next step is to make contingency plans for what you will do if the possibility actualizes. Again, make notes in a journal, where you can keep all your data and considerations in one place and need not rely on memory.

Brainstorm Alternatives

Racing through the brainstorming stage, grabbing on to the first workable alternative that occurs to you, is a mistake. Instead, take time with this step and use your journal. The purpose of brainstorming is to generate alternatives. Note in your journal any and all ways of handling the situation under consideration. Let your imagination flow. Don't analyze alternatives. Just write down ways you might respond and things you might do. Include off-the-wall alternatives. Although unacceptable, they may prompt a breakthough in your thinking and lead to creative, workable alternatives.

Try on Alternatives

Resist the tendency to make preparing for change a totally intellectual process. Instead, use all available aids, including imagination and feelings.

Try out each attractive alternative in your fantasy theater. While sitting in the audience, see yourself on the screen carrying out the first alternative plan. Play the scenario out to its conclusion. There are many things to notice. What are the pluses of this alternative? What are the negatives? What new changes does it stimulate? While watching the drama, be alert for pluses and minuses you hadn't anticipated before the viewing and for unexpected consequences of the alternative. How did you feel as you carried out the plan? Finally, notice the impact upon important people in your life. You are not an island, you know. If you fail to consider and prepare for other people's reactions, a good plan can be sabotaged by those close to you.

Periodically call an intermission so that you may leave the theater to record what you have learned about the effectiveness and consequences of the alternative. Don't procrastinate on recording this information. It slips away quickly. Repeat this process with each alternative you are considering.

Use Rehearsal and Stress Inoculation

> Don Juan: The most effective way to live is as a warrior. Worry and think before you make any decision, but once you make it, be on your way free from worries and thoughts; there will be a million other decisions still awaiting you. That's the warrior's way.
> —Carlos Castaneda
> *A Separate Reality*[7]

Once you settle on a particular plan, rehearse it. And you can simultaneously inoculate yourself against the inevitable stress the change will cause if it comes to pass.

Again, the practice and inoculation takes place in the fantasy theater. Enter your theater, and project the possible change on the screen. This time, instead of sitting passively in the audience, actively project yourself into the scenario. Do not be an observer; be a participant. Engage your senses. Feel, hear, see, smell, even taste the experience. The more real the rehearsal, the more powerful the learning, and the more effective the inoculation. For a few moments, *allow yourself to experience the anxiety*, sense of loss, and other stressful emotions that accompany change. Next, *actively enact the proposed plan and experience it working*. That is, experience events going your way (not dramatically, but realistically) and people responding as you hope. At this point, you will probably notice the anxiety and stress diminish because the plan provides some degrees of control over what is happening. You are not helpless.

Research has demonstrated that fantasy rehearsal of new behaviors is as effective as actual rehearsal. By practicing in your fantasy theater, you teach yourself what to do if confronted by that particular change. Further, by allowing yourself to experience some of the accompanying distress, then handling it successfully, you can inoculate yourself to some degree against the harmful consequences of stress. The process works much in the same way as a vaccination, which introduces a mild form of a disease in order to stimulate the body to build internal defenses.

Mental rehearsal and inoculation is an invaluable technique for handling daily life changes and crises. Anticipate the unexpected, then practice alternatives on your "mental screen." If you tend to worry, transform the frightening images. Use what James Newman, author of *Release Your Brakes*,[8] calls the "positive power of negative thinking" to prepare yourself. When something goes wrong, don't magnify it. Instead, retreat to your threater to devise a plan for handling it.

Relax

Relaxation is a stress antidote. A regenerative process, relaxing is a time of rest and refueling. Although it seems like the natural thing to do when tense, surprisingly few people know how to relax.

Breathe Deeply

When you are stressed, breathing tends to be rapid and shallow, further increasing tension. In contrast, slow deep breathing automatically relaxes you. Even a few minutes of deep breathing will produce a noticeable change in your tension level. Deep breathing can be used anytime and any place. Several deep breaths just before a difficult situation is calming and increases feelings of control, for example.

You can test whether or not deep breathing will work for you right now by conducting the following experiment.

EXPERIMENT 1

First, rate your tension level on a scale from one to ten (one is low and ten is high tension). Next, with your eyes closed, breathe deeply and slowly while counting "One . . . and . . . two . . . and . . three . . . and . . . four . . . and. . . ." On count "one," breathe in deeply; on count "and," pause; on count "two," exhale slowly and completely; on "and," pause again. Repeat the same process with "three . . . and . . . four . . . and . . . ," then go back to count "one." Keep your attention on your breathing while you continue counting this way for three minutes. Then rate your tension level again. How does the second tension rating compare with the first? If you're like most people, the breathing and counting relaxed you. When your attention wanders from the counting, let the distracting thought go and return your attention to the counting.

Breathing and counting can be used in a multitude of ways. Spending 10–15 minutes breathing and counting in the morning, for example, can protect your health and start your day off right. When used for several minutes after work, it helps you make the transition to evening and leisure. Experiment and see how you can use deep breathing. Breathing deeply for two or three minutes before entering a stressful situation can help you prepare.

Relax Your Muscles Directly

Another effective way to release stress is by alternately tensing and relaxing each muscle, one by one. You may have used this technique to go to sleep. If not, try it tonight. Here's what to do. While lying in bed, first tense, then relax each muscle. Begin with the toes, move up the legs, through the torso and shoulders; then tense and relax the hands and arms, and, finally, the neck and face muscles. When you finish, you will feel relaxed.

Used often, tensing and relaxing has great benefits. For example, while doing the exercise, assume the attitude of a scientist and *dispassionately* observe the sensation in each muscle when it is tensed and then compare that sensation to the feeling when it is relaxed. This comparison process develops your ability to discriminate between the two sensations and thereby helps you

detect tension at an early stage. This detection ability is important. Many people think they know when they are tense or relaxed. But the fact is we can be chronically tense and yet be
unaware of it. To demonstrate how quickly sensations diminish,
try the following experiment.

EXPERIMENT 2

Notice how your right hand feels. Rate the sensation
on a scale of one to ten to provide a baseline for comparison. Now tense your right hand into a fist as tightly
as you can. Study how it feels. Rate the sensation of tension. Notice what happens as you continue holding your
fist tightly tensed. Sensations in your fist quickly begin
to diminish. To experience this more dramatically, continue to hold the tension in your right hand and make
your left hand into a tight fist. Compare the sensations
in the left fist to those in the right one. The sensations
in your left fist are much higher than in the right one.
Now release the tension by shaking your hands.

With this simple tensing and relaxing exercise, you can train
yourself to identify and reduce tension.

Use Your Imagination

Fantasy or the ability to create images and mentally project
ourselves into other places is another useful tool for managing
stress. Because the easiest way to understand the process is
through direct experience, try the following experiments before
reading on.

EXPERIMENT 3

Using the screen in your fantasy theater, imagine you
are in a scenario you find particularly pleasant, such as
floating on a cloud, strolling along the beach on a summer day, or enjoying wine and cheese in a lovely secluded
park. Get into it completely. Notice what you see. Notice
odors and sounds. Feel the air on your skin. Do this for

about 60 seconds. How do you feel while imagining yourself in the pleasant scenario?

EXPERIMENT 4

Bring to mind a bummer you experienced sometime in
the past. It doesn't have to be the worst bummer you ever
had, but it should be a situation you found negative and
distasteful. For 60 seconds, project yourself back into
that scene, making it as real and vivid as possible. As you
relive the scene, notice how your body feels and how you
respond.

If you are like most people, after the pleasant scenario you
felt comfortable and relaxed, engulfed in good feelings. Whereas
after the bummer scenario, you probably experienced a number
of negative sensations and thoughts. You may have felt stiffness
in your neck, tightness in your stomach, or tension in your
forehead. How did you feel and where did you feel it as you were
reliving the bummer? Now recall the actual bummer. How did
you feel at that time? Chances are the way you felt after recalling
the bummer was very similar to how you felt when you were in
the actual situation.

These experiments demonstrate how the mind and body work
together. Our bodies are totally dependent on our minds to ap-
praise data from the senses and memories, and to tell our bodies
what is happening out there. Whatever thoughts are in the mind,
the body responds to as if they were real. This means that when
you were imagining the pleasant scenario your body said, in essence, "Whoopee, it's a beautiful spring day and I'm feeling
good!" Whereas when you imagined the bummer scenario, your
body responded as if you were back in the actual bummer.

Use this knowledge as a tool to control your mood and stress
level. Project yourself into a pleasant scenario when you want
to relax. You can use fantasy to stimulate other emotions as well.
For example, mentally reviewing success scenarios—times in
the past when you performed at your peak and received the response you desired from others—will reignite feelings of satisfaction and self-confidence. When faced with boredom, experiment with the stimulating effects of sexual and adventure
fantasies. Experiment with the ways you can use your imagi-

nation as a tool to enhance productivity, personal power, and feelings of well-being.

Build Community

A strong social support system is a stress buffer. The dynamics of how relationships impact on health are a mystery. Perhaps it is because family, friends, colleagues, and co-workers can provide encouragement, sympathetic ears, and feelings of acceptance and belonging. Mounting research data indicate that people with strong social relationships tend to live longer, get sick less often, and report they are happier than those lacking satisfying relationships. For example, in a longitudinal study of doctors that began in 1946 when they were students, Caroline Thomas[9] of Johns Hopkins University School of Medicine correlated extensive physical, demographic, and psychological data with the incidence of disease and death. Her latest results indicate that health and longevity are significantly higher among those respondents who have stamina. Stamina is resilience and the strength to withstand disease, fatigue, and hardship. Thomas believes that an open, flexible approach to life; self-esteem; a spontaneous, outgoing temperament; and a minimum of tension, depression, anxiety, and anger while under stress are important elements in the development of stamina. The doctors with stamina grew up in homes that provided emotional support, acceptance, understanding, and love. In fact, "bodily contact of all sorts is very important, especially hugs" in promoting health and stamina.[10]

So make building and maintaining strong supportive relationships a priority. Not only do they feel good and provide a context for a full life, but supportive relationships fortify against the stress of change. And don't forget man's best friend. Relationships with pets have stress-reducing benefits, too.

Think Powerfully

> For the intellect is but a machine; it makes a splendid servant yet a bad master.
>
> —Paul Brunton
> *The Secret Path*[11]

Experiments 3 and 4 demonstrate that what you're thinking and how you're thinking about it determine how you feel. Most of us would probably prefer to have a preponderance of positive emotions and pleasant sensations. Yet, all too often we succumb to thinking that creates anger, depression, and anxiety and, try as we may to think positively, negative, stress-producing thinking triumphs.

It is easy to believe that the cause of downer emotions is external, out there somewhere, when emotions actually result from what we are thinking. How often do you hear yourself thinking "He made me mad," for example? Another person cannot *make* you mad. Events cannot *make* you respond. What actually happens is that when an event occurs we evaluate it as positive or negative. Although we are constantly making such appraisals, we are largely unaware of them. Following is a classic example.

Sitting in front of a lovely fire, reading an enjoyable novel, you feel relaxed, comfortable, and secure. Then out of the corner of your eye, without being consciously aware that you are looking, you notice something move. As you leap several feet from the chair, your heart pounds and you fill with fear. As you land, you realize that it was nothing more than a draft moving the window curtain, and you think, "Oh, it was nothing." Determining there is no danger, you calm down and return to the novel.

Undoubtedly, you have experienced a variation of this scenario. It demonstrates two things. First, our minds are constantly alert, checking out the environment and noticing events that occur. And second, we make rapid appraisals or evaluations of these events. The most basic evaluation that we make at all times is: "Is there a threat?" Anytime our minds determine that, yes, indeed, there is a threat, the stress response kicks in, mobilizing us to fight or flee.

We are appraising things all the time, and yet, we are largely unaware of it. A roller coaster ride is evaluated as "fun," and as a consequence, the experience is thrilling rather than terrifying, for example. And we evaluate others' motives, too. For example, the head of a pharmaceuticals lab in one of my workshops described how his technicians often "capriciously" argued with his introducing new tests. He said it made him angry. I pointed out that "capricious" was *his* evaluation of their actions and not necessarily reflective of their motives. Perhaps their arguing resulted from the natural tendency of people to question and resist change. Later this man reported that when he thought, "I should expect resistance to change," instead of "They're playing with me and deliberately trying to sabotage my program," he no longer responded with anger. Instead, he saw that helping them to accept new tests was a challenging part of his responsibility.

> Don Juan: "Things don't change. You change your way of looking, that's all. . . .
> "The world is such-and-such or so-and-so only because we tell ourselves that that is the way it is. If we stop telling ourselves the world is so-and-so, the world will stop being so-and-so."
> —Carlos Castaneda
> *A Separate Reality*[12]

The mnemonic EAR is helpful in describing and reminding us to notice how we respond. *E* stands for the *event*—something happens or someone says something or doesn't say something. *A* stands for the *appraisal* of the event. Is it positive or negative? *R* stands for the *response*. How do we react; what do we do? In short, we respond not to the events themselves but to our thoughts about the events. The more we listen to our EARs and notice the mental process behind our responses, the more we are able to command ourselves and maximize positive emotions (see the accompanying diagram).

The implication is profound. We have little control over many events that affect us. Yet, we can change our thoughts about events and thereby change the way they influence us. Another experiment will give you more insight into the workings of the mind.

EXPERIMENT 5

A blank mind contains no thoughts, no images, no colors. Nothing at all. Try to keep your mind blank for 60 seconds.

What happened? Unless you've had intensive meditation training for a number of years, you probably discovered you could not make your mind blank. Thoughts intruded. Perhaps

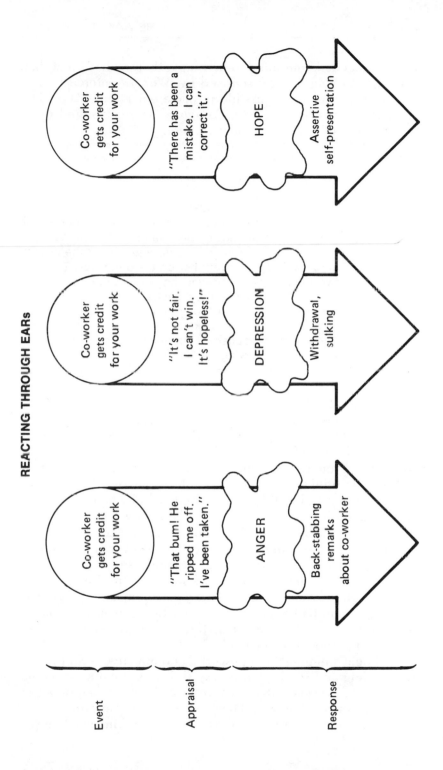

REACTING THROUGH EARs

Event

Appraisal

Response

Co-worker gets credit for your work

"That bum! He ripped me off. I've been taken."

ANGER

Back-stabbing remarks about co-worker

Co-worker gets credit for your work

"It's not fair. I can't win. It's hopeless!"

DEPRESSION

Withdrawal, sulking

Co-worker gets credit for your work

"There has been a mistake. I can correct it."

HOPE

Assertive self-presentation

you commanded your mind to be blank, then realized that that, too, was thinking. Images scurried by. Worries entered in. For most of us, it seems impossible to make our minds blank. The mind is constantly filled with thoughts and images, and these thoughts directly influence how we feel.

THE MUDDY ROAD: A Zen Story

Two monks were walking along a muddy road when they came upon a beautiful woman unable to cross the road without getting her silks muddy. Without saying a word, the first monk picked up and carried the woman across the road, leaving her on the other side. Then the two monks continued walking without talking until the end of the day. When they reached their destination, the second monk said, "You know monks are to avoid women. Why did you pick up that woman this morning?" The first monk replied, "I left her on the side of the road. Are you still carrying her?"

Chances are there have been times when you have experienced thoughts in your mind as being virtually out of control. Perhaps at 3:00 A.M., when you should be sleeping, you lie awake anxiously rerunning a bummer that has occurred or one you fear will occur. From Experiment 4, you know that a mere 60 seconds of bummer thinking had a noticeable negative effect on your mood and physical well-being. Multiply that by hours of useless ruminating. Although it is productive to review a bummer once, even twice, to analyze it and develop a plan of action, it is not productive to rerun the bummer over and over like a broken record. Nothing is solved. Instead, feeling bad, you needlessly stress your body and miss out on a lot of sleep. With practice, you can control your thoughts. This does not mean repressing or avoiding them. Rather controlling your thoughts means you determine when to think about disturbing situations and are not subjected to thoughts run amok.

Thought stopping[13] is a powerful and effective technique for intervening and stopping runaway thoughts. Like most mental techniques, however, it is easy to talk about but requires persistent practice to master. The best way to grasp how thought stopping works is to try the following two experiments. You will need a thought to stop. So once again, find a bummer to practice with. It can be the same bummer you used before or another one. It need not be a terrible bummer, but a situation that was negative and of concern.

EXPERIMENT 6

Rerun the bummer on your fantasy screen, making it as vivid as possible. Put yourself back into the situation. When you are absorbed in the bummer thought, yell "Stop!" as loudly as you can inside your mind. Notice what happens.

Chances are when you yelled "Stop!" the bummer thought did in fact stop. But only for an instant, then it returned. Consider this: What happened when you yelled "Stop!"? Didn't you command that your mind be blank? We already know from Experiment 5 that it is virtually impossible to make your mind blank. A blank mind is much like a vacuum, it fills immediately with the most available thought. So simply yelling "Stop!" is not sufficient. You must go one step further and replace the undesired thought with a more desirable one—one that will elicit positive feelings and a sense of personal power.

Bummer thoughts generally revolve around unfair or inappropriate treatment and helplessness. Such powerless thinking triggers negative emotions, as you discovered in Experiment 4. What you must do is substitute for the bummer thought a powerful thought, one that focuses on what you *can do*. The following list shows some examples:

Bummer Thought	Powerful Thought
"I blew it. I'm a failure."	"I made a mistake. I can learn from my mistakes. Next time I will. . . ."
"My boss is unfairly critical when he should acknowledge my good work."	"I prefer that my boss acknowledge my good work, but he doesn't know how."
"If she does that, I don't know what I'll do. I'll lose control and make a fool of myself."	"I'll make a plan of what to do if she does that."

Powerful thoughts are not self-deceptions. Much like the old "the glass is half empty" versus "the glass is half full," powerful thinking focuses on the positive, on personal power. Powerful thinking triggers problem solving and determination instead of anger, depression, and anxiety. Rather than avoiding the situation, powerful thinking emphasizes what you can do. To experience how this works, try Experiment 7.

EXPERIMENT 7

On a piece of paper, write the powerful thought that you intend to substitute for the bummer thought. Once again bring the bummer onto the fantasy screen for 60 seconds and relive the scenario. When the bummer dominates your mind, silently yell "Stop!" Then immediately substitute the powerful thought. Notice what happens.

Chances are you were more successful in driving the bummer out this time. But for many people, the negative thought will still return. If it does, yell, "Stop!" again, and again substitute the new thought.

The mind is often likened to a wild elephant that must be tamed. First efforts to control the elephant are met with rebellion—roaring, flapping ears, and attempted escape. You must teach the elephant that you are the master. When it tries to get away, pull the elephant back. It will roar and once again try to get away. Pull it back again. And again, and again. Eventually the elephant will learn that you are the master. Then you can unhook the restraints, climb on the elephant, and ride wherever you wish. Like the elephant, your mind—as soon as you attempt to master it—rebels, refusing to obey. You must teach your mind that you are the master. Then it will serve you well.

DEVELOPING YOUR ZEN MIND

We have two sides to our brains with different but complementary functions. Most familiar to Westeners is the left side of the brain, which oversees words, simple mathematics, and linear logic. The left side works much like a computer, using either/or categories and decision trees. In contrast, the right side of the brain controls creative leaps of logic, music appreciation, and the formation of images. These nonlinear functions are far beyond the capability of the computer. Western education has become extraordinarily sophisticated in teaching the left-brain skills of "readin'", "'ritin'," and "'rithmetic," but the paradoxical and elusive skills of the right side of the brain have been largely neglected.

Using a special brain test to analyze mental functioning during a variety of work activities, researcher Ned Herrman[14] identified two selves that correspond to the left and right sides of the brain: The "safekeeping self" and the "experimental or risk-taking self":

Safekeeping Self	Experimental or Risk-Taking Self
Structures situations; creates rules; is alert to danger; is hesitant, cautious, and fearful; avoids risks and surprises.	Prefers ad-libbing in ad hoc situations; is open, impetuous, playful, and naïve; takes risks; likes change.
Intellectualizes; evaluates; thinks deductively; prizes the known; is realistic; identifies consequences; seeks closure.	Is imaginative; feels; thinks inductively; prizes novelty; dreams; recognizes patterns; enjoys ambiguity.

The safekeeping self draws upon left-brain abilities to protect and guard us. A famous psychology experiment[15] provides an example: As a baby, Little Albert was playing with a fuzzy white rabbit when a sudden loud noise startled and frightened him, making him cry. The next time he saw the rabbit, he immediately cried, refusing to touch it because he associated it with the loud noise. Later, when Little Albert met his first Santa, he took one look at the big fuzzy white beard, began crying, and refused to sit on Santa's lap.

The Little Albert story demonstrates how the safekeeping self uses the left side of the brain for protection. Like the computer, the left brain creates categories that are used in the evaluation of new experiences. Dangerous situations are identified and responded to on the basis of their similarity to other dangerous experiences. To Little Albert, Santa's beard and the bunny's white fur were lumped into the same category—white fuzzy hair. He had learned that white fuzzy hair meant danger of a loud frightening noise.

This type of functioning has much survival value. However, it can be a liability in a rapidly changing world in which old categories become obsolete. What was formerly dangerous or beneficial may no longer be so. A dominating safekeeping self can protect us from dangers, but it can also inhibit adaptation to dramatically new situations. And adapt is what we all must do now.

The experimental or risk-taking self, which uses the capabilities of the right side of the brain, functions in a wholly different way. Because it does not use words, it does not break things into categories or think in terms of either/or. The experimental self is optimal in trial and error, which is essential for rapid learning and adaptation. Unfortunately, in the Western World our mutual belief system and our schools have overemphasized safekeeping, left-brain functions and neglected the experimental, right-brain functions. If we are to adapt to the information era, which promises to change dramatically the very underpinnings of society, we must be able to use more of the risk-taking, right-brain capabilities. The Oriental discipline, Zen, is aimed at developing these capabilities. By using the Zen mind, we are more able to handle change because we are less inclined to follow blindly the safekeeping self, clinging to an obsolete past. Instead we become more open and receptive to a new future. The teaching and practices of Zen show how to bypass the ever vigilant safekeeping self, the word-making gatekeeper residing in the left side of the brain. But because the Zen mind comes from a part of ourselves that is nonverbal, it is something that is difficult to describe in words.

Detached Concern

> A Western means of achieving non-attachment may be by having so many different "irons in the fire," so many people around, so many jobs, that no one action takes on too much importance. The Eastern way would be to remain nonattached to the fruits of *any* of one's actions, like a mirror—merely to perform the actions and observe the performance.
>
> —Deane H. Shapiro
> *Precision Nirvana*[16]

The metaphor of the mirror conveys the basic elements of the Zen mind. The mirror teaches what is called "acceptance" or "nonevaluation." When you step before the mirror, it reflects you. It doesn't evaluate who you are or engage in a lot of dialogue about whether or not it wants to reflect you. It simply reflects you. Unlike the mirror, we constantly look at the world with EARs, evaluating sensations, events, and situations. Then we respond to these evaluations as if they were the actual events. This evaluation process is part of the safekeeping self, which puts things into preestablished categories. As Joseph Chilton Pearce said, "We see through the prism of our categories."[17] We do not respond to the "real" world at all, but to preconceptions about the world instead. Our reflections are like those of a fun-house mirror distorted. And this undermines adaptability.

Try the following experiment:

EXPERIMENT 8

Step 1: Stop reading, and look around the room for yellow objects.

Step 2: Close your eyes. Name the red objects in the room.

Step 3: Look again.

Unless you are remarkably observant or you peeked at Step 2, you had difficulty naming red objects. Because your attention was focused on yellow, you blocked out things of another color. You did not "see." A crucial first step in adapting creatively is to "see."

CUP OF TEA: A Zen Story

A professor visited a Master to inquire of Zen. Anxious to get to important matters, the professor politely accepted the master's offer of a cup of tea. The Master filled the professor's cup and continued pouring as the cup overflowed. Surprised, the professor exclaimed, "The cup is full; no more will go in!" To this the Master replied, "Like this cup, you are filled with your notions and preconceptions. How can I teach you of Zen unless you first empty your cup?"

The mirror also teaches "detached concern." When the mirror reflects you, it does so with its whole "being," holding nothing back. In this way, it exhibits "concern." Its efforts are totally engaged in what it is doing—reflecting. Yet when you step away from the mirror it stops reflecting. In this way it exhibits "detachment." To be effective, people who work with people (social workers, health care professionals, police officers) must demonstrate concern. They must be willing to care about and become involved with others. But too often concern becomes overinvolvement. If the other person does not respond, the helper begins to experience burnout. In other words, not knowing how to be detached, many helpers withdraw concern and become indifferent instead.

Detached concern is a delicate balance of involvement and nonattachment. A story about Nobel prize winner Mother Theresa illustrates: When asked "How can you stand it? You work with the sick and dying, and they die anyway," Mother Theresa is claimed to have said, "We love them while they're here." Let's look closely at her words. "We love them [we are concerned] while they're here [then we let them go—detach ourselves]." Like Mother Theresa and the mirror, we must learn to let go, to be detached, and to leave what we have passed on the side of the road.

The philosophy of sportsmanship advocates detached concern. Play to win (concern), but do not worry about winning (detached). Athletes who *must* win inevitably fumble and lose. How one shoots the arrow is more important than hitting the target. Whether you are the chief executive or a newly hired clerk, whether you work with people, data, things, or authority, be a warrior, a Ronin. Strive for excellence in performance, and let go of the outcome, good or bad. Winning is fun. Enjoy it, but don't cling to it. And don't demand that you win. Let losing teach you how to shoot next time. But don't cling to losing, either, bemoaning your fate or criticizing yourself. Leave it on the side of the road, and walk on without saying anything.

> But if ever the least flicker of satisfaction showed on my face, the Master turned on me with unwonted fierceness. "What are you thinking of?" he would cry. "You know already you should not grieve over bad shots; learn now not to rejoice over the good ones. You must free yourself from the buffetings of pain and pleasure, and

> learn to rise above them in easy equanimity, to rejoice as
> though not you but another shot well.
> —Eugen Herrigel
> *Zen in the Art of Archery*[18]

Often we review things from the past, but we err in being judgmental, evaluating our performances. This mistake leads to guilt and self-consciousness. When you use your fantasy threater, it is vitally important that you suspend judgment. Do not evaluate. Instead, sit back and look at the scenario objectively, like a scientist. Let it unfold before you but don't make internal comments. Just see what is happening like a mirror "sees." When you try this, you'll find that it is difficult to suspend judgment. The safekeeping thinker persists in evaluating, putting things in categories of good and bad. When this occurs, notice that you are judging and then let the judgment go. Be a witness not a judge.

Eventually you will learn to be a witness in the moment, while you are performing. This is different from being self-conscious. The conscious mind is the left side of the brain, the thinker and evaluator. Self-consciousness puts on brakes. Trying to be perfect, we fumble. The witness sees but does not judge. The witness is you being aware of being alive now. This unfiltered awareness allows you to enjoy the moment fully and readies you for change.

Be Here Now

> For eternally and always there is only
> *now*, one and the same now; the present
> is the only thing that has no end.
> —Erwin Schrodinger[19]

The "be here now" philosophy is often associated with being irresponsible, unconcerned about the past, and making no plans for the future. But that is a misconception. Rather it is a prescription to live fully in the present moment—whatever you are doing. Try the following experiment:

EXPERIMENT 9

Become aware of the hair on your head. Notice the clothes touching your back. Feel the furniture you are sitting or lying on. Notice the sounds around you.

The degree to which you were unaware of the sensations before the experiment is the degree to which you are asleep, tuning out what is happening to you *now*.

THE STRAWBERRY: A Zen Story

A monk was walking through the jungle when he encountered a hungry tiger. Running away, he came to a ravine with a vine hanging over the edge, which he quickly climbed down. Then the monk saw a second hungry tiger below, looking up. For the moment, the monk was safe from both tigers. Then he heard a gnawing noise from above, and looking up, he saw two mice chewing through the vine. The monk did not concentrate on his pending doom. Instead he looked at the ravine wall next to where he was hanging. There he saw a strawberry plant with one perfectly ripe strawberry growing out of a crag. Just as the mice chewed through the monk picked the strawberry, popped it into his mouth and exclaimed, "Ah, delicious!"

The safekeeping self, with its words and evaluations, draws us into dialogues about the past and worries about the future. We spend precious few moments being here now. Being fully in the present moment tends to induce a curious altered state of consciousness called "expanded time." Phil Zimbardo, a Stanford University social psychologist, found in his research[20] that when students were given suggestions under hypnosis that time was expanded they tended to laugh more and to be more creative, playful, exploratory, and impressionable. Expanded time is the eternal now.

Most of us experience expanded time when we travel. Days filled with adventure and discovery feel like weeks. We are carefree, open, and aware, seeking the unknown. We notice things we would normally ignore. Each moment, like those of a child, is filled to overflowing with stimulating newness. And we let go of our normal ways of being and our egos, becoming more friendly, more adventurous, and more accepting. At these times, change is no threat; change is a thrill, an intoxicant. And in our state of open receptivity, we adapt beautifully—expanding, learning, and growing.

The opposite phenomenon often occurs when we follow routine. Months seem to dwindle into days. The time flies; our lives speed by. Faced with the sameness of routine, we stop looking and see little. Awareness narrows. We become resistant to anything that threatens to alter the routine. We learn little and grow hardly at all. The challenge is to maintain in our daily routine the alert, open joyousness experienced during travel. Learning to do this is one of the goals of Zen.

Be Yielding

> When riding a wave, [the surfer] must strive to stay just slightly ahead of it, since if he moves out too far he will not be "with it"; he will lose contact with the surging power which has been propelling him along and quickly sink . . . if he allows the wave to overtake him, he will be overthrown or "wiped out" by the wave's crushing power, since, once again, he will not be "with it."
> —Oscar Ratti and Adele Westbrook
> *Secrets of the Samurai*[21]

To be yielding does not mean to be passive, allowing yourself to be suppressed or walked upon. Instead, be like a blade of grass in the wind—bend when necessary, then spring back. Yielding means to be receptive, interacting with the world and responding to it rather than rigidly clinging to a particular position or posture.

Go with the flow. Many incorrectly believe this means fanciful undirected movement. Actually, the phrase means to capitalize on ongoing movement. Martial arts employ this principle concretely. Using judo, for example, a petite 95-pound woman can effortlessly flip a large man who attempts to attack her. The woman does not grab and throw the man. Instead, she yields to and uses his movement.

IS THAT SO? A Zen Story

> A young woman became pregnant and, fearing for her lover's safety, lied, "It was the Old Man on the hill," when

her brother demanded she reveal the identity of the father.

When the child was born, the brother took it and climbed the hill to the old man's hut. "Here, Old Man, this child is your responsibility. I am leaving the child here." The old man replied, "Is that so?"

The old man loved the child and cared for it as his own. The child was a joy and filled his hut with laughter.

After about three years, the woman, filled with regret, confessed her lie. "I want my baby!" she cried. Again, the brother climbed the hill to the old man's hut. Apologizing, he said, "I've come to take the child." "Is that so?" the old man replied.

Legend has it that the martial art jujitsu originated in China during a long, cold winter. Each day, snow fell on two trees in a field. Being firm and rigid, the limbs of the larger tree supported piles of snow. Finally, the branches, no longer able to bear the weight of the heavy snow, cracked. The branches on the smaller tree also accumulated snow, but being supple, not rigid, they bent to the ground, letting the snow slide off, and then returned to their original positions. The tree that yielded survived the winter.

In our daily lives, at work or at home, to yield means to alter goals as circumstances require. Like water flowing downstream, yield and flow around the rocks in life. Be flexible. Look for alternative and creative ways to reach your goals.

Accept Paradox

We do not play the game of Black-and-White—the universal game of up/down, on/off, solid/space, and each/all. Instead we play the game of Black-versus-White or more usually, White-versus-Black. For, especially when rates of vibration are slow as with day and night or life and death, we are forced to be aware of the black or negative aspect of the world. Then, not realizing the inseparability of the positive and negative poles of the rhythm, we are afraid Black

may win the game. But the game "White
must win" is no longer a game. It is a
fight—a fight haunted by a sense of
chronic frustration, because we are
doing something as crazy as trying to
keep the mountains and get rid of the
valleys.
      —Alan Watts
         The Book: On the Taboo Against
         Knowing Who You Are[22]

   The Western mind tends to get trapped in either/or or dich-
otomous thinking. Yet, life is not either/or; it is a continuous process. Because of the way we have been taught to think and perceive, we break the continuum into separate categories. But this
is a false separation, an overlay of the rational mind, the safekeeping self. We judge ourselves as being good *or* bad when we
are in fact both good *and* bad. We struggle over emphasizing self-
interest *or* the interest of others, when in fact they're both important. We worry about living now *or* planning for the future,
when we should live both now *and* plan for the future. As a result,
we are constantly confronted with confusing contradictions that
immobilize us. Organizations, for example, are paradoxical. Organizations, which are made up of people, seek clarity, certainty,
and objectivity. Yet people are not clear, certain, or objective,
they are changeable and subjective. Believing that these contradictions should not exist creates frustration and confusion and
attempts to conform to modes of being that are not possible to
achieve. The organization with its chain of command is structured so that no one person has too much control or power, yet
to be mentally healthy and productive, individuals must have a
sense of personal power.[23]

Shift Your Viewpoint

      Problems that remain persistently in-
   solvable should always be suspected as
   questions asked in the wrong way.
         Alan Watts
            The Book: On the Taboo Against
            Knowing Who You Are[24]

The Zen mind does not put things in paradoxes, separating black from white or the mountains from the valleys. To break out of immobilizing paradoxes, we must look at the situation in a totally new way, making what Marilyn Ferguson, in *The Aquarian Conspiracy: Personal and Social Transformation in the 1980s*,[25] calls a "paradigm shift." We must ask the right questions. For example, people once believed the earth was flat. From that paradigm, intricate belief systems about the stars, moon, sun, and their relationships to the earth evolved. The discovery that the earth was round and circled the sun was a dramatic paradigm shift—one that altered the way of life. More recently, there has been another dramatic paradigm shift. For centuries, leading thinkers adhered to Newton's mechanical theory of the universe. But Einstein's special theory of relativity upset the basic premises of Newtonian physics, turning them inside out.

We are often unaware of our basic beliefs and guiding principles. A belief most of us have accepted is that the only way to success is to climb the linear career ladder. Few people even realize that this is a career strategy; still fewer challenge it. Ronin have made a paradigm shift. They do not unquestioningly accept specialization as the only career strategy and a straight line progression as the only acceptable path.

> Don Juan: "Yesterday you believed the coyote talked to you. Any sorcerer who doesn't *see* would believe the same, but one who *sees* knows that to believe that is to be pinned in the realm of sorcerers. By the same token, not to believe that coyotes talk is to be pinned down in the realm of ordinary men.
> "In order to *see* one must learn to look at the world in some other fashion, and the only other fashion I know is the way of the warrior."
>
> —Carlos Castaneda
> *Journey to Ixtlan*[26]

When you develop and exercise your Zen mind, you can enhance your ability to make paradigm shifts—to see things in more ways than one and to ask new questions. With the Zen mind, you realize that life and work follow both the principles of science and the principles of magic.

Laugh a Lot

Laughter is a stress buffer, but as with relaxation, the dynamics remain a mystery to medical science. Humor is a tool for breaking out of paralyzing paradox, allowing us to look from a different vantage point. We gain a new perspective and release tension.

When you catch yourself taking things too seriously, use this as a signal to laugh. Think of the "cosmic chuckle" and of the absurdity of the human condition. Satirize your dilemma. Imagine yourself in a Charlie Chaplan script. As a discipline, practice finding humor in disaster. You'll find freedom there.

THE DONKEY CHASE: A Sufi Tale

Nasrudin, the playful teacher, was riding his donkey out of town when he passed one of his disciples who asked, "Where are you going?" Nasrudin simply grinned as he rode past.

Sure that the old man was up to something, the disciple jumped on his donkey and rode after him. When Nasrudin saw he was being followed, he urged the donkey on to a trot. Seeing this, the disciple kicked his donkey and chased after the old man.

Seeing that he was being chased, Nasrudin took a shortcut across a field and headed the trotting donkey into the cemetery. Pulling the donkey to an abrupt stop, Nasrudin leaped off and jumped over a gravestone. On his heels, the disciple pulled his donkey to a stop, ran over to the gravestone, and looking over it at his crouching teacher, he demanded, "Why were you running away?" To which Nasrudin asked, "Why were you chasing me?"

Notes

1. *The Ronin: A Novel Based on a Zen Myth* (Tokyo, Japan: Charles E. Tuttle Co., Inc., 1968), p. 44.
2. Both Toffler's and Wilson's observations are from Robert Anton Wilson, *Cosmic Trigger: Final Secret of the Illuminati* (Berkeley, Calif.: And/Or Publishers, 1977), p. 215.

3. Translated from *Hagakure*, trans. Minoru Tanaka, ed. Justin F. Stone (Albuquerque: Sun Books, 1975), pp. 40, 34.
4. Reprinted in Jennings, *The Ronin*, p. 11.
5. Hans Selye, *The Stress of Life* (New York: McGraw-Hill, 1976).
6. For more information on how to engineer your environment, see "Environmental Engineering," in Beverly A. Potter, *Beating Job Burnout* (New York: Ace Business Library, 1982), pp. 82–87.
7. New York: Pocket Books, 1972, p. 47.
8. New York: Warner Books, 1977.
9. Cited in John Pekkanen, "Keys to a Longer, Healthier Life," *The Washingtonian*, November 1982.
10. Sidney Cobb, professor of community health and psychiatry at Brown University, cited in Pekkanen, "Keys to a Longer, Healthier Life."
11. *The Secret Path: A Technique of Spiritual Self Discovery for the Modern World* (New York: Dutton, 1935), p. 18.
12. New York: Pocket Books, 1972, pp. 37, 219.
13. For details on how to control thoughts, see "Thought Control," in Potter, *Beating Job Burnout*, pp. 139–154.
14. W. E. (Ned) Herrman, Applied Creative Services, Lake Lure, North Carolina 28746.
15. J. B. Watson and Rosalie Rayner, "Conditional Emotional Reactions," *Journal of Experimental Psychology* (1920), No. 3, pp. 1–14.
16. Englewood Cliffs, N.J.: Spectrum Books, 1978, p. 212.
17. *The Crack in the Cosmic Egg: Challenging Constructs of Mind and Reality* (New York: Pocket Books, 1974), p. 34.
18. New York: Vintage, 1953, p. 69.
19. Cited in Alan Watts, *The Book: On the Taboo Against Knowing Who You Are* (New York: Pantheon Books, 1966), p. 99.
20. For more detailed information on this research, contact Dr. Phil Zimbardo, Psychology Department, Stanford University, Stanford, CA 94305.
21. *Secrets of the Samurai: A Survey of the Martial Arts of Feudal Japan* (Tokyo, Japan: Charles E. Tuttle Co., Inc., 1973), p. 431.
22. pp. 30–31.
23. Abraham Zaleznik, Manfred Kets de Vries, and John Howard, "Stress Reactions in Organizations: Symptoms, Causes, and Consequences," *Behavioral Science*, Vol. 22 (1977), pp. 151–162.
24. p. 55.
25. Los Angeles: Tarcher, 1980.
26. *Journey to Ixtlan: The Lessons of Don Juan* (New York: Simon & Schuster, 1972), pp. 300, 302.

7

Corporate Ronin

The corporations that will succeed and flourish in the times ahead will be those that have mastered the art of change: creating a climate encouraging the introduction of new procedures and new possibilities, encouraging anticipation of and response to external pressures, encouraging and listening to new ideas from inside the organization.

The individuals who will succeed and flourish will also be masters of change: adept at reorienting their own and others' activities in untried directions to bring about higher levels of achievement. They will be able to acquire and use power to produce innovation.

—Rosabeth Moss Kanter
The Change Masters[1]

By the early 1980s, business performance in the United States had deteriorated. No longer did we make the best and more reliable products. And what's worse, indications were that this decline would become a trend. The number of patents granted to U.S. citizens in 1980 was down more than 30 percent from the peak in 1971, and research and development expenditures had fallen steadily since the 1960s. Analysts linked the drop in innovation with the slump in productivity.[2]

If we are to turn around this decline, business must foster the entrepreneurial spirit and renew its ability to be innovative. Our changing and unpredictable times call for new responses. The challenge of innovation could be a catalyst for an American corporate renaissance.

TRADITIONAL ORGANIZATIONS STIFLE INNOVATION

Innovation usually pivots around what Thomas J. Peters and Robert H. Waterman in their ground-breaking report, *In Search of Excellence*,[3] call a "product champion," the fanatic who inspires the extra effort and pushes the project through and around the bureaucratic maze. But today in American business, there are too few of these corporate Ronin because their work style is viewed as at odds with the way that most businesses manage their employees. Ronin are regarded as too independent, and much of what they do is taken as a challenge to the status quo. Consequently, their corporate lives are filled with many hurdles and few rewards for overcoming them. It is almost as if organizations unwittingly conspire to kill the spirit of the Ronin they so desperately need.

The very structure of organizations discourages innovation. Mechanisms meant to keep the organization on its planned course inhibit change and entrepreneurialism instead. For example, functions are compartmentalized into specialities and arranged hierarchically into chains of command that create barriers to communication. The system is designed with internal controls to avoid risk, but the result is that organizations forget how to experiment and adapt. Even when innovations do emerge, they are less likely to be used.

Traditional organizations are replete with rules that fence us in. As protocol takes precedence over performance, corporate fiefdoms learn to defend themselves by using rules to withhold the information, resources, and support we need to get the job done. Because innovation in feudal systems requires going against the grain, it is not too surprising that most innovations in traditional organizations come from newcomers, outsiders, or malcontents who do the wrong thing, in the wrong place, at the wrong time. Such corporate feudalism produces a rigidity that is a disaster in an era of rapidly accelerating change. By comparison, innovative companies can adapt by shifting posture and resources as circumstances require and thereby stay ahead of change.

> By necessity for efficiency reasons some jobs have a high component of routine, repetitive do-it-as-ordered action. . . . The problem for innovation and change is not the *existence* of such tasks but the *confinement* of some people within them.
>
> —Rosabeth Moss Kanter
> *The Change Masters*[4]

Kanter[5] says that innovation comes out of successfully grappling with the challenge of combining the necessity for routine jobs with the possibility for employee participation beyond these jobs. It is possible, she maintains, for a "mechanistic production hierarchy" and a "participative problem-solving organization" to exist side by side, carrying out different but complementary types of tasks.

The primary function of a hierarchy is to maintain the organization and its production. By routinizing useful procedures, a hierarchy defines titles, pay, reporting relationships, and tasks. Opportunities tend to be limited to formal promotional paths in which power follows position. On the other hand, the participative problem-solving organizations Kanter studied are oriented toward change. In these organizations, she observed a fluidity that allows people to be grouped temporarily in a number of different ways, as appropriate to the problem-solving tasks at hand. In this parallel structure, as Kanter calls it, opportunity and power can be expanded far beyond what is available in the regular hierarchical organization. The parallel structure exists simultaneously with the hierarchy, not replacing it but rather serving different purposes: to examine routines, to explore new options, and to develop new tools, procedures, and approaches. And as the utility of new routines is demonstrated, they are transferred to the line organization for maintenance and integration.

In short, according to Kanter's findings, to be innovative organizations must have two ways of arranging people. First, they need a hierarchy with specified tasks and functional groupings for carrying out what they already know how to do and can anticipate will be the same in the future. But organizations also need a set of flexible vehicles for figuring out how to do what they don't yet know, such as how to encourage entrepreneurs and how to engage both the grass roots and the elite in mastering innovation and change.

> How . . . could the mind of the strategist, with its inventive elan, be reproduced in [the] corporate culture? What were the ingredients of an excellent strategist? . . . The answer I came up with involved the formation within the corporation of a group of young "samurais" who would play a dual role. On the one hand they would function as real strategists, giving free rein to their imagination and entrepreneurial flair in order to come up with bold and innovative strategic ideas. On the other hand they would serve as staff analysts, testing out, digesting, and assigning priorities to the ideas, and providing staff assistance to line managers in implementing the approved strategies. This "samurai" concept has since been adopted in several Japanese firms with great success.
>
> —Kenichi Ohmae
> *The Mind of the Strategist*[6]

ROOTS OF INNOVATION

More than the people working within it, the environment of the organization makes the biggest difference in the amount of innovative activity. Innovative organizations are characterized by open communication that promotes sharing ideas and solving problems; relationship ties that cut across functions, levels, and departments; and decentralization of resources. Experimentation, the most powerful catalyst for getting innovation into action, must be encouraged, and the failures that inevitably result must be accepted.

> The most discouraging fact of big corporate life is the loss of what got them big in the first place: Innovation.
> —Thomas J. Peters and Robert H. Waterman
> *In Search of Excellence*[7]

Innovation thrives best in environments in which small groups of people, usually ten or fewer, work together. Small work units promote increased participation and better communication as well as feelings of commitment and ownership over projects. In fact, small workplaces outperform big ones on almost every performance indicator. But not just any small group of people working together produces innovation. Groups function best and are most productive when they consist of volunteers from a variety of fields who set their own goals for a project of limited duration.

Rich support systems are needed to counteract the organization's built-in opposition to change. Circulating people across jobs allows people to learn a number of skills while facilitating the formation of networks. The complex ties that develop encourage employees to cut across job boundaries to work collectively with others. Companies benefit by a flexible and adaptable work force, and employees gain from added variety and the challenge of learning.

One way of bringing more of the entrepreneurial spirit into the corporation is through "intrapreneuring"[8]—establishing a company within the corporation. Although in the strictest sense, the intrapreneur stays an employee, special rules govern the interplay between the intrapreneur and the corporation. The objective is to simulate the small business environment. This innovative approach promises to yield the assets of both the large organization and the entrepreneurial venture.

THE INTRAPRENEUR

> The [intrapreneur] is allowed great freedom of action.
> . . . Once the business plan is accepted he can "borrow"

corporate money at a stated interest rate. He can buy
services from corporate staff or outsiders as he wishes,
or rent office space elsewhere if it is cheaper than the
available space, or hire full-time staff people from corporate staff departments. The only limits are that he adhere to standard corporate accounting procedures and
use corporate lawyers.

—William Copulsky and Herbert W. McNulty
Entrepreneurship and the Corporation[9]

CORPORATE RONIN AS COMPANY ASSETS

What distinguishes the Maverick Executive from *all* other executives is his
rare constellation of characteristics,
skills, attitudes, strengths, and weaknesses. His most notable marks are exceptional drive, courage, optimism, and
decisiveness. But a listing of his features would also embrace an extraordinary diversity of terms, many paradoxical: excitable and tireless, self-
confident and intolerant, suspicious and
gullible, decisive and nonanalytical,
dedicated and fickle, innovative and
conservative, superficial and profound,
persevering and nonconforming, auto-
cratic and versatile, inspiring and ruth-
less, indifferent and meddling, impetuous and rigid, obsessive and careless,
scheming and unreflective, demanding
and casual, critical and idolizing.

—Robert N. McMurry
The Maverick Executive[10]

Innovating and developing successful new products is not a step-
by-step, carefully planned, linear process. It is true that, during
planning, a target or direction is identified, but getting there is
much like sailing. Unable to sail straight into the wind, the cap-
tain navigates generally north by tacking to the northeast, then
correcting the course as the boat comes about, and tacking to the
northwest. Likewise, we will not solve the riddles of living in

an organizational world with a linear approach. We must experiment and make mistakes to discover and refine new ways of doing things.

STRATEGIC THINKING

Successful business strategies result not from rigorous analysis but from a particular state of mind. In what I call the mind of the strategist, insight and a consequent drive for achievement, often amounting to a sense of mission, fuel a thought process which is basically creative and intuitive rather than rational. Strategists do not reject analysis. Indeed they can hardly do without it. But they use it only to stimulate the creative process, to test the ideas that emerge, to work out their strategic implications, or to ensure successful execution of high potential "wild" ideas that might otherwise never be implemented properly. Great strategies, like great works of art or great scientific discoveries, call for technical mastery in the working out but originate in insights that are beyond the reach of conscious analysis.
—Kenichi Ohmae
The Mind of the Strategist[11]

The acts of a myriad of individuals drive the innovative organization. There would be no innovation without someone somewhere deciding to shape and push an idea until it takes usable form as a new product, management system, or work method. Corporate Ronin create new possibilities for organizational action by testing limits and by pushing and directing the innovation process. They have an intellectual elasticity or flexibility that enables them to come up with realistic responses to changing situations.

Doris Randall . . . was the new head of the backwater purchasing department that she feared would join personnel and public relations as the "three Ps" of women's ghettoized job assignments in the electronics industry. But she eventually parlayed technical information from users of the department's services into an agreement from her boss to allow her to make the first wave of changes. No one in her position had ever had such close contact with users before, and Randall found this a potent basis for reorganizing her unit into a set of user-oriented specialities, with each staff member concentrating on a particular user need. Once the system was in place, and hers acknowledged to be functioning as the best purchasing department in the region, she went on to expand this kind of reorganization into the other two purchasing departments in the division.

—Rosabeth Moss Kanter
The Change Masters[12]

Ronin bring many benefits to the corporation. As a result of many nonlinear moves and a wide range of experience and skill, for example, they tend to see problems in a larger perspective and understand all the important operations of the company. They bring ideas and material from different corners together in new ways. Having moved laterally within the company, Ronin have allies in different departments and at different levels, enabling them to build coalitions to get things done.

Ronin are able to envision new possibilities, and when organizational structure and protocol block actualizing their vision, they are inclined to bend the rules. For example, they have been known to transfer funds from one budget line to another, act before they receive official approval, and bootleg resources. It's this characteristic—that Ronin are not beholden to the traditional rules, the Company Way—that organizations both fear and desperately need.

LONE RANGERS

A small number of managerial entrepreneurs in unreceptive environments are what Ken Farbstein called "Lone Rangers," organization loyalists acting on their *values* to remedy what they see as less-than-optimum situations for a company and a job they care about. The person who is this kind of "bureaucratic insurgent" can be an activist reformer who remains loyal to the organization and its mission while working gradually but persistently to "convert the heathen. . . . He takes advantage of loopholes, skirts the edge of regulations, evades formal orders, and is less than fully complacent when he cannot ignore them."

> Half outlaw as well as hero, [the] innovator may be
> ready to break rules to reach a great goal. He or she may
> engage in illicit budget transfers using funds for a pur-
> pose other than the official one, hold off-site meetings
> to raise the morale of troops even though the company
> has forbidden it, create his or her own rewards systems,
> spend money before it is allocated or even get a product
> into production before receiving official approval.
>   —Rosabeth Moss Kanter
>   *The Change Masters*[13]

Corporate Ronin shape their jobs. They know how to use
power, and they can mobilize people and resources to get things
done. When infused with purpose, corporate Ronin will take it
upon themselves to damn the bureaucracy and maneuver their
projects through the system. Ronin are self-directed. And as such,
they set their own goals, and take personal responsibility for solving problems and getting feedback. The difference between career feudalists' and Ronin's types of commitment is illustrated
in the accompanying diagram.

BECOMING A CORPORATE RONIN

First Ronin experiences are often in response to practical factors
in the work environment. For example, sometimes an employee
begins to exhibit Ronin qualities when confronted with a job that
is just too large. Carving out a concrete goal requires an innovative approach. Other times, jobs are too small and employees
are bored and unfulfilled. Realizing that advancement is blocked
is a common spur to becoming a corporate Ronin.

Operating within a large organization without burning out or
becoming indentured and an interchangeable part is no small
feat. On the other hand, organizations provide opportunity. They
provide a competitive arena in which to expand experience, to
develop capabilities, to pursue adventure, and to attain excellence. Yet at the same time, working in a corporation poses a
challenge that develops and hones up skills. Operating in a corporation is a true warrior's test.

Working in an organization means contending with contradiction. Turning these paradoxes to your advantage is an adventure in becoming a warrior. The Way of the Corporate Ronin is

COMMITMENT FOR CAREER FEUDALISTS AND RONIN

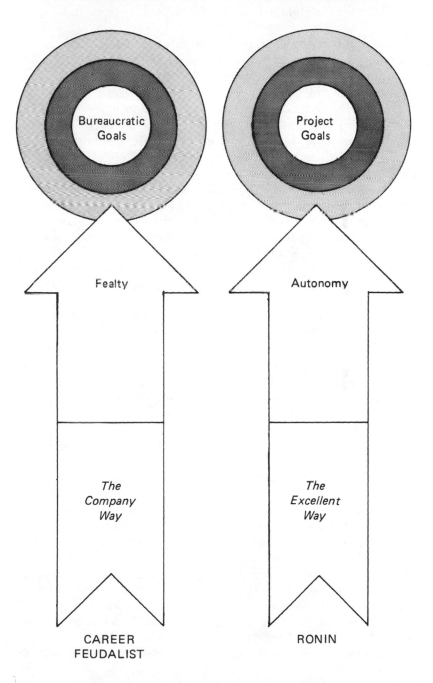

guided by the code of autonomy (directing oneself), excellence (carrying out the right action), and adaptability (remaining flexible).

The first corporate paradox is the inherent contradication between your roles as an individual and as a member of a work group or team. Inevitably, work within an organization is a team activity, involving groups of people working together to achieve goals. Yet, Ronin tend toward the extreme of individualism. The need to be a good team member and the propensity toward individualism make the corporation an excellent opportunity for Ronin to wrestle with the shadows of "meism," opportunism, and glibness. And it is an opportunity to learn to synergize and direct group efforts. Those who succumb to individualism are often ejected from the game not for poor work but for being poor team players and not adhering to the rules of the game. Others who overcompensate by moving too far to the extreme of dependence fail to resolve the paradox because they are slowly seduced into becoming indentured. Loyalty to the team is transformed into seeking approval and acceptance instead of striving for excellence.

The resolution of the paradox is achieved by utilizing the golden mean to determine the excellent action. The middle point between independence and dependence is autonomy and interdependence. Autonomy is different from independence. It means self-directed, whereas independence means not dependent. In day-to-day interactions autonomy is exercised through ongoing choices between being a rebel and standing up for what you believe versus conforming and going along.

The second paradox is the contradiction between assigned project goals and corporate demands that emanate from bureaucracy and politics. Everyone who works in an organization comes up against this contradiction. It is the damned-if-you-do-damned-if-you-don't bind that undermines motivation and contributes to job burnout. This paradox is particularly difficult for Ronin, who are motivated by striving toward the accomplishment of project goals and become agitated when they must be placed second to the Company Way. When this happens, Ronin are tempted to bend the rules and often do.

This paradox is resolved by exercising wisdom. As you recall from Chapter 3, wisdom consists of the interplay between theoretical wisdom and practical wisdom. Theoretical wisdom involves using general knowledge of the situation and its dynamics

to develop a strategy or plan of action. Theoretical wisdom is knowing ways to cause breakthroughs and to open windows in the Company Way, such as redefining goals as compatible, using higher corporate goals to supersede lower ones, going to the meta-level, identifying loopholes, or making an end run. Practical wisdom directs the development of tactics, the practical steps for implementing the plan.

The third paradox Ronin must negotiate is the concurrent pressures to both diversify and specialize. Through the track promotional structure and with job labels, organizations push us into specializing. Yet if we specialize, we simultaneously limit our upward movement, because top-management positions require diversity and broad vision.

> Broad, diversified experience in all the important operations of a company is becoming the primary qualification for upper-level jobs. . . . Your long-range strategy must incorporate lateral moves to get the experience which paves the way upward. For all . . . who have been locked into a narrow corner of their field, the smartest way to promote yourself and your career is to move sideways. . . . The shortest path to the top is not straight up, it is a zigzag field run.
> —Betty Lehan Harragan
> *Games Mother Never Taught You*[14]

The resolution to this paradox is achieved by using nonlinear planning to become a generalist with specialities. Follow the Go strategies of moving indirectly and concentrated dispersion described in Chapter 5.

MANAGING FOR EXCELLENCE

> The inherent preferences of organization are clarity, certainty, and perfection. The inherent nature of human relationships involves ambiguity, uncertainty, and imperfection. How one honors, balances, and integrates the needs of both is the real trick of management.
> —Richard Tanner Pascale and
>   Anthony G. Athos
>   *The Art of Japanese Management*[15]

Managing is a tough job. There are many responsibilities and little training in how to handle them. Obviously, most important is getting the job done—meeting production goals. The manager must build a team and draw cohesiveness and commitment from

CHAIN OF COMMAND: INFORMATION FLOWS DOWN

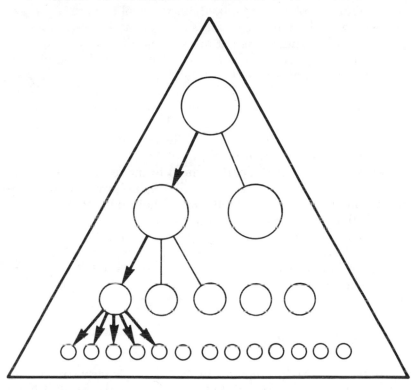

individuals. But building team spirit is not enough. Cooperation is essential to facilitate a productive interfacing of different employees.

Managers are troubleshooters. They are expected to spot problems, make decisions, and implement solutions. This requires information about what's going on. Who knows the nitty-gritty, day-by-day problems of a given job? Those at the top? No, the person doing the job knows more about that job, its problems, and their potential solutions than does anyone else. Think about it. Increasingly, organizations are realizing that employees are an invaluable source of information vital to the survival and profits of the company. Organizational structure provides for the flow of information from the top down through the chain of command, as shown in the accompanying diagram. But the challenge for companies is getting information from the bottom up to the decision makers at the top. Participation—gathering information by encouraging employees to talk about the problems they are experiencing and their ideas for solutions and innovation—is needed. And getting participation is a complex skill.

Trying to compensate, managers will attend workshops where they learn the importance of participation. The next day they go back to their staff and say, "Alright you guys, I want you all to participate!" What happens? Chances are employees clam up, because demanding participation rarely works.

Finally, managers are responsibile for supervision—directing, developing potential, teaching their staffs how to perform better on the job and preparing them to move on to new jobs, controlling, evaluating, giving feedback, helping correct substandard performances, motivating, and helping employees generate enthusiasm and commitment to work.

Concurrent with handling these responsibilities, managers typically have to juggle pressures from above and below in the hierarchy under deadline constraints with a myriad of distractions. The question is how to meet all these responsibility demands.

Feudal Bossing Rituals

Managers have few models for managing excellently. The academic models are just that, too theoretical with too little how-to on the specifics of implementation. Instead, most managers tend to rely on the real-life models around them, the corporate culture, and common sense. Consequently, many struggle with being too nice or too tough. Both approaches are suboptimal.

Nice Guy Boss

From an early age, we were taught to ask others nicely to do things by saying "Please" and to acknowledge appreciation with "Thank you." These rules work well until managerial responsibilities are assumed. Upon becoming managers, we are required to do what we have spent 20, 30, or more years learning not to do! As a manager or the boss, we are expected to direct employees, to tell them what to do. This creates a conflict for bosses that makes directing employees and commenting upon their performance difficult and awkward. Wanting employees to think of them as friends and fearing that they'll be unliked becomes a struggle.

Researchers David C. McClelland and David H. Burnham[16] boldly state, "Good guys make bum bosses." In their intensive study of 49 department heads in large American corporations, they found that nice guy managers, those who were overly concerned with being liked and appearing to be the employee's friends, "get less work out of their people and create lower morale" than did the more directive managers they studied. What is it that nice guy bosses do that lowers morale and producivity? McClelland and Burnham's research indicates that nice guys are wishy-washy. Their directives are vague, confusing, even contradictory. It's just this type of vagueness that is often cited as a major contributing factor to the burnout of motivation. Vague directives can result in an employee working on the wrong task, misunderstood expectations, and confusion about the scope and nature of one's responsibilities. As a result, completing assignments and achieving excellence are more difficult.

Giving feedback is another problem area for nice guy bosses. Just as they resist saying "Do this," nice guys are hesitant to say "You did this wrong," fearing that if they give negative feedback they won't be liked. Consequently their feedback is often confusing or withheld altogether. Employees don't know how they're doing and are deprived of the vital information they need to improve performance. In short, the nice guy's conflict over being a boss creates problems for employees. Nice guy managers tend to forget that implicit in the employment contract is the acceptance of direction and review. It's expected. In fact, successful completion of work tasks is easier when responsibility, expectations, and feedback are clear.

Drill Instructor Boss

Let's look now at the drill instructor boss (DI for short). Whereas the nice guy says, "Would you please do your work?" the drill instructor orders, "Do your work!" Imagine being in a foxhole under fire and hearing the drill instructor say, "Oh, by the way you guys, I think it might be a good idea if you get your heads down." Absurd! We'd be shot. Instead, the drill instructor orders, "Get your heads down," and we obey by dropping down immediately.

Compared to nice guy bosses, drill instructors are effective. Subordinates know what's expected and how they performed. Employees get their heads down, and the job gets done. But the drill instructor boss is far from the most effective kind of manager. Drill instructors are not effective in meeting most of the responsibilities we discussed. The drill instructor model doesn't get participation or gather information; it doesn't develop employee potential, evaluate, or provide feedback; it doesn't promote innovation.

Manager as Coach

> Being part of a team designing a new program for the company can give people a heightened sense of importance and involvement, an experience of creation that punctuates the rest of their ongoing work experience.
> —Rosabeth Moss Kanter
> *The Change Masters*[17]

Traditionally, our concepts of leadership, the chain of command, coordination, control, and functional specialization have followed the military model. Consequently, many managers are constrained by beliefs, assumptions, and perceptions about management that are rooted in the military metaphor. But workers have changed. They know more and expect more. Simultaneously, the nature of work has evolved. There are fewer rote tasks and more jobs requiring judgment, initiative, and creativity. Now with the advent of telecommuting and the electronic cottage, employees will be increasingly working off site, further challenging the old approaches to control and coordination.

We need a new management metaphor, one that allows for more individual creativity and participation. Management is a team activity, and the role of a manager is very similar to that of a coach. The single most important task for a coach is to elicit high performance from the team. Coaches do this in two ways: through training, teaching the skills needed for peak performance, and through motivation, inspiring the players to perform at their peak.

Coaches are both supportive and tough. They pace the team players in small steps to stretch their abilities. People grow by

testing the limits of their abilities against a measure. Coaches
teach players how to set specific performance goals to strive for
and how to use one's last performance as a measure to surpass.
Coaches create an environment in which stretching ability is rewarding. Coaches teach "working for" or achievement motivation. They encourage the players to exert themselves to stretch
to previously undreamed-of heights. Coaches praise progress and
give critical feedback that points out areas for improvement.

CREATE A RACETRACK: An Arena of Competition

Endow work with the characteristics of competitive
sports. And the best way to get that spirit into the workplace is to establish some rules of the game and ways
for employees to measure themselves. Eliciting peak performance means going up against something or some-
body. Let me give you a simple example. For years the
performance of the Intel facilities maintenance group,
which is responsible for keeping our buildings clean and
neat, was mediocre, and no amount of pressure or in-
ducement seemed to do any good. We then initiated a
program in which each building's upkeep was periodically scored by a resident senior manager, dubbed a
"building czar." The score was then compared with those
given the other buildings. The conditions of *all of them*
dramatically improved almost immediately. Nothing else
was done; people did not get more money or other rewards. What they did get was a racetrack, an arena of
competition. If your work is facilities maintenance, having your building receive the top score is a powerful
source of motivation. This is key to the manager's approach and involvement: he has to see the work as it is
seen by the people who do that work every day and create
indicators so that his subordinates can watch their
"racetrack" take shape.

—Andrew S. Grove
High Output Management[18]

The sports metaphor provides for innovation and adaptability.
In any competitive sport, risk is encouraged and periodic failure
expected. In business as in sports, no one wins all the matches.
Winning is a measure of accomplishment. Stretching one's abilities is the real objective.

Coaching with TASC+

> The new leader is a facilitator, not an
> order giver.
>   —John Naisbitt
>   *Megatrends*[19]

The challenge of management is integrating coaching into a tight schedule filled with demands, deadlines, and conflicting personalities. It is one thing to say, "Manage like a coach," and quite another to do so. What exactly do you do and say? And when? What is involved in creating a racetrack, the arena in which your team can productively compete? To answer these questions, we must move from the realm of theory and models to the concrete, how-to steps.

TASC+ is a guide to managing like a coach. It is used out on the daily playing field, where the action is, and not just on the sidelines. TASC+ is designed to be integrated into your ongoing, minute-by-minute interactions with employees. It does not require special meetings or additional contact. TASC+ involves setting goals, giving feedback, eliciting participation, and acknowledging good work—the four promoters of high motivation (see Chapter 2). Let's take a look.

TASC+ stands for *tell* how performance compares with what's expected; *ask* for information; *specify* action or objective; *check* performance; the plus stands for *acknowledge* "on-TASC" performance. TASC+ is flexible and lends itself to individualization. Consequently, it can be used with employees falling anywhere along the directiveness continuum from traditionally directed to autonomous.

Tell. Tell the employee what's expected or the standard. *Tell* provides the target to shoot for, the bull's eye to aim at. But a target alone is not enough. There must also be feedback so that employees know where their arrows are hitting. Thus, to be effective when telling employees what is expected, a manager must add how their performance compares to that expected.

The rule of thumb for *tell* is best illustrated by Sergeant Friday from the TV classic "Dragnet," in which Friday was famous for saying, "I want the facts, Ma'am, nothing but the facts!" Be specific in describing outcomes, such as "a completed design proposal" or "fill out eight forms per hour," or in describing

behaviors, such as "smile and greet customers when they come
to the register."

Avoid such vague guidelines as, "You should be cooperative,"
"Be friendly to customers," or "We expect you to show initiative." The meaning of vague words varies too much to know
precisely what is expected or where one stands. In addition,
strive to be objective by avoiding judgmental and emotional
statements, such as, "You look pretty sloppy," or "This is a half-
assed job." Such descriptions convey disapproval but little concrete information about what's wrong. Such poorly stated *tells*
are guaranteed to derail communication by putting people on the
defensive. Be concise. Don't ramble, repeat, or go on tangents
in which the essential message gets lost in a barrage of verbiage
that feels like a harangue. And avoid clouding the issue by justifying, defending, or apologizing. Justifying gains little and encourages arguments and attacks.

Describe one situation or one comparison to the standard at
a time. Don't piggyback with "and another thing . . . ." which
can overload and come across as a harangue. When there is no
comparison performance, simply describe the situation or expectation, following the principle of "Just the facts, Ma'am, nothing but the facts."

Ask. The single most common error managers make is to jump
to conclusions instead of asking for information. It's easy to get
into a habit of telling, telling, telling and forget that the employee
is the most valuable source of information about what is going
on with that job. It is up to the manager to tap that information.

Asking is the tool for getting information and eliciting participation. When you ask a question, pressure is put on the employee to answer. This is what's meant by "eliciting participation." By then responding thoughtfully to the employee's
answer, you actively encourage further participation.

Asking questions is also an ideal tool for developing employee
potential. Developing potential means teaching employees
skills. The Socratic method, teaching by asking questions, is considered one of the best ways to facilitate learning. For example,
if I ask you a question, does it mean I don't know the answer?
What is the reason for my asking the question? I ask because the
question makes you think. In the process, you learn and retain.

But to be effective, questions must be well phrased. Probe
with open questions that begin with "what," "when," "where,"
"how," "who," "in what way," "in which way," "under what

conditions," and avoid questions beginning with "why." Why
questions tend to put employees on the defensive, eliciting jus-
tifications and excuses instead of facts. Likewise, avoid closed
questions that can be answered with yes or no, such as, "Do you
. . .?" "Can't you . . .?" "Will you . . .?" Closed questions are
insidious because they encourage you to leap to conclusions and
to talk excessively—two communication roadblocks. Closed
questions are appropriate for prosecuting but not for gathering
good information.

Another danger of closed questions is that they are almost
always leading questions that imply the answer you expect. What
does a boss who asks "Are you looking for responsibility?" probably expect to hear? Responsibility, right? What if the boss asks,
"How do you feel about responsibility?" Although this question
is open ended, it is still leading. Compare it to "What are you
looking for?" which contains no content that suggests what the
boss thinks the person ought to be looking for. Leading questions
curtail problem solving by narrowing the focus of discussion to
what is suggested in the question.

Some examples of poor and better questions are listed below:

Poor	Better
"Did the machine give you trouble?"	"What happened?" "What gave you trouble?"
"Does the noise bother you?"	"What bothers you about this?"
"Would better directions from me help?"	"What would help?" "How can I help?"
"Are you looking for responsibility?"	"What are you looking for?"
"Do you have any questions?"	"What questions do you have?"
"Do you have any suggestions?"	"What suggestions do you have?"
"Do you think you could keep me informed with a weekly memo?"	"How can you keep me informed?"
"Why were you late?"	"What happened?" "What delayed your getting here?"
"Why did you do that?"	"What happened?" "What was the reason for doing that?"

"Do you want to get ahead?"	"What do you want?"
"Are you nervous?"	"How do you feel?"
"You're upset, aren't you?"	"How do you feel?"
"Do you think you can get this done today?"	"What can you do to get this done today?"
"Do you think you can be on time tomorrow?"	"What will help you be on time tomorrow?"
"Does the valve need to be replaced, or is it the regulator?"	"What's the problem with this?" "What caused the malfunction?"

Don't race through the *ask* step. Instead, ask enough questions to get all the relevant information. This is important. And keep an open mind. Consider everything said, otherwise employees will clam up, cutting you off from needed information. Instead, listen and ask more questions. Remember, listening is not agreeing, but it is essential for considering.

Use active listening. That is, act in such a way as to communicate, "I am listening; I want to hear what you have to say." Use body language, such as eye contact, nodding, or leaning forward. Don't rifle through papers, or let the phone or others interrupt. Finally, ask for suggestions. Remember, the person doing the job knows more about what's happening vis-à-vis that job than you do. The coaching manager's challenge is to get employees to solve problems pertaining to their work. When you stop trying to solve employees' problems for them, a tremendous burden is removed from your shoulders. You don't have to have all the answers! So ask for suggestions.

Of course, not every suggestion is a good one. Some may be unfeasible or even off the wall. Generally, there are three situations in which unacceptable suggestions are given. The employee may be trying to sabotage you by deliberately offering an unacceptable suggestion. If you respond with something like "Come on, be serious! I want a suggestion that will work," you're likely to get the retort "I knew you wouldn't listen, so why bother!" Other times the employee is naive, not realizing that the suggestion is unworkable. If the suggestion is discounted without consideration, the employee will probably feel foolish and clam up. Finally, the suggestion may actually be a good one and it is *you* who can't see its creativity! Here the employee probably considers you closed minded, even rigid.

How can these pitfalls be avoided? Instead of discounting unfeasible suggestions, ask a question designed to reveal the flaws. "How would that work?" "How would you get that funded?" "How would you get that by JB?" If the suggestion was meant to sabotage, the bomb is in the saboteur's lap. Naive employees, on the other hand, don't feel put down. Instead, when attempting to answer, they discover what's wrong with the suggestion. When the suggestion is a creative one, the employee has an opportunity to argue its creative aspects, and you can evaluate it without looking old-fashioned or closed minded.

Specify. In the *specify* step, information and suggestions gathered during *ask* are translated into a plan of action. It's vital that the action be described in specific terms. Indicate who will do what, under what conditions, and to what extent (how long, how many, how fast, to what degree). Vaguely stated plans lead to problems of interpretation and accountability. For example, "Try to work harder" puts on pressure but doesn't say what is regarded as harder work. Does hard work mean to write longer reports, or to put in overtime, or to speak up in meetings? A vague *specify* can point the employee in the wrong direction.

Concentrate on short-term steps to handling the situation or meeting the expectation described in *tell.* Focus on what will be completed or performed today or this week. Use small, specific step to help employees pace themselves in accomplishing long-term goals. A side benefit is that, in the process of working out the small steps, employees learn how to break distant goals into discrete, doable steps to be taken today. As a result, self-starting and follow-up skills are enhanced.

A well-stated *specify* helps accountability. A coach wouldn't say, "Try to run faster." The coach would add a concrete measure to the objective, "This time strive to make the run in 2 minutes 15 seconds." Likewise, "Increase your speed from seven forms completed per hour to eight" is better than "Work faster this week," because it is easy to determine when the objective has been met. Here is the step in which you create an arena of competition. Instead of plodding along with no markers of accomplishment, the measure makes the evaluation of progress possible. An objective just a small step away encourages stretching. *Specifies* that have no concrete measure deprive the employee of essential performance feedback. Once again, it is much like asking the archer to improve shooting, but providing no specific target and not telling him where the last arrow fell. Under such conditions, performance rarely improves and motivation rapidly evaporates. Use quantitative terms because they provide an observable measure of accomplishment. Both you and the employee can tell when performance is "on-TASC."

When the plan of action pertains to a particular behavior or performance, describe it in terms of its *doing*—of specific actions. If a screenwriter, for example, described a character as "acting nervous," director and actor might have conflicting intrepretations of how to act the scene. To minimize this problem, scripts describe characters' action on the *doing* level: "He paced back and forth, frowning and wringing his hands frantically." Describe the small step specifically enough to give the person a picture of what he is to do. Instead of "Be more friendly to customers," say "Greet customers with a smile as they enter the shop and ask if you may assist them." Describe what is wanted rather than what is wrong. "Don't announce it before checking with me," becomes "Check with me before announcing it."

Negotiating the plan and its details with the employees is better than directing them. You have an opportunity to draw upon the employees' experience and knowledge as well as encouraging their commitment. Additionally, this is your opportunity to teach employees to self-start and take more initiative. In early uses of TASC+, you assume most of the responsibility for working out the details of *specify*. Keep in mind that you are simultaneously teaching the employees how to *specify*. Gradually shift to using more questions and thereby guide the employees in specifying their own small steps.

Check Performance. Visualize the coach standing on the sidelines, stopwatch in hand, checking the runner's speed. Checking is the manager's responsibility. Frequent checking allows quick action at the first sign of trouble, before a serious problem develops. And it makes the manager accessible for questions and guidance. Sometimes *check* is called "management by walking around." Check at different times. Avoid making a rigid routine, such as dropping by every afternoon at 3:00 to count the output, which encourages employees to look good at those times.

When possible, use charts and graphs. They are welcome additions to any arena of competition. Posting performance graphs can motivate in a number of ways. High performers are obvious, and others become aware of these superior performances. Average and poorer performers learn how they stand relative to others, making realistic goals easier to define. And posted charts increase peer acknowledgment, thus removing from the supervisor the burden of being the sole source of acknowledgment. Posting the performance of individual players highlights individual contributions and stimulates intragroup competition. It's often used effectively with sales, for example. To solidify the team, on the other hand, it is more effective to post group performance charts. This stimulates intergroup competition.

But to be charted, the outcome or performance must be clearly defined. Even if you don't use charts, the ability to do so is a good measure of the strength and probable success of the small action step.

Encourage self-charting in which employees rate and record their own performance. Self-charting stimulates players in any game to compete with their own previous performances. It is a powerful motivator for stretching. When employees chart their own performances over several days or weeks, patterns emerge and progress becomes evident. Research has indicated that when companies implement self-charting, performance of the variable charted improves dramatically. Self-charting also provides immediate feedback, which encourages self-acknowledgment for "on-TASC" performance and stimulates correction of drops of output.

Acknowledge. Many people believe that money is the most powerful reward for good work. Actually, the most potent, consistently available reinforcer is attention. Wanting to be acknowledged is universal. In fact, a strong argument could be made that promotions, raises, and perks are reinforcing because they are symbols of acknowledgment. We use them as concrete measures of our ability. Yet, it is easy for managers to get caught up in daily demands and become stingy in giving positive attention.

Giving attention doesn't take long. In fact, whenever interacting with others, we constantly give and withhold attention, usually without much deliberate thought. And because we don't think about it, it is easy to get caught up in paying too much attention to the actions we don't want repeated instead of those we do. For example, it is easy to snap at late employees while ignoring those who are on time or to criticize poor performers while ignoring those who live up to our expectations. Coaches, on the other hand, realize that acknowledgment is a critical step in training and motivation.

Directly acknowledge on-TASC performance by commenting on specific actions. Avoid vague superlatives. "Good job!" gives little feedback. Don't fall into a routine of mindlessly saying "Thank you." It's too easy to do this without giving genuine attention. Comments pointing out specific actions are far more effective. "This report is thoroughly researched and well presented" is far more effective than "Good report. Thanks."

Tailor acknowledgments to the individual. Use the employees' metaphors, and speak in terms of their issues. For example, if an employee is ambitious, a comment such as "That's the kind of idea that'll help you get ahead around here" can be highly reinforcing. To a more socially oriented employee, "You've done a lot to improve communications" would probably be more effective. Focus on on-TASC performance by paying attention to ways in which the person is performing as desired. Pay attention to on-TASC actions, those that move toward accomplishing the plan of action negotiated in *specify*. Vary when, how often, and what actions you acknowledge. Anything that becomes routine is soon discounted. But worse, when following a routine, we tend to stop paying attention. Give acknowledgment publicly. Having work acknowledged in front of others (also in newsletters, on plaques, and so forth) can be very rewarding to employees. Harness peer pressure and peer attention in the service of on-TASC performance. Encourage employees to acknowledge and reinforce each another. Peer acknowledgment removes the manager's burden of always having to be there and helps encourage team spirit and a strong social support system. Likewise, encourage self-acknowledgment, the cornerstone of high self-esteem. It helps people get through attention dry spells. And knowing how to acknowledge oneself is essential for self-starting and self-directing.

On following page is a recap of guidelines for TASC+ performance.

Managing Ronin

Managing Ronin sounds, at first, like a contradiction. Ronin seem so independent and even headstrong. And, indeed, traditionally Ronin have collided with both nice guy and drill instructor bosses because their self-starting style disrupted the established way of doing things and threatened managerial control. The trick is to give them free rein while guiding the thrust of their work. TASC+ provides a means of resolving this paradox.

With TASC+, autonomous employees take the lead in setting their goals and in working out and implementing their action

Do	**Don't**
Tell	
Describe what the person is doing.	Infer motives or feelings.
Be specific and concrete.	Be abstract and general.
Be objective.	Be judgmental.
Use performance indicators (quantitative words).	Use absolutes: always/never.
Describe one standard or expectation at a time.	Describe more than one standard or expectation at a time.
Be concise.	Ramble, repeat, go off on tangents.
State facts.	Justify, defend, apologize.
Ask	
Use open-ended questions.	Ask leading or closed (yes/no) questions.
Seek facts.	Ask "why" questions.
Get all relevant information.	Jump to conclusions.
Keep an open mind.	Argue.
Use active listening.	Be impatient or distracted.
Ask for suggestions.	Tell or judge.
Specify	
Be specific.	Be vague.
State what is wanted.	Say only what is wrong.
Negotiate with employee.	Tell employee.
Check	
Vary when and how much.	Check by routine schedule.
Use charts/graphs, including self-charts, if feasible.	Ignore charts/graphs.
Acknowledge	
Tailor to the individual.	Use platitudes or generalities.
Focus on on-TASC performance.	Acknowledge irrelevant performance.
Acknowledge following performance.	Acknowledge before performance.
Vary.	Always say or do the same thing.
Acknowledge publicly.	
Encourage peer acknowledgment and self-acknowledgment.	

steps while the manager checks the direction of their work and the progress of its delivery. In this way, managers translate Ronin creativity into on-the-job applications and harness their autonomy into the service of innovation.

Remember, you are a coach and your job is to move your team to peak performance. With Ronin, the first objective is to help them become good team players: to coach and guide them in the rules of the game and reward them for throwing the ball to other players.

But not all employees are Ronin. You must create an environment in which people who may be vastly different from one another will cooperate in playing ball. Some of your staff may prefer strong direction and to avoid decision making and change. Most are probably somewhere in between the Ronin and the career feudalist, struggling with conflicts arising from being an individual in the organizational world.

TASC+ is a tool managers can use to coach employees with dramatically different styles. It provides a structured yet flexible way to guide the work without making Ronin feel encumbered. Simultaneously, TASC+ provides a process for keeping informed and for overseeing autonomous employees' work. TASC+ takes maximum advantage of self-starting skills and employee creativity, and provides a way of eliciting participation while focusing on problem solving. At the same time, TASC+ can be adjusted to employees who require much more direction than do corporate Ronin. TASC+ guides managers in being more active during *specify* with employees lacking self-directive skills. By asking questions and breaking goals into action steps, TASC+ provides a way to help these employees develop problem-solving and self-directing skills. Begin by being directive during *specify*, and over time guide employees in taking more active roles in shaping their project goals and accompanying small steps.

> Some researchers . . . argue that there is a fundamental variable that tells you what the best management style is in a particular situation. That variable is the task-relevant maturity (TRM) of the subordinates, which is a combination of the degree of their achievement orientation and readiness to take responsibility, as well as their education, training, and experience. . . . Varying man-

agement styles are needed as task-relevant maturity varies. Specifically, when the TRM is low, the most effective approach is one that offers very precise and detailed instructions, wherein the supervisor tells the subordinate what needs to be done, when and how: . . . a highly structured approach. As the TRM of the subordinate grows, the most effective style moves from the structured to one more given to communication, emotional support, and encouragement, in which the manager pays more attention to the subordinate as an individual than to the task at hand. As the TRM becomes even greater, the effective management style changes again. Here the manager's involvement should be kept to a minimum, and should primarily consist of making sure that the objectives toward which the subordinate is working are mutually agreed upon.

—Andrew S. Grove
High Output Management[20]

CORPORATE RONIN AND COMPANY PROFITS

Ronin contribute to company profits in three ways: productivity, innovation, and adaptability. Being self-starters and working for goals they have defined, autonomous employees offer a high productivity potential. This potential can translate into company profits if their greater motivation is harnessed and directed with the proper management strategy.

The second way Ronin contribute to profits is through innovation. Their diversified experience combined with strategic thinking increases innovative breakthroughs, such as the discovery of profitable loopholes.

The third way Ronin contribute to company profits is through adaptability, being able to respond creatively to changes in technology and the marketplace. Their diversified experience and transferable skills enable them to assume a variety of roles as needed, and their creativity encourages finding workable alternatives.

The potential exists for an American corporate Renaissance, with its implied return to greatness. Because recent economic conditions have been so unfavorable for

American business, leaders should be motivated to
search for new solutions—and to engage their entire
work force in the search. I argue that innovation is the key.
Individuals can make a difference, but they need the tools
and the opportunity to use them. They need to work in
settings where they are valued and supported, their intelligence given a chance to blossom. They need to have
the power to be able to take the initiative to innovate.

—Rosabeth Moss Kanter
The Change Masters[21]

In times of transition, a Ronin archetype appears as part of
the ongoing cycle of stagnation and rebirth. With the Ronin lies
hope for a corporate Renaissance, because they have the potential to stimulate innovation and revitalize the corporation. Har-
nessing this potential is the challenge managers face.

Many of the factors that have been stifling productivity and
job satisfaction are being superseded by new structures. Confusion and uncertainty will inevitably accompany this transition.
As Naisbitt, author of *Megatrends*, said, this is a yeasty time—
the time of the parenthesis. For Ronin, it is a time of exciting
possibilities—a time of adventure.

Notes

1. *The Change Masters: Innovation for Productivity in the American
    Corporation* (New York: Simon & Schuster, 1983), p. 65. © 1983
    by Rosabeth Moss Kanter.
2. Ibid., p. 40.
3. *In Search of Excellence: Lessons from America's Best-Run Com-
    panies* (New York: Harper & Row, 1982).
4. p. 180.
5. *The Change Masters.*
6. *The Mind of the Strategist: The Art of Japanese Business* (New
    York: McGraw-Hill, 1982), p. 5.
7. p. 200.
8. The Foresight Group is pioneering this model in its intrapreneur-
    ing school. For information, contact Gustaf Delin, Fram-Gruppen,
    Grufkontoret Persberg, 632 00 Filipstad, Sweden.
9. New York: AMACOM, 1974, p. 94.
10. New York: AMACOM, 1974, pp. 6–7.
11. p. 4.

12. p. 219.
13. pp. 99–100.
14. *Games Mother Never Taught You: Corporate Gamesmanship for Women* (New York: Warner Books, 1977), p. 169.
15. *The Art of Japanese Management: Applications for American Executives* (New York: Simon & Schuster, 1981), p. 105.
16. "Good Guys Make Bum Bosses," *Psychology Today*, December 1975, pp. 69–70.
17. p. 369.
18. New York: Random House, 1983, p. 170.
19. *Megatrends: Ten New Directions Transforming Our Lives* (New York: Warner Books, 1982), p. 188.
20. New York, Random House, 1983, p. 174.
21. p. 370.

Suggested Readings

Alter, JoAnne, *A Part-Time Career for a Full-Time You*. Houghton Mifflin, Boston: 1980.

Applegath, John, *Working Free: Practical Alternatives to the 9 to 5 Job*. New York: AMACOM, 1982.

Arbose, Jules R., ed., "Intrapreneurship: Holding on to People with Ideas," *International Management*, March 1982.

Aristotle, *The Ethics of Aristotle: The Nicomachean Ethics*, translated by J. A. K. Thomas. London: Penguin Classics, 1953.

Blank, Raymond, *Playing the Game: Strategies for Your Career*. New York: Ace Business Library, 1981.

Bolles, Richard, *What Color Is Your Parachute?* Berkeley, Calif.: Ten Speed Press, 1978.

Brown, Paul L., *Managing Behavior on the Job*. New York: Wiley, 1982.

Browne, Harry, *How I Found Freedom in an Unfree World*. New York: Avon, 1973.

Caple, John, *Careercycles: A Guidebook to Success in the Passages of Your Work Life*. Englewood Cliffs, N.J.: Spectrum, 1983.

Castaneda, Carlos, *The Second Ring of Power*. New York: Simon & Schuster, 1977.

_____, *The Teachings of Don Juan: A Yaqui Way of Knowledge*. New York: Pocket Books, 1974.

Chapman, Elwood N., *Scrambling: Zig-Zagging Your Way to the Top*. Los Angeles: Tarcher, 1981.

Connellan, Thomas K., *How to Improve Human Performance: Behaviorism in Business and Industry*. New York: Harper & Row, 1978.

Copulsky, William, and Herbert W. McNulty, *Entrepreneurship and the Corporation*. New York: AMACOM, 1974.

Delin, Gustaf, and The Foresight Group, *Intrapreneurship: An Opportunity for Business Development in Large Corporations*. Corporation for Enterprise Development (2420 K Street NW, Washington, D.C. 20037), 1981.

De Ropp, Robert S., *The Master Game: Beyond the Drug Experience*. New York: Delta Books, 1968.

———, *Warrior's Way: The Challenging Life Games*. New York: Delta/Seymour Lawrence, 1979.

Dyer, Wayne, *Pulling Your Own Strings*. New York: Crowell, 1978.

Edelwich, Jerry, and Archie Brodsky, *Burn-Out: Stages of Disillusionment in the Helping Profession*. New York: Human Sciences Press, 1980.

Ellis, Albert, and William Knaus, *Overcoming Procrastination*. New York: Signet, 1977.

Farber, Jerry, *The Student as Nigger*. New York: Pocket Books, 1970.

Ferguson, Marilyn, *The Aquarian Conspiracy: Personal and Social Transformation in the 1980s*. Los Angeles: Tarcher, 1980.

Freudenberger, Herbert J., *Burn-Out: The High Cost of High Achievement*. New York: Anchor Press, 1980.

Gardner, John W., *Self-Renewal: The Individual and the Innovative Society*. New York: Colophon Books, 1965.

Grove, Andrew S., *High Output Management*. New York: Random House, 1983.

Harragan, Betty Lehan, *Games Mother Never Taught You: Corporate Gamesmanship for Women*. New York: Warner, 1977.

Hegarty, Christopher, *How to Manage Your Boss*. Mill Valley, Calif.: Whatever Publishing, 1982.

Herrigel, Eugen, *Zen in the Art of Archery*. New York: Vintage, 1953.

Hewes, Jeremy Joan, *Worksteads: Living and Working in the Same Place*. Garden City, N.Y.: Dolphin/Doubleday, 1981.

"Intrapreneurial Now," *The Economist*, April 17, 1982, pp. 48–52.

Jacobs, Dorri, *Change: How to Live with, Manage, Create and Enjoy It*. New York: Dorri Jacobs, 1981.

Johnson, Warren, *Muddling Toward Frugality*. San Francisco: Sierra Club Books, 1978.

Kanter, Rosabeth Moss, *Men and Women of the Corporation*. New York: Basic Books, 1977.

———, *The Change Masters: Innovation for Productivity in the American Corporation*. New York: Simon & Schuster, 1983.

Kennedy, Marilyn Moata, *Career Knockouts: How to Battle Back*. New York: Warner Books, 1980.

Keyes, Ken, *Handbook to Higher Consciousness: The Science of Happiness*. St. Mary, Ky.: Living Love Publications, 1975.

Korda, Michael, *Power! How to Get It, How to Use It*. New York: Random House, 1973.

Lefkowitz, Bernard, *Breaktime: Living without Work in a Nine-to-Five World*. New York: Penguin, 1979.

Losoncy, Lewis, *Turning People On: How to Be an Encouraging Person*, Englewood Cliffs, N.J.: Prentice-Hall, 1977.

McGill, Michael E., *The 40 to 60 Year Old Male*. New York: Fireside, 1980.

McMurry, Robert N., *The Maverick Executive*. New York: AMA-COM, 1974.

Mandino, Og, *University of Success*. New York: Bantam, 1982.

Masada, Yonji, *The Information Society of Postindustrial Society*. Tokyo: World of Future, 1980.

Mayer, Nancy, *The Male Mid-Life Crisis: Fresh Starts After 40*. New York: New American Library, 1978.

Michelezzi, Betty, *Coming Alive from Nine to Five: The Career Search Handbook*. Palo Alto, Calif.: Mayfield Publishing, 1980.

Musashi, Miyamoto, *The Book of Five Rings*. New York: Bantam, 1982.

Naisbitt, John, *Megatrends: Ten New Directions Transforming Our Lives*. New York: Warner Books, 1982.

Newman, James, *Release Your Brakes*. New York: Warner Books, 1977.

O'Connell, Sandra E., *The Manager as Communicator*. New York: Harper & Row, 1979.

Ohmae, Kenichi, *The Mind of the Strategist: The Art of Japanese Business*. New York: McGraw-Hill, 1982.

Pascale, Richard Tanner, and Anthony E. Athos, *The Art of Japanese Management: Applications for American Executives*. New York: Simon & Schuster, 1981.

Pearce, Joseph Chilton, *The Crack in the Cosmic Egg: Challenging Constructs of Mind and Reality*. New York: Pocket Books, 1974.

Pelletier, Kenneth, *Mind as Healer; Mind as Slayer: A Holistic Approach to Preventing Stress Disorders*. New York: Delta Books, 1977.

Peters, Thomas J., and Robert H. Waterman, Jr., *In Search of Excellence: Lessons from America's Best-Run Companies*. New York: Harper & Row, 1982.

Pines, M., Elliot Aronson, and Ditsa Kafry, *Burnout: From Tedium to Personal Growth*. New York: The Free Press, 1981.

Pirsig, Robert M., *Zen and the Art of Motorcycle Maintenance: An Inquiry into Values*. New York: Bantam, 1975.

Potter, Beverly A., *Beating Job Burnout*. New York: Ace Business Library, 1982.

_____, *Changing Performance on the Job: Behavioral Techniques for Managers*. New York: AMACOM, 1984.

_____, *Turning Around: Keys to Motivation and Productivity*. Berkeley, Calif.: Ronin Publishing, 1983.

Ratti, Oscar, and Adele Westbrook, *Secrets of the Samurai: A Survey of the Martial Arts of Feudal Japan*. Rutland, Vt.: Tuttle, 1973.

Reps, Paul, *Zen Flesh, Zen Bones: A Collection of Zen and Pre-Zen Writings*. New York: Doubleday Anchor Books.

Riesman, David, *The Lonely Crowd*. New Haven: Yale University Press, 1969.

Rifkin, Jeremy, *Entropy: A New World View*. New York: Bantam, 1981.

Ronco, William C., *Jobs: How People Create Their Own*. Boston: Beacon Press, 1977.

Rosen, Gerald M., *The Relaxation Book: An Illustrated Self-Help Program*. Englewood Cliffs, N.J.: Prentice-Hall, 1977.

Rosenthal, Ed, and Ron Lichty, *132 Ways to Earn a Living Without Working (For Someone Else)*. New York: St. Martin's Press, 1978.

Sarason, Seymour B., *Work, Aging, and Social Change: Professionals and the One-Life-One-Career Imperative*. New York: The Free Press, 1977.

Scheele, Adele M., *Skills for Success: A Guide to the Top*. Los Angeles: Morrow, 1979.

Schumacker, E. F., *Good Work*. New York: Harper Colophon, 1979.

Scott, William, and David Hart, *Organizational America*. Boston: Houghton Mifflin, 1980.

Seligman, Martin E. P., *Helplessness: On Depression, Development, and Death*. San Francisco: Freeman, 1975.

Shapiro, Deane H., *Precision Nirvana*. Englewood Cliffs, N.J.: Spectrum Books, 1978.

Sheehy, Gail, *Passages: Predictable Crises of Adult Life*. New York: Bantam, 1977.

_____, *Pathfinders: Overcoming the Crises of Adult Life and Finding Your Own Path to Well-Being*. New York: Bantam, 1982.

Siu, R. G. H., *The Craft of Power*. New York: Wiley, 1979.

Toffler, Alvin, *Future Shock*. New York: Random House, 1970.

_____, *The Eco-Spasm Report*. New York: Bantam, 1975.

_____, *The Third Wave*. New York: Bantam, 1980.

Vennga, Robert L., and James P. Spradley, *The Work Stress Connection*. New York: Ballantine/Self-Help, 1981.

Watson, David, and Roland Tharp, *Self-Directed Behavior: Self-Modification for Personal Adjustment*. Monterey, Calif.: Brooks/Cole, 1972.

Weaver, Peter, *You, Inc.: A Detailed Escape Route to Being Your Own Boss*. New York: Dolphin, 1975.

Wilson, John Oliver, *After Affluence: Economics to Meet Human Needs*. New York: Harper & Row, 1980.

Yankelovich, Daniel, *New Rules: Searching for Self-Fulfillment in a World Turned Upside Down*. New York: Bantam, 1982.

Zukav, Gary, *The Dancing Wu Li Masters: An Overview of the New Physics*. New York: Bantam, 1979.

Index

Act of Will, The (Assigioli), 112
After Affluence (Wilson), 88
American Society for Training
    and Development (ASTD),
    148
*Aquarian Conspiracy: Personal
    and Social Transformation
    in the 1980's, The*
    (Ferguson), 183
Archimedes, 69
Aristotle, 74
    on ethics, 66–67
    on freedom, 73
    on goodness, 68–69
*Art of Japanese Management,
    The* (Pascale and Athos), 198
Assigioli, Robert, 112
Athos, Anthony, 198
autonomous-directed person, 65–
    66

baby-boom generation
    expectations of, 1, 6–7
    underemployment of, 123
Bateson, Gregory, 124–125
Beating Job Burnout (Potter), 42,
    108, 125
Bolles, Richard, 106, 108, 113
Book of Five Rings, The
    (Musashi), 24
*Book: On the Taboo Against
    Knowing Who You Are, The*
    (Watts), 182
Bridges, William, 138
Bright, Louis, 84
Browne, Harry, 72, 138, 144
Brunton, Paul, 100, 166

budo, 61
bujutsu, 60
bureaucracy, 32–33
Burnham, David, 201
*Bushido: The Way of the
    Samurai* (Yamamoto), 156

Camus, Albert, 31
capital-intensive industries, 16
Castaneda, Carlos, 25, 68, 78, 80,
    83, 110, 161, 168, 183
causality, and motivation, 42–45
Cavafy, C. P., 26, 95
Change Masters, The (Kanter),
    186, 188–189, 193–194, 202,
    215
*Character and Social Structure:
    The Psychology of Social
    Institutions* (Gerth and
    Mills), 83, 84
*Coming Alive from Nine to Five:
    The Career Search
    Handbook* (Michelezzi), 108
complacency, as enemy of Ronin,
    80–81
composite careers, 138–139
computer technology, 18–20
concentrated dispersion, 132–139
confidence, as enemy of Ronin,
    79
Copulsky, William, 191
Craft of Power, The (Siu), 133,
    146, 150

decentralization of the
    workplace, 16

demotivating work situations,
  46–53
De Vichy-Chamrond, Marie, 93
de Vries, Manfred Kets, 36
diversity
  in attitudes toward work, 3
  in the workplace, 16
Don Juan, *see* Castaneda, Carlos
Dyer, Wayne W., 92

EAR (event, appraisal, response),
  168
economy, U.S.
  sluggish, 6–8
  uncertain, 123
Eco-Spasm Report, The (Toffler),
  18
electronic cottage, 21–22
empowerment of employees, 53–
  57
energy crisis
  nonrenewable resources in,
    15–16
  results of, 17
*Entrepreneurship and the
  Corporation* (Copulsky and
  McNulty), 191
Even Cowgirls Get the Blues
  (Robbins), 27

Farber, Jerry, 83–84, 85
fear, as enemy of Ronin, 77–79
Ferguson, Marilyn, 183
feudalism, career
  adverse effects of, 5, 32, 37–38,
    46, 50, 53
  characteristics of, 15, 18, 31–34
  innovations in, 188
  schooling and, 43–44
feudalists, career, 59
flexibility
  in workplace, 16, 20
  yearnings for, 3–4
  see also versatility, of Ronin
Fruedenberger, Herbert, 50

Fuller, Buckminster, 154
Future Shock (Toffler), 19–20,
  33, 65

*Games Mother Never Taught
  You* (Harragan), 198
Gardner, John, 15
Gerth, Hans, 83, 84
Go, Chinese game of, and career
  strategy, 125–127, 136, 140,
  146, 198

Harragan, Betty L., 13, 198
Hart, David, 12, 14, 83
Herrigel, Eugene, 177
Herrman, Ned, 173
Hewes, Jeremy J., 22
hierarchical structures in
  organizations, 15, 18, 31–34
High Output Management
  (Grove), 203
hobbit fantasy tales, 77–78
Howard, John, 36
*How I Found Freedom in an
  Unfree World* (Browne), 138,
  144

information era, 123
innovation, 192–194, 214–215
  discouragement of, 187–191
In Search of Excellence (Peters
  and Waterman), 187, 190
"intrapreneuring," 190–191

Jennings, William D., 76, 153
job burnout, 38–40, 123–125,
  176
Johnson, Warren, 16
Journey to Ixtlan (Castaneda),
  183
jujitsu, 181
jutsu, 60

Kanter, Rosabeth M.
  on belonging to a team, 202

on innovation, 193–194, 215
on mastering change, 188–189
on opportunity structure, 8–9
Kesey, Ken, 37
*Knowing the Score: Play-by-Play
   Directions for Women on the
   Job* (Harragan), 13
Korda, Michael, 131, 139

labor-intensive industries, 16
ladder, corporate, bypassing,
   131–132
   see also linear career
Lennon, John, 84
Lichty, Ron, 4, 107
linear career
   midlife crisis in, 57–59
   path of, 1–2, 5
   strategy of, 2, 11, 17, 35, 123
   track of, 17, 32
linear careerists, 25–27
Lombardo, Michael M., 135
Lonely Crowd, The (Riesman),
   61

management
   general techniques for, 198–
      212
   of others, 50–52
   of Ronin, 211–214
   of self, 92–100
Many Dimensional Man (Ogilvy),
   73
Masada, Yonji, 65
"Matching Personal and Job
   Characteristics" (U.S.
   government publication), 107
Maverick Executive, The
   (McMurry), 191
McCall, Morgan W., Jr., 135
McClelland, David, 201
McMurry, Robert N., 191
McNulty, Herbert W., 191
Megatrends (Naisbitt), 1, 21, 133,
   143, 204

Michelezzi, Betty, 108
midlife crisis, 57–59
Mills, C. Wright, 83, 84
Mind of the Strategist, The
   (Ohmae), 189, 192
mobility tracks, 7–9
Moshe, 157
Mother Theresa, 176
motivation
   causality and, 42–45
   demotivation situations and,
      46–53
   empowerment of employees
      and, 53–57
   of self, 92–100
Musashi, Miyamoto, 24

Naisbitt, John, 1, 21, 133, 143,
   204
National Speakers Association,
   148
networking, 149–152
Network Revolution, The
   (Vallee), 21
networks, affect of
   computerization on, 18–20
Newman, James, 162
New Rules (Yankelovich), 7
Nicomachean Ethics, The
   (Aristotle), 66

"Occupational Outlook
   Handbook, The" (U.S.
   government publication), 107
Occupational Temperament
   Inventory, 102–105
Ogilvy, James, 73
Ohmae, Kenichi, 189, 192
*One Flew Over the Cuckoo's
   Nest* (Kesey), 37–38
*132 Ways to Earn a Living
   Without Working (For
   Someone Else)* (Rosenthal
   and Lichty), 4, 107

*Oppressed Middle: Politics of
  Middle Management, The*
  (Shorris), 14
Organizational America (Scott
  and Hart), 12, 83
Organization Man, The (Whyte),
  11
organizations
  bureaucracy in, 15
  control in, 11–13
  discouragement of innovation
    in, 187–191
  totalitarian threat of, 11, 14, 17,
    22
  understaffed, 127–130
other-directed person, 64–65
  see also self-direction
overspecialization, 17

Palladin, 24, 90
Pascale, Richard T., 198
Pearce, Joseph C., 175
Peters, Thomas J., 38, 187, 190
Potter, Beverly A., 42, 108, 125
power
  as enemy of Ronin, 79–80
  methods of, 118–119
*Power: How to Get It, How to
  Use It* (Korda), 131, 139
Precision Nirvana (Shapiro), 174
product analysis, 141–145
Pulling Your Own Strings
  (Dyer), 92

Ratti, Oscar, 61, 123, 180
Reed, William, 19
Release Your Brakes (Newman),
  162
Riesman, David, 61
Rifkin, Jeremy, 16
Robbins, Tom, 27
Ronin
  career path of, 59, 127, 183
  change and, 22–27, 156–157
  contributions to corporations
    by, 28, 192–198, 211–215

five enemies of, 76–83
personal power of, 117
self-direction of, 34, 44, 65–66,
  196
striving for excellence as, 176
thought control of, 55
versatility of, 92, 124, 135–136,
  192
Way of the, 70, 73, 76, 79–80,
  194
Zen, discipline of, and, 55
Ronin, The (Jennings), 76, 153
Rosenthal, Ed, 4, 107

samurai, 92
schooling
  career feudalism and, 43–44
  description of, 83–88
Schrodinger, Erwin, 177
Scott, William, 12, 14, 83
Second Ring of Power, The
  (Castaneda), 83
Secret Path, The (Brunton), 110,
  166
Secrets of the Samurai (Ratti and
  Westbrook), 61, 123, 180
self-acknowledgment, 95
self-direction, 61–64
  autonomous, 65, 72
self-fulfillment, 3, 34, 44
self-knowledge, 54
self-managing, 92–100
self-realization, 4–5
  in linear career track, 35
  as Ronin, 22–27, 156
Seligman, Martin, 45
Selye, Hans, 157
Separate Reality, A (Castaneda),
  161, 168
shadow, as enemy of Ronin, 81–
  83
Shakespeare, 54
Shapiro, Deane H., 174
Shorris, Earl, 14
Siu, R. G. H., 133, 146, 150

solar power, and future industrial
    society, 16
stress
    definition of, 40–42
    laughter as buffer for, 184
    management of, 54, 157–172
"Stress Reactions in
    Organizations," *Behavioral
    Science* (Zaleznik, de Vries,
    and Howard), 36
Student as Nigger, The (Farber),
    83–84

TASC+ (tell, ask, specify, check,
    and acknowledge), 204–213
Teachings of Don Juan, The
    (Castaneda), 78, 80
Tennyson, Alfred Lord, 90
Third Wave, The (Toffler), 18
Thomas, Caroline, 166
Toffler, Alvin
    on characteristics of
        bureaucracy, 33
    on future of organizations, 19–
        20, 65
    on future of society, 16, 18
    on technology, 154
totalitarian threat, of
    organizations, 11, 14, 17, 22
tradition-directed person, 61–62
Transitions (Bridges), 138

understaffed organizations, 127–
    130

unemployment, 8

Vallee, Jacques, 21
versatility, of Ronin, 92, 124,
    135–136, 192
visibility, 145–149

Waterman, Robert H., Jr., 38,
    187, 190
Watts, Alan, 182
Way of the Ronin, *see* Ronin
Westbrook, Adele, 61, 123, 180
What Color Is Your Parachute?
    (Bolles), 106, 108, 113
"What Makes a Top Executive,"
    Psychology Today (McCall
    and Lombardo), 135
Whittier, John Greenleaf, 108
Wilson, John O., 2, 88
Wilson, Robert A., 154
Whyte, William, 11, 15
Worksteads (Hewes), 22

Yamamoto, Tsunetomo, 156
Yankelovich, Daniel, 7

Zaleznik, Abraham, 36
Zen, 172–184
    see also Ronin
Zen in the Art of Archery
    (Herrigel), 177
Zimbardo, Phil, 178